TIME, FREEDOM, AND THE COMMON GOOD

SUNY Series in Systematic Philosophy
Robert Cummings Neville, Editor

TIME, FREEDOM, AND THE COMMON GOOD

An Essay in Public Philosophy

CHARLES M. SHEROVER

State University of New York Press

Published by
State University of New York Press, Albany

© 1989   State University of New York

For information, address State University of New York Press, State
University Plaza, Albany, N.Y., 12246

Library of Congress Cataloging-in-Publication Data
Sherover, Charles M.
    Time, freedom, and the common good: an essay in public philoso-
phy/Charles M. Sherover.
    p. cm. — (SUNY series in systematic philosophy)
    Bibliography: p.
    Includes index.
    ISBN 0-7914-0178-2. — ISBN 0-7914-0179-0 (pbk.)
    1. Political science — Philosophy. 2. Common good. 3. Liberty.
4. Phenomenology. 5. Pragmatism. I. Title II. Series.
JA71.S44 1989
320'.01'1 — dc19   89-4337
                                                                  CIP

10 9 8 7 6 5 4 3 2 1

CONTENTS

Make up your minds that happiness depends on being free, and freedom depends on being courageous.

— Pericles

One set of men ... abandon freedom because they think it dangerous; [the others] because they hold it to be impossible. ... these dangers are the most formidable as well as the least foreseen of all those which futurity holds in store. ... Let us, then, look forward to the future with that salutary fear which makes men keep watch and ward for freedom.

— de Tocqueville

Every man is a consumer, and ought to be a producer. He fails to make his place good in the world unless he not only pays his debt but also adds something to the commonwealth.

We think our civilization near its meridian, but we are yet only at the cock-crowing and the morning star. . . . The movement in this direction has been very marked in modern history.

— Emerson

To the students

of Tiananmen Square

Preface

We are today living through a dramatic turn in history. At great personal as well as social risk, many people, rulers as well as subjects, are abjuring old ideologies as they rediscover some of the virtues of freedom. Finding that alternative social practices have proven ineffective in promoting the social goods that most children of free societies take for granted, they claim to be wending their ways, with reluctance or enthusiasm, to an accommodation with the universal appeal of freedom. At the same time, many individuals from diverse countries around the world carry on a practice that marks the modern age: the attempt to leave the land of one's birth in order to migrate to lands in which the opportunities associated with free institutions are perceived as inviting.

Yet among those who have enjoyed a large measure of that freedom, which those deprived of it desperately seek, we find our public philosophy in disarray. Conflicting platforms set out irreconcilable claims for public redress of special grievances and conflicting prescriptions for their solutions. Particular problems are treated as intrinsically independent of the others, and particular solutions are proposed without much regard for their wider effects on the rest of the social body.

What seems needed, in a time of some conceptual confusion, is a clear set of normative priorities. Without them, we seem condemned to continually face our diverse problems on an *ad hoc* basis, seeking to solve each separately without regard to its impact on the others. We need to recover a common over-view, a systematically developed public philosophy, enabling us to relate our particular situations, issues and controversies as they impinge on each other so that we can build our future with foresight instead of merely drifting along. To forge a public philosophy that ties particular issues together into a systematically coherent vision would empower us to set out a clear set of priorities to guide our responses to the problems confronting us.

This essay attempts to secure the foundations of a public philosophy adequate for our time — by uncovering fundamental features of our being-together in an organized society and thereby rethinking the heritage of outlooks and doctrines that brought us to where we now are. We should then be able to elicit from these considerations some central guiding principles by which to build the future that will be our legacy to the generations that will succeed us.

This attempt to comprehensively rethink the principles of a free society was first sketched out in an article entitled, "The Temporality of the Common Good: Futurity and Freedom," published in *The Review of Metaphysics* in March 1984. Several colleagues and friends were good enough to share with me their criticisms, objections, and suggestions for development. Of all who were gracious enough to share their thinking with me, I am particularly indebted to those whose specific queries, criticisms, and admonitions, as well as comments on related efforts, directly led me to develop specific segments of this essay: Jeffrey Barnouw, Frederic Bender, Nicholas Capaldi, John Caputo, Howard Cell, Thomas Flynn, J. T. Fraser, Sam Macey, Peter Manchester, Glenn Martin, K. H. Schaeffer, Frank Schalow, Walter Volkommer, and Michael Zimmerman. In accord with the nature of human dialogue, I would hope, but do not expect, that my responses will have satisfied all of their varied objections, even as I remain indebted to them for having prodded my own reflections.

To complete this attempt, I must confess, has required some perseverance. For their warm encouragements to me along the way I am especially grateful to William Barrett, Jude Dougherty, Hilail Gildin, Drew Hyland, and David Sidorsky — no one of whom may be held accountable for anything that is said here. An earlier version of this essay was meticulously reviewed by two friends, Michael Alix and Harold O. Martin, whose very specific editorial suggestions proved crucial to me in developing this final statement. I appreciate the editorial comments of Robert C. Neville, the inquisitive copy-editing of Kay Bolton, and the help of the SUNY Press staff under the direction of Marilyn P. Semerad, in bringing this effort of mine to public view. I am also thankful to Hunter College for a sabbatical leave which enabled me to complete this essay.

Needless to say, but nevertheless necessary to add, grateful as I am to all who helped me develop what is set forth in the pages that follow, the responsibility for what is said and what remains unsaid and undeveloped is mine alone.

C.M.S.

Introduction:
Public Philosophy of Polity

This essay in public philosophy seeks its roots in the developing realities of the human condition. For, if a public philosophy may rightfully speak to the conditions of its time, it needs to faithfully address them. Out of its perceptive comprehension of the historical reality of the public it addresses, it may then speak in a systematic way and elicit normative principles that permit a coherent evaluation of the problems at hand and ways in which they may be faithfully resolved.

This quest for central guiding principles is crucial. Until we employ a cohesive set of underlying principles to discern the problems of our time, we stand in danger of acquiescing before conflicting calls for reform that, taken together, can only result in a self-destructive and "amateurish vivesection practiced on the tortured body of [our] society."[1] The aim of this essay is to suggest a way to rethink our guiding social principles, to develop an overview that provides within its outlook a set of guidelines enabling us to evaluate programs and proposals in a coherent manner and thus proceed to develop the future with some degree of confidence in the norms we seek to embody in our actual social practice.

Many may disagree with Kant's thesis that our ultimate evaluational standards, or moral principles, cannot be derived from actual experience. But, however they are developed, we must surely accept his insight: a practical course of action "which is based on *empirical principles of human nature*, and which does not consider it beneath its dignity to shape its maxims according to the way of the world, *can alone* hope to find a solid foundation" for putting those moral norms into concrete practice.[2]

1

This essay seeks to develop such "empirical principles of human nature" by consulting the nature of our being-together in a complex system of social organization. It proceeds on three presumptions, each of which can be briefly set out here and are hopefully demonstrated in the inquiries which follow: A. We are not historically autonomous but carry with us a heritage of development that provides our intellectual equipment for assessing and solving our problems. B. Our developed social orders exhibit three pervasive modes of social being that when taken together describe us both as individuals and as societal members. C. These three modes of social being carry normative import and must be honored if our diagnostic assessments are to be valid, if our prescriptive proposals are to have relevance. These three considerations frame the structure of this inquiry.

A. At the outset we need to recognize that we start from a history that is intergenerational. Our outlook is securely anchored in what earlier generations taught us. Our current perceptions are imbedded in earlier ways of looking to a future — a future which has only recently come to be conceived as intrinsically hopeful. The ideas we use to perceive and sort out the possibilities before us are inherited norms which now provide the

> evaluations beginning from which even our doubt and our contestation [of them] becomes possible. We can perhaps 'transvaluate values,' but we can never create them beginning from zero.[3]

Our current evaluations of our current situations come out of what we have been taught — what we have accepted, what we have learned to call into question — and the ways in which we reshape this heritage in order to more coherently face the problems and possibilities which lie before us.

Our republican form of government and our allegiance to a democratic society[4] come out of a long historical development which must be acknowledged as we carry it on — just because it has propelled us onto the stage where we find ourselves. Our basic notion of our being-together in a social setting comes out of the modern development of an old Greek idea, the idea of a *polis* or politically organized city. It reached its original heights in classical Athens: as described by Aristotle, it conveys the idea of a *polity*, a community that lives in accord with its own inherent principles of civic membership. Originally conceived in terms of free citizens who governed their own city,[5] the Roman Stoics "exploded the framework of the [Greek] polis which had been beyond argument by Plato and Aristotle,"[6] and extended it to cover the whole of Roman civilization, the historic core of the western world.

This heritage has provided us with the concept of 'polity,' a notion of an organized society as a body-politic in which each member finds the reality of individual life. Encapsulating the notion of social freedom in which each citizen participates to form an individual life, the idea of 'polity' looks to resolving the problems that impend on its future, as an inherently communal obligation.

Obviously, the original Greek notion of a 'polis' — which presumed that citizens knew each other, had personal friendships animating political debates, and maintained a close net of inter-personal relationships binding the whole society together into a cohesive whole — no longer has any real existential meaning for a world increasingly composed of industrialized nation-states. We have already become too large and too complex. Nevertheless, the concept of polity, even deprived of the social intimacy which imbued it in the towns of ancient Greece, has continued to function as the ideational core of every free society, no matter how enlarged. It has brought to us the notion of a coherent society built upon a free citizenry, organized around shared evaluative norms and objectives, common purposes, and generally accepted criteria for assessments of what is important enough in its situational problems to require determination by its citizens.

The contemporary development of the idea of the 'polis', as Dallmayr has noted, is the "public space constituted and maintained" by the actual practice of the community of citizens that sustains it. It depends "not so much [on] personal intimacy as [on] a public relationship steeped in mutual respect and a willingness to let one another 'be'."[7] The 'polis' is not 'the State' but the organized community which places *some* of its activities under the aegis of its political state. The 'polis' encompasses our whole *public* life — our arena of interaction with others, not only in politics but also in our familial, cultural, recreational, and economic pursuits. Framing the life of the community as such, 'polity' (as the organizing principles of a 'polis') is a useful concept for eliciting principles which should be guiding a free citizenry — referring always to the conduct of citizens in that 'public space' within which we necessarily function together. This is, as Rousseau argued, not to encompass the whole of man, but only his public face.[8] We find ourselves, even as free citizens, to be members of a complex of communities in which our individuated interests find expression.

This area of private lives that organized communities make possible is at once liberating and constraining; the ways in which this is done provides each citizen with a test by which to evaluate the common social order. Conceiving organized society as exemplifying this expanded notion of 'polity' provides a way to evaluate the modes of social functioning by the kinds of personal lives it permits and encourages.

B. When we look into the life of a polity, a society organized for the individuated lives of its members, we find that three basic statements describe its structure: 1. All individuality is nurtured by and manifested in social organization; 2. Individually and socially, all human activities are temporally organized; 3. Both depend for their concrete coherence on recognized evaluative and decisional freedoms. These three statements assert that three fundamental concepts, principles, or 'existential categories' of actual social life — *society membership, temporality,* and *freedom* — join to structure any human society we know. No one of these is found to function without somehow entailing the other two. The ways in which their functioning is dispersed and shared among society members while yet integrated within a particular society provide a systematic organizational description of the nature of that social order.

In order to discern each clearly in what it implies and portends, we need first to 'abstract' each of these three 'categories' of our social being from the social milieu in which they come to light. Doing this is the task of the first major segment of this essay — *Three Principles of Polity.* Only after these three socially constitutive principles have been brought into view can we properly turn to develop their full meaning as they coalesce in the actually functioning dynamic tensions of a free society.

In developing these three 'principles', 'categories', or 'empirical norms' of our being-together in organized society, I mean to draw on some fairly recent philosophic thinkers —American pragmatists and European existential-phenomenologists — who have, while addressing other concerns, pointed up this tri-une portrait of human nature only rarely noted before as prime. In trying to comprehend the nature of 'human nature' as it actually manifests itself in its historically empirical endeavors, they have joined together the social nature of all human individuality, the pervasively temporal nature of all human experiencing, and the social experience of an organized freedom on which the fruitful integration of sociality and temporality depend.

Rather than focus on the ways governors should govern, what is suggested as a new mode of departure is a turn to the nature of the governed. It is *they* — 'we the governed' — who must finally pass creative judgment on the possibilities of the future to which we dedicate our time. What should be of primary concern are *the ways* in which social policies impact on individually lived experiences. In contrast to some traditional political theory, I propose to look at social organization, not from the point of view of the governors as much as from the vantage point of the governed, who have a deep personal interest in maintaining a society which claims to be free. Rather than 'feed down' a doctrine of social governance, we should generalize the nature of individual *perspectives* onto social phenomena — and find our criteria for social obligations in those perspectives.[9]

In the light of such recent thinking about the nature of human existence, this essay seeks to rethink some of the lessons of the heritage that is ours and to bring this rethinking to bear upon the possibilities which define the genuine options we now seek to resolve. Any defensible prescriptions for the governance of human beings, as the tradition of political thought has always insisted, must accord with the perceived nature of man; relevant philosophic thinking about the nature and goals of polity has traditionally tested itself by its particular evaluative understanding of human nature. A comprehensive view of the structure of human social life suggests criteria to be employed in deepening and enhancing the potentialities humans bring with them as they face the possibilities of their future.

C. This last consideration suggests that an authentic descriptive understanding is pervasively evaluative. It is inherently normative in that it suggests consequent imperatives to guide the evaluative judgments that enable us to form our future out of the experienced present. As the rules of grammar set norms by which to judge how a language is being used, as the rules of chess or football prescribe ways in which the game should be played, so a physician's insightful diagnosis into an illness carries with it dispassionate norms for evaluating alternative curative procedures. Just so, to the extent that a description of man's social modes of organization is insightful, it inherently suggests ways in which its operative procedures may be properly evaluated and norms against which its ameliorative efforts are to be matched.

The second major segment of this essay — *The Dynamic of a Free Polity* — is concerned to set out, in the light of historical development, some normative criteria which the description of these three social categories suggest. And the final segment — *The Discipline of Freedom* — reverts to specific present questions of public policy by setting out the socially moral imperatives which these preceding discussions seem to suggest. If the three elicited characteristics of human living — *sociality, temporality,* and *freedom* — are prominently displayed in the experiences we each share, then these surely suggest ways in which the norms they incarnate or exhibit may be secured, enhanced, applied.

By clarifying each of these three undergirding aspects of our individual lives, as the 'existential categories' by means of which we interpret our living together, we can elucidate their significance, which we find meaningfully revealed as normative guideposts, when we turn from the ways we individually live our lives to our politically organized social involvements. When we have brought these structures of our social living into light we naturally elicit normative imperatives for carrying them forward.

As we develop these three principles of polity which govern our socially-involved individual lives, we can readily anticipate their normative outcome: 1. A societal membership that is too tightly organized promises a suffocating conformity; one too loosely organized invites anarchy; its moderated course is a democratic polity. 2. A temporality too tightly drawn results in the slavery of clockwork regimentation; one too loosely structured produces social lethargy; its moderated course is responsible government that in representing their citizens' wishes leaves the temporal disposition of its citizens' time to their own determinations while setting social requirements in accord with their own general assessments and the common concerns they need to address. 3. A freedom that is too loose degenerates into license; one too restricted quickly reverts to tyranny; a moderated course is to welcome citizen initiatives while setting a communal boundary to the way those initiatives may function, and a standard of practical 'effects' for gauging them.

Presuming that all individuality has been shown to be possible only in organized society, the discussion seeks to unfold these three principles: 1. The social membership of each, when concretely embodied in the 'dynamic of a free polity' develops into a 'citizenship' that brings each participant into the life of the social body; each citizen is then called to an acknowledged responsibility to contribute to the building of a common history. 2. The social nature of temporality invites individual freedom to construct a future that social parameters hold as open as possible, while limiting the freedom of each so it may be equitably shared; to accomplish this, as Hamilton already suggested, a free society requires a republican principle of representative governance inherently restrained in governing the temporality of its citizens;[10] the concern of citizens to secure their own open temporality requires them to specify the powers of their governors in order to ensure the power of their own freedoms; each citizen is then called to help form the common agenda for developing their mutual future. 3. The generality of freedom places a premium on enhancing the free time of free citizens generally expended on concerns of livelihood or leisure — permitting the social body to reap benefits from, while deliberately depending upon, the free initiatives of its members; these activities, by individuals and by the social body, must then be pragmatically evaluated by anticipating how their exercise may specifically be anticipated as benefiting the entire community.

❧

These considerations depend upon our explicit acknowledgement that, in taking the heritage we bring out of the past into the formation of the future — which is our present task — the most glaring inhibiting fact is the essential finitude of the human outlook. We cannot bring into view our entire past so that we can immediately draw upon *all* its relevant experiences while we plow into the possibilities depending on our decisions for resolution. Even more certainly, we cannot foresee the concrete future outcomes of our most carefully thought-out actions — for too many contemporary developments, of which we must be oblivious, may be reasonably expected to feed into the actual social future we are presently developing. In all the decisions we find ourselves compelled to make, we are bound to the ambiguity of relevant extent and the hope of careful preparation. The wisdom of humility before the extensive past and the indefinite future suggests that, however our principles may suggest courses of action, we ought to pursue them in a spirit of moderation — just because we can never be sure that we are truly 'on track'.

These considerations join again to suggest that the paradoxes of the liberalist tradition thrust it forward in opposed directions, thus bringing its contemporary pertinence into question. Its doctrine of 'absolute rights' logically demands libertarian development which can only invite an anarchy, enabling the oppression of the many by a powerful few, thus eroding these 'rights' for most. At the same time liberalism has managed to wed itself to a new egalitarianism, that paradoxically calls it to advance collectivist programs inherently requiring an elitism that would effectively de-equalize its citizens and simultaneously curtail their individual temporal freedoms. The root of this programmatic confusion lies in its superficial view of the nature of human existence — that ignores the three 'existential categories' of social being this essay develops. In contrast to liberalism's conceptual dilemmas and consequent programmatic confusions, this essay seeks to voice an alternative authentically democratic tradition that, taking the interests of all into the scope of its concern, is inherently conservative: It dedicates itself to maximize concrete freedoms and to govern its quest for progress with the restraining courage of prudential caution which a lived concern for the integrity of each individual requires.

The good of each, Aristotle had already urged, motivates each as each perceives it. In a free society, the community of motivation forms that nest of aspirations and evaluative criteria joining citizens together to seek their 'common good'. These basic social principles or 'categories' of social existence structure that common good by functioning together in a purposeful harmony. Explicating ways in which this is done provides a comprehensive outlook permitting us to enrich their development by taking up the problems and opportunities of our social situations in a coherent manner.

Our quest for this common good, which we must always share together, may be enlightened and guided by the normative guide-lines these principles of our social being suggest. Each of these three basic characteristics of lived social experience describes rudiments of the socially embedded experience of each of us and, thus, what we each seek out of our essential social involvement. Taken together, they describe the nature of a free polity, set out criteria by which a people free to make their own evaluative judgments may judge the efficacy of their social order, and then discriminate from all alternatives the specific kinds of policies they elect to pursue. These three social 'categories' of our being-together developed in the historical practice of those societies which effectively took their conjoint meaning seriously by bringing them into modern dress. Out of this historic development, their normative force emerges.

Each of these principles embodied in a free polity, individually experienced and socially demonstrated, grounds admonitions for further advance. Taken together, they suggest ways to advance our mutually sought common good, within the scope of which the good of each is to be found.

Part I

❧❧

Three Principles of Polity

Fortunately, in facing our problems we do not have to start 'from scratch'. We carry with us a tradition of thought that, having faced similar issues in the past, brings us an instructive record of accomplishments and failures. This legacy of experience that has nurtured us shows that our problems are not entirely new; they generally have a past on which we can draw as we attend to them.

We find ourselves today as custodians of a heritage of thoughtful experience and a responsibility to utilize it for the tasks that now face us. This heritage, thoughtfully used, enables us to avoid repeating earlier errors of judgment while opening the opportunity to solve problems that may have baffled earlier tries, as we creatively forge ahead into a new and hopefully brighter future. By thoughtfully appropriating our historic heritage in the light of current situations, we provide ourselves with coherent guidance into an at least dimly seen future. Our uses of this cultural legacy in the decisions we actually make will constitute the heritage we bequeath to our successors.

At least three basic themes run through the core of the social fabric. Each one contributes to the ways in which the social body is experienced by its constituents: 1. The idea of societal membership delineates each individual as intrinsically involved with a community and its common good, upon which the good of its members ultimately depends. 2. Each person's life, as the life of the encompassing community itself, is consumed by temporal activity: the pervasively temporal structure of all individual and social experience needs to be acknowledged so that we are able to understand its import. 3. Each of our lives, on every level, is vitalized by the experience of freedom; whether explained or just accepted, explicit recognition of its extent helps to provide guidelines for how it may best be enhanced.

These three cardinal notions mark the life of each of us and function together in our lives. Their recognition helps us to take in and comprehend the nature of our individual social involvements and the life of the organized society to which we belong. By explicitly seeking to reinforce the conditions of life they set forth, we can derive normative standards by which to evaluate the specific options we are continually called upon to decide.

Before we can explicate their meaning for the polities in which we are always engaged, we need to see how each contributes to our concretely individualized social experiences. By first discerning each in some abstraction from the others, we will see how they join together to form the lives we live in the organized societies to which we belong. As fundamentally descriptive, they yet suggest evaluative standards and directives for us to employ in the policy decisions we must continually make.

Chapter **1**

Membership

Succinctly giving voice not only to the force of the intellectual tradition but also to socially experienced fact, John Donne had described our individual situation plainly enough:

> No man is an Iland, intire of itselfe;
> every man is a peece of the Continent, a part of the
> maine; . . .

> any man's death diminishes me, because I am involved
> in Mankinde;
> And therefore never send to know for whom the bell
> tolls;

> it tolls for thee.

We do not need to 'buy' any conceptual scheme, such as Hegel's masterfully systematic subordination of life to logic, in order to appreciate the fact that each person finds individual life — existence, values or norms, problems, hopes and fears — in the context of membership in a social order. One's own self is only found insofar as one fully acknowledges one's affiliations in the whole gamut of the social levels in which one is engaged.

Yet we have all been imbued with a vague notion that we are each somehow ultimately independent individuals, somehow unrooted in society, history, tradition, or custom. This is a rather new view that can be traced back to the decisive break with the intellectual tradition so eloquently voiced by Donne, the break that René Descartes,

Donne's contemporary, effectively initiated, the break that marks the beginning and shape of much of the modern era.

Effectively, if only implicitly, repudiating the notion of socially rooted individuality, Descartes brought several strains of earlier thought together into a new outlook: a mechanically structured physical universe governed by laws which do not govern our minds but which our minds are nevertheless somehow deemed competent to faithfully observe. Individual existence, Descartes urged, is to be discovered neither in an active involvement with physical objects nor with other persons, but in detached acts of individual thought. He provided its ongoing slogan: 'cogito ergo sum' — *I* think therefore *I* am. One's identity is to be found not in intrinsic involvement with others, but in the detached self-examination of the thinking self. One's experience was seen to be rooted *not in 'we', but in 'I'*.[1]

Seeking cognitive certitude concerning the mathematical nature of the physical world in which we dwell, Descartes proposed that the individual mind should cleanse itself of all inherited beliefs about the nature of nature; only after passing the test of individual reason were we to accept as true those beliefs that meet the test of conceptual clarity demanded by pure reason. Effectively, if only implicitly, he proclaimed a doctrine of the 'sovereignty of individual reason', a call for a rational evaluation of particular doctrines about the nature of the world that must first pass muster in the court of individual judgment before one rightfully accepts them as certifiable fact.

The primacy of individual thought was proclaimed by Descartes against the authority of traditional beliefs — against accepted authority, custom, and inherited standards of judgment. Each individual is to evaluate these against the standard of reason somehow innately planted in each individual mind. Except to suggest a vaguely enunciated theory of 'innate ideas', Descartes never explained just how we are to develop the analytic capabilities and evaluative tools by which to do this — without a rich education society provides for us. Apart from this question and from his own interest in advancing the new physics of Galileo, Descartes' principle generated a whole new way of looking at political and social questions.

This Cartesian program, whatever may be said for it as a new scientific methodology, was developed in the 1600s when the inherited political order had already started to disintegrate. It comes, then, as no surprise that those of his more influential readers, who were as concerned with political as with metaphysical and scientific questions, took from his principle a conception of individual being as autonomous and essentially prior to any social engagements. Whether Descartes would himself have countenanced this development is doubtful.[2] But the principle of the 'I think, I am' rapidly took political expression in a virtually unprecedented doctrine of social-atomism, a doctrine that a society is a casual aggregation ultimately reducible to the particular individuals composing it. This view, central to the historic liberalist tradition, found its first systematic formulation in the work by Thomas Hobbes, who used it to justify an absolute state.

At least two ironies present themselves in this observation. First, Hobbes, a father of modern materialism, was one of the foremost contemporary critics of Descartes' exemption of 'mind' from the laws believed to govern physical 'matter'. The second is that although Hobbes' atomistic individualism provided his justification of absolutist government, it soon became one of the chief conceptual instruments of modern liberalism. Hobbes' social-atomism provided Locke, Bentham, Jefferson, and even Mill with the conceptual instrument for the development of the core of liberalist doctrine. Still present in contemporary debates,[3] this doctrine of social-atomism provides one prime source of the conceptual confusions encumbering many current controversies.

For present purposes, Hobbes' radical notion can be simply stated. The separate individuality of each person is somehow original: A society is but an organized aggregate of these ultimately disparate individuals, similar to the aggregate of the particular atoms that forms a material body; individuals freely come together as a matter of convenience and agree on a mode of governance for what they perceive as their mutual advantage. Writing in a time of civil turmoil, Hobbes urged that the prime interest of each individual is peace and stability. To attain this end he proposed that all individuals agree to place themselves under the protection of an absolute state, the prime function of which is to deny their liberty in order to enforce the peace.

A generation later, John Locke picked up this notion of the state (the political arm of the society) as but a convenience agreed to by disparate individuals for their mutual protection. This philosophic presumption provided the heart of Locke's political legacy. It formed the heart of the new liberalist tradition that regards the sole function of the society's government to be the protection of already presupposed innate individual rights — rights which Locke described in no more detail than individual rights to that "life, liberty and estate," designated as "property," which each individual presumably carries with him as he moved into organized society.[4]

Against the tradition — which stems from Aristotle and which has been given modern development by a host of writers not usually linked together — this new thesis of social-atomism portrayed society as akin to a material body that can always be broken down into its component units. Society is conceived as an artificial creation of, and thereby reducible to, disparate individuals somehow already endowed with specific needs and rights whose protection defines the limits of justifiable governmental authority. The alternative view which social-atomism sought to replace, emerged from classical sources; it insisted that a society is essentially prior to the particular individuals who compose it; one's society provides the context of meaning by which individuals come to see themselves as those whom it has nurtured and developed; society teaches its members to seek their own matured responsibilities *as members* of a polity the activities of which are to be justified as the instrument enabling them to seek their common good together.

This theoretical debate, extremely critical and also immensely practical, addresses itself directly to the nature of the common good. Tied to questions of our temporality in our pervasive encounter with time, it exhibits our way of integrating present, past, and future into a coherently constructive outlook. Tied to how we may rightfully specify 'rights', this debate speaks to their justification and function — whether these are *prior to or consequent upon* social 'obligations' — and whether they are absolute or situationally conditioned. Tied to questions of freedom, this debate focuses on the relation between 'negative liberty' and 'positive freedom'. Such questions join to evoke a norm of appropriate government, address undercurrents of current debate, and bear on contemporary controversies concerning social policy. They thus suggest guidelines by which to evaluate — and seek direction out of — some chief controversies of our day.

To develop this debate and the implications it suggests, we need to invoke the tradition of western political thought in which the concepts of democracy, republicanism, and freedom developed. The motive — a concern for the health and longevity of our republic and the furtherance of the republican principle — should impel us to rethink our basic political principles in order to discern more clearly the possibilities they present for our own continuing development of them. This is done on the ground that Machiavelli's political realism had urged: before losing ourselves in innumerable specific proposals, we should first seek out those first principles that have provided the impetus and thereby the precepts which brought us to where we now are; imaginatively invoked, they provide direction for revitalizing our republic as we use them to more effectively form our future within their scope.[5]

i. The Greek Innovation

Our idea of democracy was devised by the Greeks. Certainly the ideas of citizen-sovereignty and decision by majority voting did not emerge from earlier cultures. Indeed, most of the basic concepts we still use to formulate and describe our political experience derive from them.[6]

The unique Greek experience of a small and cohesive self-governing town, the *polis*, provides our varied words concerning civic affairs: 'political', 'police', 'policy'; from their notion of rule-by-the-'people', or *demos*, comes our word 'democracy'; their concepts of 'mixed government' were already voiced in the later writings of Plato and in Aristotle's *Politics*. From them the Romans developed the idea of 'republic' *(res publica)* — eventually retrieved to animate the Constitution of the United States and most other more recently developed systems of constitutional government.

It is, therefore, not strange that Aristotle's attempt to provide dispassionate descriptions of the ways in which different kinds of governments function, written at the sunset of the Athenian experience, still serves as a prime text on the science of governance. We may still profit from the lessons taught without forgetting that they come out of a society radically different from our own — and yet our ancestor. Out of their experience we can draw enduring lessons for governmental practice while we adapt these lessons to our own present problems.

We thus start from a long historical experience on which to draw. Our present socio-political scene emerges from a historical development which commenced on the Greek peninsula. By looking back onto the historic development which has brought us to where we are, we not only achieve some insight into how we have developed but also what we have become. We quickly find that many of our problems are not really new, that they have, in many ways, been encountered before, and that we need not repeat all the mistakes that have been made along the way.

ii. The Aristotelian Legacy

Aristotle's *Politics* summed up the Greek political experience of citizen government. It starts with a pregnant sentence that will follow us to the end:

> Every state [*polis*] is a community [*koinonia*] of some kind, and every community is established with a view to some good; for mankind always act in order to obtain that which they think good (1252 a).

The essential similarity of social and individual experience is illustrated by the parallel opening of his manual for individual ethics:

> Every art and every inquiry, and similarly every action and pursuit, is thought to aim at some good; and for this reason, the good has rightly been declared to be that at which all things aim. (1094).

Aristotle thus set forth two prime theses which should still guide us: (i) individual and community activities are both structured in much the same way: each shares a commonly defined objective, namely the quest for what is deemed to be good, and each is concerned with the process of achieving it; and (ii) human reasoning is purposive. Human *rational* activity, on both an individual and a social level, is *prudential*: it is organized by the activity of intelligence in selecting appropriate means to govern pending future activity; intelligence voices a vision, not merely of a distant endpoint, but of the continuity of actions designed to take us from the present situation to realization of what we presently hope to accomplish.

Rational human activity we can then say, if we think through its meaning, is temporally organized — it functions in the present by the light of a future possibility, presently assessed as attainable by appropriate effort. Human rational activity, always socially structured, is organized with a view to a future state of affairs which is presently conceived as possible. Human rational activity, whether individually or socially conceived, is to be understood as purposive behavior: human rational activity is *presently* structured by a *present* understanding of possibilities not yet realized but which are *now* envisioned as attainable by adequate human effort. This essential temporality of human activity was never explicated by Aristotle.[7] But a contemporary reading would suggest that he implicitly perceived the temporal structure of our experience — which utilizes its past within the context of the present to construct a future now conceived as possible. To examine the import of this temporal structure, we will duly proceed; we will see that it augments the thesis that individual experience is inherently social in nature. But before doing so, we need first come to terms with this thesis that denies radical separation of individual experience from social context.

iii. The Primacy of the Social

In order to understand how a society works, Aristotle urged, we must first start by comprehending the whole. The state (or polis) comes into existence as a community that attempts to meet "the bare needs of life" but continues "in existence for the sake of a good life" (1252b). Looking beyond the rudimentary "supply of daily needs" (1252b), while presumably still continuing that concern, the association in community is built on the need for foresight "by the exercise of mind" (1252a). Proceeding in development beyond a "barbarian" mode of "royal rule" (1252b), "the state [polis] is a creation of nature, and man is by nature a political animal" (1253a), i.e., inherently a member of a polis. The polis, or organized society, is so completely "prior to the individual, since the whole is of necessity prior to the part" (1253a), that "he who by nature and not by mere accident is without a state" is either "a beast or a god" (1253a). The organized society is not only logically prior to any existent individual; it is also and for the same reason, in any individual experience, "prior to the family" (1253a) even if its historic development may be seen as having emerged out of the association of families.

This priority of the social could be argued out on diverse grounds. Aristotle chose to base his argument on the fact of rationality expressed in speech. Only insofar as we can reason with each other can we develop normative guidelines to govern our activity. For it is out of the community of reasoning together that the differentiations emerge between the "expedient and the inexpedient," of "any sense of good and evil, of just and unjust" (1253a). From our discussions of means and ends, we are enabled to form common concepts of "justice [which] is the bond of men in states," for "the administration of justice ... is the principle of order in political society" (1253a).

By reasoning with each other, we learn to communicate with each other; from this process, we come to develop an area of mutual concerns, a concept of our common good and of the moral insights it provides. The moral norms we see as binding upon ourselves — the notion of a system of justice that incorporates common understandings of what may and may not be done, even the ability to intelligently evaluate alternative courses of action — are socially rooted. What Aristotle suggested is the idea that our entire picture of ourselves — as moral beings who have options to pursue ends — is socially produced. The development of moral conscience, as of pragmatic considerations, emerges from societal experience and is essentially a social phenomenon.[8] All reasoning requires a community whose members communicate with each other. As a *common* language is requisite for this, the fact of language, itself, then exhibits the fundamentality of the social. And, as a community finds itself, not in contemplation, but in specific joint actions, these actions themselves are dependent for their possibility upon the community of language.[9]

It is understandable that Aristotle saw linguistic community as intrinsic to an organized polis. Even today we see, especially in emerging nations, that the sense of community is usually built around a common linguistic heritage. Yet, conflicts of different linguistic communities in multilingual states (such as India and Canada), together with conflicts of religion, still define many of the inner tensions they experience. Individuals generally identify themselves with a particular language and an assault on it is often taken as both a personal affront and a political issue.

In small societies, common linguistic community seems necessary for the unity of a polis. But this is not always true: The Swiss confederation encompasses four geographically distinct linguistic communities. In larger societies, we today find notable exceptions: Canada encompasses two, India, the Soviet Union, and some of the new African nations encompass many. In the United States, the recent influx of Hispanic immigration with resultant centers of Spanish instead of English has created similar social identifications and consequent antagonisms.

On the other hand, linguistic unity does not necessarily propel political unity, even though it may delineate cultural ties. One need but witness the number of Spanish-speaking countries in Latin America and the number of English-speaking countries scattered over the remains of the British Empire.

Yet something remains essentially true about Aristotle's perception. In most multilingual states, membership in a specific linguistic community serves as a magnet for the social cohesion of its participants, often with the deepest of emotive bonds. Many of the inner tensions of such states clearly manifest the conflict of these communities with each other. And this is understandable — just because any particular person identifies the particularity of one's own self with the language and community in which one has been raised and taught to think, with the language through which one sees and understands the nature of the world in which one's own self is found.

Each of us has been born into and has grown up as a member of a particular community of family, friends, and teachers who use a particular language for communicating with each other. That language, at the outset, defines any nascent individuality within a distinctly social context; it builds into the communication of even the simplest needs and desires a common vocabulary and group of idiomatic expressions which provide a common set of metaphors as shorthands for daily use; its grammatical structures provide the categories by which we organize all our thinking about the persons and things composing the world as it is experienced. As one learns to use it, the conceptual structure of one's language serves to shape the way in which one's world is seen.

Each of us was born into a particular cultural and religious tradition from which we first learned how to make and accept evaluative judgments given to us as binding. Within the scope of these judgmental values, we learned how to set norms to govern our conduct, develop our social judgments, and guide our daily living.

Traditionally, most societies have coupled religion with language — as expressing the degree of agreement requisite to form the social bond. Heretics were thus condemned as social malefactors, and a diversity of sectarian beliefs was abjured. It is well to remember that only within very recent times has religious diversity come to be accepted as compatible with a cohesive society. Locke's celebrated "Letters on Toleration" (1689–1692) did *not* call for universal toleration. The British Toleration Act of 1696 still excluded Catholics, Jews, and Unitarians — all English-speaking — from free worship.[10] At the time of the American Revolution, and for some time thereafter, religious diversity was differently limited, as a number of states continued to maintain their own ecclesiastical establishments.[11] The notion that a society can function harmoniously and be governed equitably without religious uniformity is relatively new; it is still abjured in large portions of our contemporary world. And the question still remains as to how far even the freest society can permit religious practices that seriously offend its operating values.[12]

iv. Layerings of the Polis

The allegiance to a community — politically, linguistically, or religiously defined — as the context within which individuality is to be found — clearly manifests the thesis that individuality is rooted in the social, that social membership is prior, within human experience, to any notion of differentiating individuality. Indeed, more pervasive and important still, is the fact that each individual is born, and each finds oneself growing up and conducting an individual life, *within* a historically developed and politically organized society.[13]

However the society is organized, whether fairly free or repressive, each person finds himself within a political entity with a multitude of overlapping and subordinate functional structures. Whatever particular freedoms and constraints may characterize it, that political entity sets out in advance, in the whole as in its various layers, the parameters and the scope of possible individual decisional options within it.

In the American scene, for example, we each live under a structure of federal government, and within its encompassing reach, a hierarchical layering multitude of political structures — state, city, and county governments, different administration districts for allocation of water, school, fire-control, and conservation entitlements and responsibilities. Each of these political structures has some kind of accepted authority over some of our activities and each demands some kind of obligation from us (in the forms of protected freedoms and rights to freely discuss, disagree, vote, and litigate; prohibitions on certain activities; mandatory adherence to requirements and tax assessments, within the scope of previously specified regulatory authority).

The prime time and attention of each of us, however, is concerned with the particular economic unit that provides the source of livelihood and commands the prime attention of daily life. These production, distribution, or service agencies function in a largely informal network that yet structures the economic life of the community. These economic units engage the prime focus of attention of the individual members of the community by engaging their time in employment — and also by inviting others to patronize their efforts when making the innumerable consumption decisions that engage a good part of leisure time. Each of these units (individually discernible by paycheck-issuing responsibility if no other) is itself socially layered by differentiations of managing authority and employment responsibility. In some fields, we find further differentiation in economically subordinate associations such as labor unions, management conferences, and professional societies.

Each of us lives as a member of a number of purely voluntary associations: churches built on religious allegiances, groups explicitly focused on socio-political disputes, and leisure time clubs devoted to cultural, athletic, and other recreational activities. In each and all of these, we act and live in hierarchical layers of optional decisions and responsibilities. We select or accept, in each realm, leaders who guide us and those whom we choose or regard as charged with special responsibilities to which we feel ourselves bound to respond. In some we may be 'Chiefs' and in others plain 'Indians' — but the status in one is rarely felt as impinging on that in another. One's portrait of one's own life is that of mixed places in varied social pantheons. The character of each individual life is usually seen in the way the many variations of status blend into a single personality.

And minimally, each individual person's own integrated experience of this intricately variegated social scene emerges from at least two purely nonvoluntary and predominant influences, which no one of us could have been provided the option of selecting: the language in which one is reared that provides the medium for one's conscious activity, and the family unit that provides one's initial world outlook and ways of evaluative perceptions.

v. Emergence of Self-Consciousness

This observation of our pervasive sociality — which we each experience as the bedrock of that individuality we are taught to develop and take pride in — is not particularly novel. But its philosophic implications for an assessment of contemporary concerns need to be accorded their due. Their reach is more pervasive than a merely sociological account of a social milieu might suggest.

The primacy of the social extends beyond the particularity of language, religion, and organized social structures, as Josiah Royce, eloquently argued.[14] The idea of the social does not arise from our separate selves: it is itself what enables these separate selves to develop. For it is one's society that provides one's conception of self-consciousness, of the idea of individuality itself, and indeed also of physical nature.

The distinction between self and others is itself social in origin. Self-consciousness is already a social product that our continual experience of ourselves among others in an individuating culture teaches us to develop. The Cartesian statement of self-awareness, 'I exist', finds "its origin for me in social intercourse ... [and] is secondary, for instance, to language" — "who I am, I have first learned from others before I can observe it for myself."[15] The distinction of myself from others, the continuity of self-consciousness, Royce argued, depends

> upon a series of contrast-effects, whose psychological origin lies in our literal social life, and whose continuance in our present conscious life, whenever we are alone, is due to habit, to our memory of literal social relations, and to an imaginative idealization of these relations.[16]

Thus, "*It is not the analogy with ourselves which is our principal guide to our belief in our fellows. ...* a vague belief in the existence of our fellows seems to *antedate* ... the definite formation of any consciousness" of the self.[17] We each seem to develop not only the idea of individuality, but of self-consciousness as well, in a *process of gradual differentiation* from those with whom we find ourselves at the outset. The idea of the self is *not immediately* given. It is progressively developed in the time-laden process of maturation, within the scope permitted, authorized, and encouraged by the matrix of social functioning to which we belong — with family, classmates, colleagues, friends.

Human sociality, Royce continued, is not only prior to the emergence of a notion of the self that arises out of the contrasting differentiation of the self from others; it is also the source of our conception of physical nature. Our concepts about the nature of nature only emerge out of our social experiences. Our social belief in our communion with our fellows "*is logically prior to our interpretation of Nature*" just because what we mean by 'nature' is what "*we conceive as known or as knowable to various men.*"[18] The physical world, which we all take for granted and presuppose as prior to our own being, is itself discovered by us, and understood as such by us, as the outcome of social experience. Only by comparing my fellow's response to some outer phenomenon with my own, can I first discover the physical reality which is common to both of us. To use Royce's example, I first learn that my fellow responds to the shining sunlight much as I do; I soon learn that others share this experience when I do not, that it is reported to have been experienced before I was born, and in lands I have not visited.

Lest there be doubt of this general thesis, consider that our contemporary routine acceptance, in defiance of all 'common-sense', of notions of a global Earth and of the heliocentric solar system are products of our society's current teaching; intrinsically counter-intuitive, most of our ancestors would have rejected both of these current commonplaces as absurd.

My 'order of discovery' of the world is first my fellow, then myself, and finally the physical world of nature as what we share between us:[19]

> The general principle, 'Whatever is, is somehow linked to others' so far amounts to the assertion that *whatever is, is in the world with others*.[20]

Before I can develop any notion of self-identity, I develop a notion of common sociality, of belonging together with others. Within that perspective of a mutuality of membership in a social order, I develop my own comprehension of my own individual self as an individual perspectival differentiation from it by living with other people in a world of nature we inhabit together.

vi. Individuality as Membership

This central point, which many regard as obvious, has had to be elaborated. But only because a liberalist tradition persists in perceiving individuals as originally autonomous beings who bring a somehow already-developed sense of moral and social outlook, particular rights, and matured individual desires with them as they 'enter' into a social order. This point is crucial to any serious consideration of human society because it is by means of social and political *pre*scriptions[21] that a society sets out standards to govern the parameters of the individualities it develops and sanctions, and within which individual society members are expected to function. If man is, by nature, essentially a social being, then any concept of social-atomism, and any teaching which takes its departure from a concept of individuality as prior to social moorings, is addressing a fictional notion; it cannot address the historical human reality of a generally prescriptive society in which we each find ourselves.

One reason, perhaps, for many conceptual confusions shrouding so much contemporary socio-political discussion is that the clichés of a social-atomism are flaunted while claiming to address the problems of socially rooted and socially involved individuals. Traditional political philosophy accepted the necessity for working from a concept of 'human nature' because it was concerned with the governance of truly existent human beings. In contemporary philosophic parlance, this is to say that political philosophy's relevance is to be rooted by forthrightly addressing the question of the *essentially* social nature of human existence, of 'social ontology', or the question of the fundamental meaning of what it means to-be-human in-a-world with others. Only after the foundational social structure of the lives of its individual members has been exposed to view, may a theoretical assessment of the human situation justifiably proceed to develop evaluative standards or prescriptive norms for individual members to pursue.

The developed individuality of any particular person is a developed *response*, not merely a mechanistic 'reaction',[22] to the bio-social environment, in all the ways it has borne upon him. This response may appear as unmitigated allegiance, qualified loyalty, or even complete disavowal of membership in the social order. In whatever way individuals may respond to their social milieu, *they are responding to it*, and are thereby answerable, even to themselves, only by some reference to it. No individual starts in a vacuum, lives in a vacuum, evaluates in a vacuum. Every social response is a response to a socially presented problem, question, or issue. No matter how idiosyncratic, therefore, a human being's living activity may be, it is inherently socially bound. Our currently well-vaunted individualism is not something with which we each start: as William Sullivan has said, "As a moral ideal it is itself a collective achievement."[23] It is a socially induced boast that we proudly proclaim.

Our social responses to others are not merely physical. They are pervasively evaluative. Because rational activity is purposive, we need to understand motives, goals, and the evaluative standards employed before we can judge the efficacy and, in most cases, the acceptability of a particular act. When we act as morally responsible beings we seek to understand the other's motive in order to comprehend the action to which we find ourselves called to respond. As I judge another's motive, I form my own. My interaction with others is, then, an "inter-subjective" compound of motives, as I interpret them — mine in response to my understanding of the other who prompts me to respond. In similar fashion, I cannot "understand a tool without knowing the purpose for which it was designed ...[or] an institution, if I am unfamiliar with its goals."[24] Particular actions, as institutions, are judged insofar as they contribute to achievement of the goals or evaluative loyalties that define them. A society is judged by those fundamental core values or normative standards espoused as its 'dream', and particular proposals for reform as they cohere with them.

That set of unifying values and goals which binds a society together is its conception of its common good — as what brings all into that over-all endeavor within the scope of which each should be enabled to find one's own good. Each of us has come to where he now stands because of the social upbringing that developed him. As any individual goes about pursuing personally desired goods, that person is dependent upon ambient social institutions and on the enablement of the sustaining health of the society itself.

Our social and political problems are those of existent human beings, no one of whom would be the same if born or raised as a member of another social complex. We are not, then, somehow self-existent atoms who merely 'happen to be' as we 'now' find ourselves. We are each born into and ever remain *members* of the historically developing society to which we continue to belong, no matter how conformist or deliberately disengaged we might become. "No man," Donne pointed out, "is an island." No one stands alone. We each enter, from the outset, by virtue of our actions, even in the loosest community, into each other's lives. And however solitary our pursuits might be, they will affect others and will depend on the social fabric for their own good fortune.[25]

We may well begin from here — from an assessment of social and political problems that honors this essential facet of the sociality of human nature — to bring to light the ramifications of the common good we seek together. To disregard this centrality of social membership and its ramifications can only leave us with the conceptual confusions which stimulate this exploration. We have then so far achieved one negative result: no social philosophy which neglects or denies this primordial social base of individuality can be germane to our contemporary concerns. Whatever else a relevant public philosophy may proclaim, it must, if it is to have relevance, acknowledge at the outset the social matrix out of which individuality develops and in which it is always rooted.

We each start life as *members* of a complex social order. We each live in it or seek membership in another. The total time span of an individual's life activity is a sequence of judgments, failures, and successes — responses and actions within a social matrix. Individual life is lived by society members. And the life of membership is formed by history, the constraints and encouragements of the social order, the temporal engagements into which we enter, and the exercise of free judgmental decisions we continually make along the way. This primacy of society membership, augmented by the principles of time and temporality — and of the freedom which enables them to function — will lead us to the principle of citizenship.

But the nature of our social time and our individuating temporality must first be explicated. We each live our social membership as the individuated time of an individual's social life. Accordant with its structure, we form our evaluations as criticisms, as goals, as correctives of ever-new present situations. The dynamic import of our temporal experiences — and the ways in which they function — is not always clear. For our common time builds our cohesion with each other, while it roots itself in and encourages the temporalities by means of which our individualities are brought forth. We must turn to explore this theme — for each of us is continuously taking up a past and looking to the future: our pervasively social experience is time-bound and is always inherently temporal.

Chapter **2**

Temporality

Time governs our lives. We celebrate the anniversary of birth and on some future but unknown date expect to die. Of neither do we have any direct knowledge: the first we accept as an authoritative report to us; the second is, within life experience, unknown and unknowable. Between these two terminal dates a time-governed life is lived. This duration, or lastingness of individual life, is lived within the social parameters of a socially accepted 'objective' time frame; but each is lived by means of individuating temporal perspectives.

When we think of time at all we generally think of clocks and calendars. Only by using them can we coordinate our activities with others. Only so can we lay out detailed plans for ourselves. Indeed, our lives are geared to them. And certainly, our highly technological society could not function without precise time-measuring devices.

But just *what* is the 'time' that these devices measure for us? Much philosophic disputation has been expended on whether time is 'real', an 'illusion', or a 'form' of the human outlook. Whatever it may in itself ultimately prove to be, our lives are governed in its terms.

Our life experiences can be described as 'encounters' with time. From the point of view of lived experience, we are each temporal beings, beings who must continually take account of the on-coming-ness of time. Our ways of doing this constitute our 'temporality'. This 'temporality' constitutes the being or 'who' we each bring to our social and political lives and, most centrally, to our own personal concerns. Our understanding of this temporality should then be seen as of social and political importance. That this import has rarely been noted is a regrettable fact of our intellectual history.

The ways in which this temporal cast of human experience functions, the way in which it is structured, needs to be explicitly examined. Doing so highlights many features of our lived experiences and underlines the import we attach to our experience of human freedom. This pervasive structure of the ways our inherent temporality forms our lives, points us to ways in which we can understand how we and others participate in the contemporary socio-political events of our time, and how we manifest our social concerns.

i. Time and Temporality

When we talk of time today, we generally presume the evenly paced progression of a needle across a dial, or the steady succession of digitally marked moments. Our generally accepted notion of clock-time is that of a twenty-four-hour span exactly divided into 1,440 evenly paced minutes (and these into seconds, etc.). But this notion of mathematically identical 'moments' is very recent. It derives from the invention of the mechanical clock in thirteenth-century Germany. In a way, the mechanical clock proved to be one of the most significant inventions of all time, for it was with the invention of the mechanical clock that the development of modern technology began. By developing and refining the gears and 'escapements' that marked those early clocks, this development of the mechanical arts — the study of friction, of precise metalwork, the advantages of different metals for different uses and conditions — provided the early laboratories that developed the technology which would feed into the industrial revolution, and led clockmakers to initiate the factory system; perhaps more crucially, their novel product cultivated "the sense of time crucial to the organized collaboration of large numbers of people."[1]

The mathematical equality of each moment collides head-on with the way the passage of the hours had been universally understood, with all previous custom and belief, with the accumulated wisdom of all previous generations. For most of human history, time was measured not by calibrated 'moments', but by the perceived movement of the sun across the heavens. The sundial, not a mechanical clock, was the key to the farmer's hours. But in winter and in summer, the duration between sunrise and sunset varies: dividing the day and night each into twelve-hour periods — their durations yet vary with the season, and vary differently in different latitudes. Thus, in the Northern Hemisphere, the duration of the twelve hours of a summer day was deemed longer than that of a winter day. In all premodern times — stretching back to ancient Greece and ancient China — the *duration* of each 'hour' depended on which day and in which season it transpired.[2] If there be any doubt about this, just pace the hours of a sundial with those of a wrist watch.

Indeed, one of the problems of the early clockmakers was to adjust the precision of a mechanical clock to the varying twelve daylight hours of agricultural life. Finally, the clockmakers stopped trying to make such technologically complex adjustments; and society, accommodating to this technological failure, slowly regeared its notion of the passage of time to that of the evenly paced clock. Accompanied by the gradual introduction of other mechanical contrivances, clock-time generated a series of social tensions and at least minor upheavals. The introduction of a mathematically divisible time frame, necessary for even the rudiments of modern technology, generated a social revolution of human habits and customs: it took first hold in the cities, which were removed from direct contact with the life of the land, and brought their inhabitants to guide their time by an intrusive mechanical contrivance — the town hall or cathedral clock chimes — rather than by habitually living by the light of the sun. Unnatural as this first appeared to be, it is somewhat remarkable how quickly the new precision of clock-time came to regulate social behavior. Indeed, the new clock-time provided one of the new inducements for learning how to handle numbers as well as becoming literate. This essentially urban progressive acceptance of the new clock-time, and the social practices that ensued from its use, was one mark of the crucial historic break between the new urban and the traditionally rural modes of life; as such, it helped to break the hold of feudal values on the new urban centers from which the new democratization was to come.[3]

Our modern technological society is necessarily governed by the clock, by a notion of time as evenly passing and infinitely divisible. Descartes, indeed, reflecting the new technology of his time, repeatedly argued that these ultimately successive 'moments' by which we now calculate time, are not only 'absolutely true', but are fundamentally axiomatic: Each moment is not only irreducible; it is an ultimate atomic point in the structure of the universe, devoid of any intrinsic continuity with, or dependence upon, any other moment.[4]

It was not long before this thesis of 'absolute moments' was brought into question by both Locke and Leibniz. Although these two represent the two polar points of departure from which developed the

division of subsequent philosophic thought into two distinct streams
of development to the present day, they both declined to take this
Cartesian metaphysic seriously. Locke argued that our concept of time
arises, not from the world itself, but from the 'train of ideas' in our
own thinking minds, which he yet seems to have conceived as a succession of evenly spaced points.[5] Leibniz, in a number of papers,
argued that (i) time is a continuum, not a series of specifiable points;
(ii) it is not a 'thing', but the basic way in which things are related to
each other; (iii) it is thereby the way in which we, as human observers,
integrate our understanding of the universe in which we find ourselves; and (iv) the attributes of past, present, and future are to be
found *in* each one of us as a living biography.[6] Kant finally brought
these two viewpoints together in three essential theses: (i) quantifiable
time is merely the way in which human beings are able to relate separate events to each other; (ii) time is presupposed as a continuity of
process no matter how we 'number its moments'; and (iii) what time
really is, in and of itself, we have ultimately no way of knowing.[7] Left
as an ultimate "secret" beyond our possible comprehension,[8] it is still
seen as universally binding all of our experiences.

These three thinkers — despite their differences and affinities on
this theme of time — made major contributions to modern theories of
republican government.[9] But they neglected to note the distinction
between the 'time', which presumably marks the world as we experience it, and *the way in which we* experience 'time', the way our 'temporality' functions in lived experience.

The radical 'breakthrough' in developing a coherent philosophy
of our temporal experience of time was made at the end of the nineteenth century by Henri Bergson.[10] His central insight was that the
way in which we understand the time of things is not the way in which
we understand our own continuing experience of the passage of time.
He drew the contrast between the relentless onward march of clock-
time — which essentially reports, not the passage of time but the
changing spatial position of the Earth in relation to the rest of the
solar system, and the ways in which we experience the duration of the
events in which we are involved. The leisurely flow of a chess game or
a picnic, the spans of attention in a baseball game, the boredom of a
long protracted meeting or the tedium of a routine job, the exhilara-
tion at the performance of an exciting musical composition or the cli-
max of a hotly contested football game, the deadly beat of 'waiting in
line' for some bureaucratic function — these are all experienced dura-

tions which are not, in our experience of them, quantifiable; *as experienced*, they are not reducible to the abstract 'moments' of clock-time measurement, even as they transpire within the clock-time coordinated system of organized society.

It is these experienced durations that mark our judgments of the time of our lives.[11] These casual everyday experiences all attest to the radical difference between the measured clock-moments that are actually 'consumed' and the experienced duration of particular events as they are enjoyed or regretted. Our time is lived, on a social level, not only by the mathematically "arbitrary division of time" which governs our collaborative efforts,[12] but also — and more centrally, perhaps — in the changing paces of lived experience.

In different and independent ways, American pragmatists and European phenomenologists carried this insight forward. They developed the distinction between the 'objective time' of the physical and social world on the one hand, and, on the other, the temporal outlook by which we each interpret to ourselves the temporal *meaning* of time for us. For the most part, their language is forbidding; their insights, however, bear rich fruit when brought into the purview of our present concern.[13]

Our interrelations with others, especially in a modern society dependent upon technological means to bring people together into cooperative endeavors, is marked by the necessary coordinating function of a common metrical measure of time. But the ways in which we appropriate and utilize this common social time, the ways in which we essentially structure our personal lives within its context, are not measured in these terms. We experience our own 'experiencing' in the more personal terms of temporality — the ways in which we meet social time and incorporate it into our lives. Temporality is then 'experiential', that is, it marks the ways in which we find our own individuality by deciding how to accord ourselves with the time structure of our social world.

We each live a life which began with a birthdate we do not really know, but of which we must be told. We each anticipate a death at some 'point' of time which is presently unknown. Yet the 'between' connecting these two terminal points encompasses the days of our lives. Between these two terminal points, of which we can have no direct knowledge, we each live a life — boring at some 'points' and exciting at others. We have our highs and our lows; we all have experiences which seem to drag on 'forever' and others which we wish could be extended 'longer'. Experiential time is not the steady beat of a pendulum ticking away its seconds. Experiential time is the continuity of the ebbs and flows of experienced living. Dates mark terminal points. Life transpires between them. It is this 'between' in which human temporality is manifested; it is in this 'between' that experiences are had, that life is appreciated as flowing — rich and thick or dull and thin, fulfilling or frustrating, rewarding or punishing, hopeful or despondent.

Our language is hopelessly misleading in this respect. For example, we all use the word 'now' — which is literally untrue when taken as referring to a precise moment in time: for literally any 'now' has already passed, as William James once observed, while one is still in the process of saying it.[14] But 'now', in normal parlance, claims to report not an ultimate 'moment' but the speaker's living present — his own relationship to a contemporary event which transpires over a 'stretch' of clock-time moments, and thus includes what is literally over, together with the on-coming-ness of what is about to be.

A clock does not really tell us what time truly *is*. Functionally, it serves to tell us how to temporally coordinate our events with each other. The *meaning* of my time ensues from my understanding of 'what is going on', 'what I must do', how other events are related to mine and to each other within my perspective. The *meaning* I read into the chronological time that governs our coordinated activities is rooted in how my thoughts and hopes and fears, recollections and anticipations, meld together as they delineate the actual existential situations in which I continually find myself. This meaning is always *mine*, even as it directs me to engage with, or disengage from, particular involvements with others.

When we address the meaning of personal experiences, our attention is directed, not to the steady succession of separate moments, each mathematically calibrated, but to the continuing temporality of lived experience. How do we face this continuing encounter with 'temporality' or 'lived time'? How do we make decisions about a future always unknown and literally unknowable? How do we take up our own past, or our society's past — each being more voluminous than anything we could possible muster in any 'moment' and yet always somehow present in our present decisions? How do we understand our *present* even as its moments are ticking away, always with some of it literally 'over' and some of it yet to begin? How do we plan for a future of which, in the most literal sense, we can have no present experience at all?

Such questions compel us to ask about our own temporality: how we temporally function as living beings, how we do indeed face our continuing encounter with the on-coming-ness of time. This temporality constitutes the existential situation of any human being, regardless of how he 'counts the moments' of his time. This is the question of the 'structure of human temporality'.

ii. The Temporality of Decision

Acknowledging the context of 'clock-time' in our social world, let us turn from any question about the nature of time itself to the ways in which we face its continuing import in our lives. For the ways in which we do this form the ways in which we ultimately bring ourselves to correlate with others. In examining this very personal mode of temporality we find ourselves individuating our experiences. And it is these individuated experiences which we bring with us to our perceptions of our present social and political concerns.

Every day we each find ourselves in a number of problematic situations — in which personal decision is called for. Indeed, when one analyzes one's own 'yesterday', what immediately emerges is that it was a succession of *decisional* 'points', most hardly noticed in passing, perhaps a few of readily acknowledged significance.

Some of these seem to have been fairly trivial: Should I take the bus or the train? Should I order apple or blueberry pie? Should I plan on fish or meat for dinner? Should I read this book or that — do I have time to read both? No 'great' moment seems to be involved in such decisions — but if the train had had an accident, or the pie or fish were contaminated, or the chosen book had changed my outlook on its topic, the decision, lightly taken in prospect, could have turned out, in retrospect, to have far-reaching implications for my next few days, weeks, months, or even years.

Some of these situations may have called for obviously important decisions — concerning a new job, school, investment, or important purchase. Each such decision obviously marked out a new turn in my life.

Indeed, some situations seem invested with importance but carry no real promise of significance: I felt obligated to vote; but does it really matter? Yet, if the voting had been very close, my one reluctant vote might conceivably have made a crucial difference.

In any of these situations I faced alternate possibilities for a future that appeared to me as undecided. And in each situation I felt compelled by the flow of time to make a decision. Time always seems to be coming at me with a force that cannot be resisted. Not to decide is itself a decision — with which I must henceforth live. I seem to have no option but to decide, and continually decide — whether on levels trivial or profound.

None of these choices I had to make appeared infinite in scope; each was among the few alternatives available. In each case my decision making was limited to what was seen as available, and in each case — for whatever reasons — I felt *compelled* to decide as I did.

How did I make these decisions? Most were made without conscious thought — by habit. Yet, when I think about it, I realize that my habits have gradually built up through previous choices made along the way.[15] By conscious preference? (I have always preferred meat to fish.) By personal custom? (My mother always made a great apple pie — will this one prove to be as good?) By consideration of public judgment? (How would it look if I drove a yellow car?) Occasionally, I find that I did not just unthinkingly choose, but carefully considered the anticipated outcome of the particular options before me and made a deliberated decision from among them.

In each situation I feel called upon to resolve, I am, in my immediate present, facing alternative possibilities for a future condition that is dependent upon my decision about which possibility should come to be. To the extent that I take the problem seriously and deliberate about it — instead of deciding impulsively — I am weighing alternatives for what is not-yet but which I presently judge to be within the range of my possible options. I can do this or that — either one or any of the alternatives — but not both or all. The pressure of time says 'only one now'. Maybe later, I will have another turn; but at this juncture of time I must decide on one course of action to the exclusion of all others. That decided-upon action exhibits itself as a course of successive acts "in accordance with a plan of projected behavior."[16]

How do I decide this? I may bank on habit, custom, tradition — and implicitly hope that they will suffice to guide me to the decision before me. I may decide to 'run with the crowd', with the fashion of the current moment. Or I might decide to defy them all and choose what *I* really prefer. However dependent my decision may be upon the precedents of the past or my expectation of the judgments of others, my present decision *is* a decision about the future, about what is not-yet but which I now judge to be within the range of what can-be. And because time always seems to be 'coming at me', I am never relieved of having to make decisions about the oncoming future that is within my ken.

I can make no decisions about the past; that is over and done with. I cannot make decisions about the immediate present, for the present situation is what I find myself already involved in. I can only make a decision about what is 'now' not-yet, about the future. Indeed, my evaluations of my present situation, of what needs to be done with it or about it, are "prognoses . . . which open the area of the possible, they provide points of attack for plan and action, they bring us into the broadest horizons, they enhance our freedom with the consciousness of the possible."[17]

In this judgment of the nature of the present situation, I am presenting to myself limited options within my grasp; and I discern them as telling me what I can do about my present situation, where I can go from 'here', what is yet pending for decision. As Aristotle had already pointed out, "no one *deliberates* about the past, but about what is future and capable of being otherwise" (1139b).

All decisional questions come to me in the form 'what should *I* proceed to do about this?'. All decisional options open to me require decisions about 'what should come next?'. The responsibility is mine and that responsibility I must live with, no matter what decision I finally make. Our acts of decision — trivial or profound — are, then, always linked with the responsibility we must accept for having made the particular decision we have made. Whatever be the activities to which we commit ourselves, the course of behavior undertaken in the name of that commitment "depends upon what [can be] expect[ed] from the future, upon the picture we form of chances and certainties. The goals of our activity are set within the area of that which we deem possible."[18] Indeed, we each "look at the present from the viewpoint of the future as from the past. The ideas we have of the future guide the manner in which we look into the past and the present."[19] Whatever problem we see the present as presenting is in the light of the possibility for development we see it as offering, and the particular aspect of past experience we recollect as germane. As I make a decision about 'what is to be done', as I invoke past experience to offer guidance, I decide upon my response to the situation as I thus understand it and "become responsible for the future"[20] to which my decision leads.

I can protest or accept the immediate present; I can protest the past — if only 'they' would have taken the other alternative! But *my* decisional parameters only refer to what has not yet been decided, what now appears open to my deliberate decision. My animating interest in considering the alternatives before me is 'how can I, and, within their scope, how *should I decide* what yet may be?'. Doing so obviously depends upon my experienced freedom to do so, to act in accord with my own foresight. Kant explained this well:

> Men are more interested in having foresight than any other power, because it is the necessary condition of all practical activity. . . . Any desire includes a (doubtful or certain) foresight of what we can do by our powers. We look back on the past (remember) only so that we can foresee the future by it; and as a rule we look around us in the standpoint of the present, in order to decide on something or prepare ourselves for it.[21]

Continually looking forward, I bring into this time-bound decision — whether consciously or not — the being that I have so far, by a multitude of earlier decisions, made myself to be. I express in any decision my whole self, the being that has resulted from my biographical becoming. As such, I face a future thrust before me by whatever situation I see myself as being in. I cannot always choose my options but must decide from among those that now appear available. And I decide as the being I now find myself to be.

Into this decision-making process, I bring my whole past self. But I cannot possibly review consciously my 'whole past' — mine, as well as my nation's and its cultural ethos, to the extent that I reflect them. And, indeed, I never make such a decision 'raw'. For I bring with me into any decisional situation my entire biographical development and all that that entails. This life history that is peculiarly mine is offered these few particular current options and I have no alternative but to decide from among them or decide to 'fold my hands' — "suppress the emergent images of possibilities and let things take their course,"[22] let come what may. Not to decide is to abdicate the ability to make a decision — and that, too, is a decision always open to me.

Consciously I reach into my experiential past as it surfaces in my present — as into a backroom supply closet — for whatever seems germane to the options before me. I selectively use my past in order to make my decision about this immediate prospect for the future. But however I decide, I am making a decision about the future. I may decide that what is before me is inevitable — welcome or not, it is something to which I should resign myself. I may decide that this choice is indeed within my power and that the decision I make must be mine — even if I ask someone to tell me what to do.

Occasionally I may be graced with the vision of a long-term project — not an immediate decision but one about a long commitment into what is not-yet — which reaches in its hopeful anticipation far beyond my present. Such a commitment 'projects' me, hurls me forward, into a vision of a future possible state which I determine to render actual — as when I choose a course of education or a new employment. I then order my series of actions so as to attain it, always hopefully keeping in mind that the ways in which I choose to proceed will not produce self-defeating side effects along the way.

However I perceive my present situation, however I respond to what it seems to offer, depends upon my own interpretation of the meaning of the present. Close friends might well interpret the current situation in which we find ourselves together differently from the way I do. I might well just 'go along' with them. Or, at some juncture, I might find myself echoing Luther's call: "Here I stand; I can do no other:" I must read this situation *my way*, in terms of the specific possibilities *I* see it as offering that *I* cannot, in good conscience, decline to accept. In fidelity to the self I find myself to be, this is the way I feel called upon to act. I thus close off all alternative possibilities and commit myself to a singular course of action.

Whether 'running with the crowd', standing off from it, or deliberately going against it, I have resolved upon my interpretation, my understanding of the possibilities the situation opens to my perception. Whether under an explicit 'call of conscience' or the judgment of prudential reason, I find an imperative to decision or commitment that I cannot refuse. My commitments are then my own — and I cannot avoid making them. Whether I decide to 'waffle' or commit myself, it is 'I' who has to decide. And I must live with what comes out of each of my decisions.

I find myself, then, continually faced with the necessity of making decisions — of seeming consequence or of none at all — without ever truly knowing how they will turn out. I find myself continually called upon to interpret my situations and act upon them. I am continually interpreting my situations to myself; and I continually seek to resolve whatever dilemmas or options I feel myself facing. Nothing appears to remove from me the burden or opportunity to constantly make these interpretive decisions along my life's way. Hence, *if I find myself continually making these interpretive decisions, then I must be able to do so.*

However this perception may be metaphysically explained — or explained away — this experiential temporality is *my experience* of freedom. This experiential freedom, this constant demand that I exercise my ability to make interpretive decisions about whatever the facts at hand may mean, this ability to integrate my perception of 'the facts' into an interpretation of their meaning, is something I cannot ignore. And neither can I displace my feeling of responsibility for the decisions I have made. In my experiential horizon, to use Erich Fromm's famous phrase, there is no 'escape from freedom'. For even if I abjure the right or opportunity by yielding it to another, it is I who have decided to yield it; and I am, thereby, morally bound to the actions of those to whom I have decided to yield it.

Whether, as some would hold, I am merely acting out a 'role', or whether the decisions I am making are truly mine, I experience them all as personal quandries which I must face. My experience of freedom in the press of temporal demands for decisions is not, then, merely a casual array of choices before me that I can abjure or accept. I am always facing the necessity of having to decide. Whatever else my experienced freedom may be, *my freedom, as I experience it, is this temporally constituted necessity of having to make innumerable interpretive decisions*, picayune or important, about the use of oncoming time.

However else I conceive my self to be, I identify myself with the temporal horizon I find open to me — with the necessities I must face beyond any interpretive decision I may make, and with that open area of presented options, either welcomed or regarded as 'fated' but among which I find that I must decide. Recognizing this continuing presentation of mandated acceptances and open decisions, and thereby my ability to project my expectations or anticipations into a future that is yet to be known, is how I find my self-identity.[23] I am not only what I have been; I find my own self as this unique being in this present circumstance who is bound to go on because of these particular necessities and these particular open options that are somehow left *to me* to resolve.[24]

I conceive myself as this particular biographic being who is bound by a finite array of possibilities, as being called upon to make just these choices and decisions which are mine alone to make, and to accept just these responsibilities for decision which are mine alone to accept. I find myself as this individual being who brings a singular past experience to bear into each decisional present. I identify myself with my area of finite freedom which defines my open future; and in this I find, for myself, the existential meaning of my own existence. I find my own being in the necessities and freedoms that define my present situation to myself. I find myself in those temporal 'futurities' which I see as mine to open or close.

iii. The Pervasive Presence of Futurity

It may be objected that not all experiences are future oriented. Some experiences may focus on the past or the immediate present, but a crucial degree of futurity, of decisional option, is ingredient to all. The question 'what should we do about this current situation?' appears to be involved in any present assessment. And the 'what should be done?' or 'what shall be done?' points to what is not-yet but can be.

To establish this point and elicit its significance for our present concern, let us briefly consider each of three basic kinds of human interpretive situations.

a. Esthetic Experience

When I stop in awe or wonder to gaze at a beautiful sunset or a beautiful painting, I am not usually conscious of the continuing pulse of time — except to arrest it. I am caught up in a seemingly temporally seamless duration of esthetic response or religious awe (which Kant termed the experience of the 'sublime'). My attention seems fully consumed by the object commanding my gaze.

Is this truly a nontemporal experience — as some estheticians and mystics have often claimed? Doesn't my present experiential moment connect what I now see with what I have seen before? Doesn't it *press* to maintain a *continuing duration* against distraction from future interruption? And if, while presently enthralled, I am conscious that this experience must itself finally end, isn't my continuing entrancement itself something of a protest against its impending future closure? Doesn't the meaning I read into this consuming presentation focus my projected integration of my past experiences, the present activity, the education of the esthetic norms I been taught to look out for, and also my hope for its continuing into the at-least proximate future? And, when this experience has itself ended, don't I note its end and yet carry the experience with me as an orientation to possible recurrences? Don't I find this experience, not only as a discontinuity within the continuity of experiential flow, but also as projecting forward criteria which should be sought in experiences yet to come.[25]

My esthetic temporality is defined for me by what I allow myself to appreciate — by judgment of acceptance, neutrality, or repudiation. This area of possible esthetic experience denotes the extent of the esthetic freedom I find myself experiencing. Insofar as society's censor circumscribes my possible area of esthetic experience, it 'fences in' my possible esthetic temporality, my freedom for possible esthetic experiences, and thereby precludes what it forbids from my possible future area of judgmental experience.

b. Cognitive Experience

Essentially similar is any 'cognitive experience' whereby one makes a claim to having attained knowledge. Like the esthetic, it calls for a deliberate suspension of the personal in an acknowledged focus on what is 'objectively' seen; it calls me to depersonalized acknowledgement of the cold 'factuality' before me. But is it that impersonal? It requires me to *deliberately* ignore what is deemed irrelevant to its claim of truth. It focuses on a carefully selected portion of the total presentation. It brings into its report the judgmental factors of 'important' and 'unimportant', 'relevant' or 'irrelevant' — for it cannot possibly report every detail while it necessarily focuses on what it deems as germane to the essentially selective focused (and thereby partial) reports it provides.

Scientific objectivity, as popularly pictured, eschews all 'subjectivity' and only asks us to recognize 'the facts'. Which facts? Not the myriad of detail in the panorama before us, but those that are selectively judged to be relevant or important to the focus of the particular query. Judged by what criteria? By selectively evaluating the components of any scene in the light of a scientific attitude of dispassionate inquiry, I am already using interpretive criteria. These interpretive canons provide my understanding of the 'meaning' of what I recognize as important to my investigative concern. Without such interpretive criteria to guide us we could discover nothing, not even set out to do so.

Picture a physicist, chemist, biologist, and poet looking at the same oak tree in the yard. Each, as such, will provide radically different descriptions of the 'one tree' they view together. Clearly, the interpretive criteria each uses provide the kinds of questions each of them asks and the standards of acceptability for the answers offered.

Any why, we may ask, did each undertake the particular professional investigation? Was it not because some specific information was required for another task, because the investigator himself expected to profit from a successful report, or even because he just wished to fill in missing data? Without consulting the goal of the investigation, can we really understand why it has been conducted in its own way? Even the most dispassionate investigator is engaged in a rationally planned, purposive enterprise: without some notion of the goal foreseen, without understanding the interpretive criteria one has committed himself to honor, neither he nor I can explain just what the investigator is doing or justify the procedures systematically followed in doing it.

Any claim to dispassionate objectivity depends on a rigorous personal commitment to depersonalized truth, acceptance of specific judgmental criteria, and allegiance to a specific set of investigatory procedures. Any investigation involves the commitment of a stretch of oncoming time in order to be pursued; it requires an incorporation of specific possibilities of a specified futurity into a continually moving present. Before it is undertaken, it requires an assessment of the possibilities for doing what is deemed requisite for the investigation; it means acting, in a 'spread' of a sequentially moving present, according to what that assessment of still-open possibilities permits. Systematic investigation of the sort that science epitomizes and that many of our own daily fact-finding queries incarnate, is a double temporal commitment: (a) to the use of oncoming time in the light of what can yet be attained, and (b) to use the intervening spread of time to interpret whatever data is uncovered. The commitment to seek knowledge, on any level, depends upon the experiential freedom of the investigator to organize his activity in accord with his own pursuit. He finds his being, as investigator, in the free disciplined use of his own temporality.

Every investigation — however technical or popular it may be — starts from earlier answers which have raised new questions, and each new question, when asked, points ahead to an answer that can only be sought in what is still futural. Any investigation is thus rooted in the social milieu out of which the investigation itself arises and a future to which it looks. And unless it be the idiosyncratic investigation of a hermit, it will feed back into those circles of discussion from which it arose, raising new questions for continuing exploration.

Any investigator, to be successful, must have access to the equipment necessary to pursue his inquiry and the freedom to do so. Any quest for knowledge, for cognitive attainment, relies upon a social structure that protects and sustains it. That social structure must, indeed, provide the investigator freedom to use his time, and the equipment he needs. It must also protect his commitment to depersonalized truth by allowing his report to emerge — 'let the chips fall where they may'. The investigator's society must keep open his access to free discussion — out of which the investigation arose — with his colleagues along the way, and allow him to explain his results when he is ready to offer them. The time of the investigator is the time of his own free commitment to using his temporal imagination — playing with possibilities not yet actualized, projecting himself into conceivable experiments not yet undertaken — so as to function in a state of protected investigatory and discussional freedom. His use of his time is then, one might say, his utilization of a socially protected freedom to temporalize his concern in his time-consuming project and to pursue its necessary temporal procedures, out of and then back into free dialogue.

As Heisenberg observed,

> Science is made by men, a self-evident fact that is far too often forgotten. ...Science rests on experiments; its results are attained through talks among those who work in it and who consult one another. ...[S]cience is rooted in conversations...In these conversations...[h]uman, philosophical or political problems will crop up time and again, and...science is quite inseparable from these more general questions.[26]

All science, as epitomizing cognitive activity, depends upon a socially educated ability to selectively integrate past information into the present commitment to future attainment of new knowledge or insight. It equally depends upon the free access to information — on the free temporality of uninhibited and informed discussion and free access to information that is requisite for discussion.

Systematic investigation epitomizes the essential core of what we mean by cognitive experience. On every ground and at every stage of its progression, systematic investigation or cognitive inquiry is socially grounded in an open temporal field. It immediately involves the investigation with others — historical or contemporary — in a temporal exercise of self-disciplined freedom to commit oneself to a stretch of oncoming futurity. Any such project is then a free, socially ensured, temporal exercise that presumes an open future.

c. Moral Experience

More generally, any practical or moral situation dramatically exhibits this continuing temporal engagement. When I am faced with a task to be undertaken, a conflict of desire or obligation, a problem demanding solution, I find myself facing the question 'what should I do?'. That 'should' directly refers to the future, to what is not-yet but presently judged feasible. The past, we may say, is over and done with; the immediate present is what is now actual. Concerning neither of them do I have any option but acceptance. But a situation discerned as presenting a problem demands that I (a) ask 'what should I do about this?' and (b) decide how to project myself forward into oncoming time to act upon my response.

Aristotle, as we have seen, had argued that "no one *deliberates* about the past but about what is future and capable of being otherwise" (1139b). As Peirce stated it, "future conduct is the only conduct that is subject to self-control."[27] A situation, discerned as problematic, defines itself in the guise of the future as being somewhat open, as presenting a finite range of alternate possibilities or options. My intelligence seeks to delimit these possibilities — to distinguish what may-still-be from what cannot-be. Unless I am to wash my hands of any decision and 'let come what may' (itself a time-bound decision), I must project a course of action designed to bridge the temporal interim between the immediately present 'moment' and the realization of the possibility I commit myself to actualize.

Any act that is not merely reactive is a deliberative practical act that is responsive to, and thereby guided by, a present vision of what is not-yet but may-be, and that I think should-be. Out of my whole experiential past, I can only elicit what immediately seems germane to my present decisional task. Practical acts, coming out of my response to the 'should', are clearly future-oriented acts. They project out of the actuality of the present and the relevant past into what is — in the most literal sense — presently unknown and unknowable. They are a commitment of myself by myself into the unknown.

When I make an evaluative prognosis of those possibilities I deem to be viable, I am not starting *de novo*. I bring with me the whole canon of moral judgments and priorities I have already been taught to honor, even as I may have amended them in the process that has so far constituted my life. As Ricoeur has succinctly told us:

> we are born into a world already qualified in an ethical manner by the decisions of our predecessors . . . we are always already preceded by evaluations beginning from which even our doubt and our contestation become possible. We can perhaps 'transvaluate' values, but we can never create them beginning from zero.[28]

The evaluational framework each person brings along is already historical, which is to say 'temporally developed'. Evaluative norms are not only generated out of the past experience of the culture we carry forward; they are instruments we each sharpen in use as we face our temporally defined problems.

The meaning I read into my present problematic situation is not merely the 'result' of my past conjoined to the immediate present. As the past is closed and unchangeable, so my present has already closed off some possibilities I may have preferred to pursue and it is effectively already fixed as unalterable fact. My present, as I see it calling for decision, is defined for me by the offerings of the future which it holds out before me. My present vision of possibilities is always an invitation that calls upon me to decide just how I should selectively integrate some of these open possibilities with my present factual situation as I discern it.

The 'what should I do?' must be answered selectively and also decisively just because oncoming time demands decision. It is not an abstract intellectual matter. It requires definite commitment to the course of oncoming actualization. My choice is to decide, and to resolutely commit an oncoming stretch of futural time as my one way to produce a specific future state, to the exclusion of all others.

My resolute decision, my resolve, is not restricted to any description of my present situation that a cold analytic intelligence might provide. Such a description could only tell me what actually *is*; it cannot tell me just what I *should do* about it. My evaluation of possibilities and resolution to act — to act in a specific way — goes beyond bare facts. It incarnates 'values' or 'norms' into the interpretive framework I bring to bear. These norms of 'good and bad', 'right and wrong', 'important' or 'unimportant' — in each case, by some defensible standard — provide the rationale for any evaluative discernment.[29]

Deliberate action is a commitment to an interpretation of the meaning of the facts — as illumined by an evaluative norm. If the propriety of the action is questioned, it is appeal to that norm which provides its rational defense. If someone asks me why I do not just take an unguarded object I crave, I reply that 'stealing is wrong'. When I am told that no one would know I took it, I repeat, '*I* would know; and I know that stealing is wrong'. Perhaps I stop and help a blind person cross the street when I am in a hurry. I am asked why I do this. I reply that one should take time out to aid those who need one's help. Each of these simple actions is a judgment about the use of time in the light of normative evaluations of the possibilities presented; each decision is the imposition, in these cases on me by me, of an evaluative norm in the light of which I interpret the situation at hand as requiring of me the action I performed.

Without such norms to guide temporally open behavioral situations, it is difficult to see how the rationality of any decision could be defended, much less coherently formed. The use of such evaluative norms, as prescriptions for decisions to act, cannot function without the temporalized use of intelligence. Whether one justifies an action as leading to a desired goal or as 'standing by' evaluational standards regarded as binding, the invocation of evaluative norms is requisite in justifying the goal and the commitment to it, or the standards for 'right' actions by which one judges what one is doing. In either case, the use of intelligence is required to rationally evaluate the ways in which one's commitment can best be served.

This consideration raises the question of 'prudence'. Aristotle had already taught that prudential reason is a central virtue because it is requisite to responsible behavior. Only as enlightened by a vision of further goal, by a notion of 'virtues', 'motivating maxims', norms, or similar evaluative standards can one intelligently assess a particular situation as requiring some action to rectify its deficiencies. Only by means of such evaluative standards can one use intelligence to set out a course of action and the precise steps it entails. Just because our actions nearly always involve others, it would seem that prudence in decision and action is a moral responsibility of free men.[30] But before prudence can be exercised, one must have already developed a fairly coherent set of interpretive criteria, even if somewhat 'preconceptually', by which one can discern the possibilities of a present situation and determine the direction in which those available possibilities — as the impetus to decisive action — are to be taken.

However one may decide to formulate evaluational standards — whether by justifiable goals or by justifiable kinds of actions — such standards are needed to guide us to coherent action into the future. Whatever else moral reason may entail, it is concerned in calling us to action; it is, thereby, primarily concerned not with what has-been, but with the offerings of the future presently judged as open to our own discriminative determination, our evaluative judgments.

The commitment of my temporality to a sequence of actions designed to effect some chosen outcome — whether an actual state of affairs or the incarnation of chosen values into the then-current matrix — depends upon my experiential freedom to do so. The degree of control I have over my own temporality exhibits the possibilities of my experienced freedom. Although my 'living with others' mandates a mutuality of that freedom — traditionally read as 'liberty not license' — I find myself as a free being with control over my temporality, to the degree that my living with others permits.

iv. Social Temporality

Individual temporality, as we have seen, is directed to the future while it is rooted in societal membership. On whatever level, the individual exercise of temporality presupposes the temporality of one's society. One's ability to decide on courses of action necessitates his being able to seize upon selected possibilities before him; as a factual matter, it depends upon the support and protection the society provides for one's freedom to do so.

That my society provides the context within which my temporality is exercised is quickly apparent. For my society is itself temporally constituted.

It shows, most prominently, in my language. Any language is not merely a mode of communication. It is an instrument for generational development, for taking up, carrying forward, and passing on the historical heritage out of which 'we' emerge. It is the necessary condition for the accumulation of knowledge, customs, and evaluative norms to be handed on. The language that binds a community together is its means for maintaining itself, in its living present, as a bond that is continuous with the past that it sees itself passing on to its posterity.

This transmittal is not passive. In the process of living, that cultural tradition and the language which conveys it undergo refinement and reshaping. New circumstances bring about new emphases, and evaluative priorities are revised. A culture continually reinterprets, in the light of current problems, the meaning of its own past, as new parameters are inconspicuously being set out within which new expectations and anticipations develop.

Every community has an ancestry and a genesis. It is animated by its own special heroes and myths, evaluative norms and priorities, interests and commitments. These developing aspirations carry it forward while forming the 'binding cement' that provides it with a notion of its own identity. It is, as Burke reflected, something of an agreement of the present generation with the past that produced it and the future it sees itself as presently building. As an individual sees oneself linking ancestors and heirs — so a society sees itself as a historic process that "has a past and will have a future. Its more or less conscious history, real or ideal," is not separable from it but essentially ingredient to its self-definition.[31] It sees itself, even if never quite explicated this way, as a temporal process, as a "being that attempts to accomplish something in time and through the ongoing deeds of its members."[32] A society's continuity and fidelity to its own self-perception both depend upon the ways in which individual members continue to interpret their common heritage, and the possibilities they foresee themselves sharing together. The 'civil religion' it inculcates in its children, as in its adult members, includes a reverence for its heroes, traditions, and customs; the general binding evaluative norms by which it judges successes and failures; the motives it approves; the aspirations it honors; and its mode of integrating the multitude of subcommunities within itself that consume the temporally structured attention of its members.

An organized society is, then, to use Royce's term, a "community of interpretation," a community that acknowledges a common heritage and shares general evaluative norms in looking ahead to what yet can-be. Each organized society has its own subcommunities — and, again, each of these is bound by a common sense of historical development and forward-looking aspiration, in terms of the particular interest that draws its members together. Generally speaking, a free society prides itself on its internal pluralism, not only of language, race, religion, economy, or conviction, but even more so, it sees its strength in the strength of the subcommunities or 'intermediate bodies' within it. For in the activities of these subcommunities — and not in those associated with government structure — the average citizen, in his daily rounds, spends most of his time, and to those activities devotes most of his active concerns.

To the extent that the members of each of these subcommunities identify with the general outlook of the society — identify themselves with its history, accept its folklore, live by its customs, share its problems and its aspirations — they bind themselves into the identity of a common 'we'. They then regard themselves as members of a greater whole, in the 'between' that bridges its heritage to its future. Only within this temporally framed outlook can they conceive of a common good, a good which they must somehow forge together and in which each is to find his own.

This temporality is pervasive. It is exhibited in each of the institutions that can be delineated in the social fabric. Each came into being because of a need or opportunity that was experienced in a past present. Each functions successfully only as it appears to continue to be doing so. When some irate citizen calls the need for a particular governmental agency into question, he is effectively suggesting that the originally discerned need that justified its creation no longer exists, that its bureaucratic functioning has turned to needs other than those for which it was originally ordained, or that it no longer appears to be serving any useful (future-oriented) purpose.

Each nongovernmental agency — be it a service or charity institution, a manufacturing or sales organization — was originally created to serve some socially discerned need, of product or service, in its formative present. To the extent that either market considerations or governmental sanctions are currently operative, each surviving unit is successfully meeting a socially discerned need, while commanding the prime attention of those engaged in its functioning.

When technology opens new possibilities of usefulness, new economic units are formed to address those possibilities of anticipated future demand. Some already existent units may expand their horizons to encompass these possibilities. Economic activity may indeed be based on a 'profit-motive'; but that motive depends for its conceivable success on intelligently anticipating possible uses for what the enterprise discerns as eventually needful — not in the eyes of the dispassionate external observer, perhaps, but needful in the eyes of those who might conceivably be willing to patronize it. Economic decisions are essentially anticipatory in nature; when not under a command-economy, they entail a continuity of judgment about future possibilities and a commitment of resources to meeting anticipated 'demand' for them.

When private economic organizations suffer reverses or failures, they do so because of mistaken anticipations of emergent possibilities, or by not attuning themselves appropriately to address them. They thus resist the onward historic temporality of the continuing present by insisting on performing with habits designed to anticipate what was originally their perceived future. Or they break down as part of a social disequilibrium that the government was perhaps expected to forestall. When an economic enterprise falters, it radically alters the future prospects, not only of those who have conceived or directed it but also of those dependent on supplying it, those marketing its products, and those it has employed and who have, with varying degrees of voluntary association, staked their own personal futures on its success.

Each individual, whatever his status may be in a productive or service enterprise, also functions as a consumer. As such, he values the time he has expended to earn the consumption power he is able to exercise — and the time he must expend in order to exercise it. Economic statistics often equate the 'work-hours' of labor needed to acquire a particular consumption-product with its monetary price; but can they evaluate how much personal time an individual must expend in order to acquire the desired object? Is it possible to compute how much time the consumer must spend in researching alternative products, standing in purchase-lines, or otherwise engaging personal time in order to acquire the desired product? Such 'transaction-time cost', in addition to the time of labor in acquiring the power of purchase, is part of the price an individual pays for what he consumes. The time for (a) acquiring purchasing power and (b) the time for making the purchase, both combine to form the real 'price' an individual expends for any product and the 'property' he has achieved when he possesses it. And whatever other ramifications his ownership may have, his property in the desired object saves him additional acquisition time when he is ready to use it. A rationally conceived purchase is a deliberate expenditure of the time it took to earn the 'purchase price' plus the temporal allotment of the time the social mechanism requires to make the purchase itself, and is an anticipatory saving of that time expenditure in the future.

However we may presently function, we are living within an emerging computer age. And these new accessories of our business lives, and often of our personal lives as well, provide an additional 'input' of 'transactional-time'-saving. For essentially what a computer does is save the 'transaction-time' for the accumulation, digestation, and interpretation of information in accord with the evaluative standards that we prescribe. The computerization of contemporary business and production procedures is essentially a time-saving technology which enables each of us to do more in a given span of 'clock-time' than previously envisaged as possible. Just how one utilizes this new time-saving capability is, again, dependent upon one's temporal outlook.

However engaged an individual may be with the various social institutions — including those producing his income and the markets in which goods are purchased — that govern the time of individual life, a person's self-identification is primarily in reference to family and friends. These generally evoke the first loyalty and firmest commitment. But one's family, in much the same way, represents a bit of temporal development. Its coming-into-being can be dated, as can each of the prime events that mark its way. It regards itself, as does every other subsociety, as somewhat autonomous and self-contained within the encompassing social order. Each person comes out of two prior streams of development, functions by their integration, and usually looks forward to producing heirs.

A family may, itself, represent some special cultural heritage within the whole, which it carries forward in its own modified way that orients to the demands of its social world. It imposes on its children its own outlook — its own fidelity to the special heritage it may adhere to, its own customs, mores, and evaluative ways of handling future contingencies. And, above all, it inculcates the priority of futurity in its essential organization — for it is essentially built on the principle of 'parenting', a quintessential instance of future oriented caring — in which every family member participates as provider or recipient.[33]

Voluntary organizations exhibit a similar pattern. A church takes up a particular religious heritage and seeks to preserve it for its communicants in order to guide their moral development. A chess club is organized because a social need is perceived for the players of the game and is guided by the ways it foresees their desires. A little-league ball club is organized to teach children rules of sportsmanship while providing exercise and organizing time to be spent with playmates and parents in leisure-time enjoyment. A political action committee or environmental group comes into being to forestall dangers it anticipates or to influence the development of future events.

On whatever social level, all organization and all purposive activity is temporally structured. Each has been brought into being in order to organize some aspect of the conceived future. Each has taken up past experiences, surveys their meanings in the living present, and focuses on what it sees as possibilities for what is not-yet. In no free society do any of these organizations expect to exercise any monopoly of direction, planning, or control.

v. Temporality in History

Organized human activity, as temporally organized, is then historical. It is embedded in a society's historical development. Its specific forms have a datable chronology and invoke antecedent experience, as the present outlook of each is consumed to resolve or redirect some specific problems of the future it faces. Just what 'the present situation' *is* can rarely be precisely defined — just because it is a complex mix in which 'past' and 'future' are hopelessly entwined.[34] We read the meaning of the past in terms of the futural possibilities which it has presented to us, just as the possibilities which we now foresee have emerged out of our past development; we find ourselves, at every decisional juncture, deliberately seeking out how to meld them.

Rooted in historical development, an individual's specific acts are generally directed toward others or envisioned as encompassing others. One understands the acts of others primarily insofar as they impact on oneself. We each can only understand the rationale of what others do insofar as we can grasp the motives or norms which seem to animate them, or the purposes they appear to be seeking, what they are trying to accomplish. I cannot understand the institutions which encumber my life if I do not comprehend their functions, their goals.

> I do not understand a tool without knowing the purpose for which it was designed, a sign or a symbol, without knowing what it stands for, an institution, if I am unfamiliar with its goals, a work of art if I neglect the intentions of the artist which it realizes.[35]

My understanding of the subsocieties and the various activities that dominate my individual life — as my understanding of the government, a supervening agency representing the 'we' we claim to be — is subject to my comprehension of the values sought, the norms by which they function, the purposes intended, the social benefits that are promised. The institutions with which I deal in my daily rounds, each seem to provide goals in which I can share. They also define ways of doing this by means of the constraints that I find it necessary to accept if I am to participate in the benefits they promise.

On whatever level I seek to examine my own life, I am concerned with possibilities of temporal commitment. Some of these I gladly welcome; others I reluctantly accept — only because no alternative seems feasible. But I define my own being to myself and to others by the temporalities to which I, myself, have chosen to adhere. Sometimes the range of my options is wide; sometimes very narrow, indeed. But given all the circumstances and conditions, my decisions are ultimately mine. Or at least I experience them as being mine. In most cases, I can think of alternative streams of development I might have preferred; or, I can conceive of alternate temporal commitments I might have made. By and large, however, I find my own self in terms of streams of my own temporal commitments, which are always bound into social time. No one of these is exclusive: *We are social beings whose lives all severally flow together.*

Whoever I may be, however I may have come to this particular existential situation, I do so within this social matrix that has its own story but which I somehow take into myself as mine. My life, my identity, is seen by me in just this particular set of temporal engagements that define me to myself within the broader context of my society's time, its ongoing history. I am this biographical development in this present historical situation, the time-formed context for the complex of past experiences out of which I have emerged while looking forward, with hope or foreboding, to those possibilities — presented by the social context or by my own individuated efforts — I now see as hovering before me, and from among which I still must decide.

My own particular acceptance of my current situation depends, in large part, on how freely I feel I have been able to determine the options that have brought me to my present situation — and how wide the parameters appear before me for making decisions about what shall yet be. As we have seen, the question of temporality inherently incorporates the question of freedom — as socially liberating and constraining while, to the extent that my personal temporality is permitted to function, it marks the emergence of my individuality as a distinctive being within my social order. Socially provided and individually appropriated, my temporality depends upon my use of my freedom. And this freedom is the freedom of my temporal options enabled by my social order. To the temporality of the socially buttressed individuation of freedom we can now turn.

Chapter 3

Freedom

We face our current situations in temporal terms. We discern them, evaluate them, and respond to the demands or opportunities we see them as offering by interpreting each one as a nexus between what has been and what my yet be. Our temporal activity is thus both interpretive and decisional — regarding the future and selectively appropriating past experiences that seem germane. If each of us continually functions in this way, each must somehow be able to do so. The exercise of this capability exhibits the personal experience of freedom.

However else freedom may be understood and explained, it is concretely experienced in the degrees of control one is able to exercise over one's time. We reach into the past and interpret the meanings particular strands now seem to hold. We acknowledge restrictions on what we can do henceforth; within these boundaries, we comport ourselves in accord with decisions made along the way. It is, perhaps, just because self-identity is so fused with personal temporality and the experience of freedom this temporality expresses, that freedom is so highly valued.

Freedom is universally demanded, beyond any common agreement on how to explain it or just what it entails. To what extent we can accurately describe its embodiments, much less precisely define it, is a fundamental question still disputed.[1] Yet it is quickly evoked in any serious protest, and irreconcilable policies and programs are justified in its name. Vague and almost undefinable, the call for freedom yet touches something basic in us. As Karl Jaspers observed, "all peoples, individuals and political regimes demand" it; but just what it is or represents, and the proper ways to achieve it are all questions that provoke "at once a wide divergence of views. Perhaps the deepest human

antitheses are determined by the mode of men's consciousness of . . .
[freedom, and in its name] almost everything is desired by men."[2]

This is not only a philosophic but also a historical judgment: the
question of the meaning of freedom (as political liberty) dominated
political discourse for the twenty years preceding the American
Constitutional Convention:

> there was a wide range of opinion: almost the only thing generally
> agreed upon was that everybody wanted it. Everything else — what
> liberty was, who deserved it, how much of it was desirable, how it was
> obtained, how it was secured — was subject to debate.[3]

Whatever freedom may involve, it is understood by us as describing both individuals and societies. The traditional discussions have
tended to treat these two dimensions of freedom as radically distinct
from each other. But the meaning of either personal or political freedom cannot be meaningfully *experienced* in any concrete way without
continual reference to the other; like the two sides of a coin, each side
is different but entails the other. We speak of freedom as personal, religious, social, economic; of freedom to think for oneself, to speak and
hear others speak, to assemble in order to deliberate, advocate or
protest, vote, and decide; to plan ahead; to relocate or emigrate; to
choose a profession, a job, or a school for ourselves or our children; to
hold our own opinions; to choose our own forms of recreation; to
enjoy life as each can; to protect our own privacies; to meet our responsibilities; to control our own lives; to acquire and use property. None of
these freedoms, no matter how private, is devoid of social sanction or
consequence and thereby entirely personal; none of these freedoms, no
matter how socially oriented is operative without a companion notion
of personal freedom.

In life as lived, the two necessarily go hand-in-hand. The individual freedoms one presumes to exercise are those freedoms either
explicitly protected by the organized society, the state — or beyond
its allowable control. The social freedom of the society itself depends
on the protected autonomy of at least some of its citizens — insofar
as each is vested with some decision-making authority. Without
explicit limits on this authority of governmental officials, while yet
requiring governmental protection of freedom's use, it is difficult to
see how the generalized idea of individual freedom could become
existentially meaningful.

i. Emergence of the Idea of Freedom

If the debate about the meaning of freedom is a modern debate, this seems to have more to do with developments of history than with any sudden emergence of a new insight. As a metaphysical question, freedom indeed may well be, as Arendt urged, "the last of the time-honored great [questions] to become a topic of philosophic inquiry at all."[4] Why this question has only recently emerged as a central issue may be variously explained. It may well be that the increasing complexity of modern society coupled with the totalitarian attacks on free political states, has raised it to the forefront of thought. If so, this consideration only buttresses the thesis that social and individual freedom are inseparable.

As a serious political concept, Jaspers noted, in a book first published in 1949, "freedom has only been tried in the West."[5] Only during the second half of the twentieth century — after the Second World War — has it finally become a universally extolled norm.

For whatever historic reasons, the idea of freedom appears, in many basic ways, to have been an early Greek notion. Although not a central question, the idea of personal freedom, at least in the sense that a man could reform his own behavior, was already presumed in the moral admonitions of the presocratic thinkers. But the idea of freedom as a social concept forcefully emerged in the 'golden age of Greece', which had developed — over the one and one-half centuries following the reforms of Solon, a merchant and lawgiver who lived about 600 B.C. — into the democratic polis for which Athens was to become legendary under the leadership of Pericles. And it was Pericles who directly raised this theme: in his famous "Funeral Oration," he first reminded his fellow citizens that, in contrast to other Greek societies, "our political life is free . . . and we are free and tolerant in our private lives." He then admonished them: "Make up your minds that happiness depends on being free, and freedom depends on being courageous."[6]

His address is especially noteworthy because the idea of freedom as such was rarely brought to the fore in Greek thought, even though it was generally presumed. One reason may well be that the distinction of 'voluntary' as against 'involuntary' was taken as self-evident. With neither a notion of an omnipotent deity who could control the future, nor the new mechanistic determinism of nature of the 17th century — both of which were to call freedom into question — they saw no need to labor what was deemed obvious. Socrates presumed the capacity of reason to freely think through questions of meaning and truth. Plato presumed the ability of each to perceive 'the true good' and adapt oneself to its requirements. The distinction between 'voluntary' and 'involuntary' redounds through Aristotle's *Nichomachean Ethics* which depends on the distinction for its own rational coherence and was spelled out in political terms in Aristotle's *Politics*.

Some men, he observed, are free and others not; this seemed obvious in the evidence around him. In making the distinction between those who were free and those who were not, he set out the norm of 'constitutional government', the 'idea of polity' itself, the norm against which functioning governments are to be tested.

The distinction between those who are-free and those who are-not-free is crucial to Aristotle's entire political discussion. Despite the lapse of some two thousand years and the gradual transformation of the city-state into the nation-state, the political delineations he developed upon this distinction still seem to hold: between those states governed *for* the good of the whole free citizenry or the 'common good' ('constitutional government'), and those ruled for the benefit of the rulers (whether an individual tyrant, a tyrannical group, or a tyrannical majority).

Prime principles from his work still aid us to formulate guidelines for the governance of free citizens: the generally recognized need for a bar to both minority- and majority-tyranny; discrimination between types of governmental powers; the standard for distinguishing policies that favor only the majority from those that forward the interest of the society as a whole; the need to avoid dividing the social whole into the very-poor and the very-rich in order to maintain social cohesion; the consequent need for a dominant middle class as requisite for the social cohesion that enables free government to function; the need to include *all* citizens within the concept of the common good so that the loyalty of each to the common concern may be ensured. These principles still guide us. They may occasion controversy in terms of institutional embodiment or legislative enactments but are rarely contested in any society that takes the notion of its freedom seriously.

It may be considered ironic that Aristotle, who provided in his study of Greek political practice the prime text from which the theory of the free state has developed, also defended the Greek institution of slavery. As a child of his time, it may not seem so strange that Aristotle, as virtually all thinkers preceding the onslaught of the modern age, had accepted the idea of slavery as a factual matter. The dialectical nature of human thought, which Plato pointed out, shows us that a person usually perceives what an idea involves only when it is contrasted to its conceived negation: thus, the Greeks in the process of inventing the notion of 'freedom' seem also to have invented its contrasting-concept of 'slavery'. In the pre-Greek world, this distinction hardly existed. Except for the few rulers, all were virtual slaves. "By the very act of creating a free man, [the Greeks] found themselves producing a servile class."[7] Chattel slavery may have originally arisen as a humane alternative, as Montesquieu speculated, to the practice of slaughtering those who were vanquished in battle.[8] However chattel slavery may have come into being, it seems clear that the delineation of freedom, as the voluntary self-originating activity of free men, was developed in ancient times as a contrast to those who were not permitted to exercise this human capacity.

This contrast was most sharply and quite cruelly developed by the Romans, who carried these notions of both free citizenship and slavery onto a more universal ground. While doing so, however, they not only forged the notion of 'republic' (as the *res publica* or 'public property' or 'common wealth') which we use today to describe a government whose officials are freely selected by its citizens. The notion of 'being free', as a crucial socio-political concept — because it was self-evident that some were free, by either custom or proclaimed legal entitlement — progressively became, with the developed Roman Republic (especially as voiced by Cicero), and subsequently in Caesar's Empire, the first sign of citizenship.[9] Not until the mid-1700s, was the issue squarely faced. First Montesquieu and then Rousseau drew the delineation of freedom against slavery as an absolute divide. Freedom was still defined in contrast to slavery, and insofar as slavery was unconditionally condemned, together they thereby first *universalized* the right to free citizenship.[10]

The Roman extension of citizenship through its domains carried with it the notion of individual freedom as the power of self-control. Freedom was seen as something not only civic but also inherently individual — as distinguishable from the free citizenship of the civic association. This may have come first from Epicurus. It also came, perhaps more prominently, from the Stoic philosophers who dominated Roman philosophic thought — such as Epictetus, Seneca, and Marcus Aurelius. They all shared a common preoccupation — how to attain inner peace by liberating oneself from the vicissitudes of the world: the freedom to decide for oneself what one did and did not have the power to control, and the ability to adjust one's own life accordingly, an ability which, in accord with the Greek acceptance of the distinction of 'voluntary' and 'involuntary', did not appear as a philosophic problem for learned disputation.

The second, and certainly most influential, notion of individual inner freedom emerged from the tradition of Biblical thought by way of the new Christian dispensation.[11] Enunciated by St. Paul, a contemporary of Seneca who enjoyed a Hellenic education as a Roman citizen, the notion of personal freedom was finally sanctified. Eschewing the bondage of ritualistic obedience, St. Paul, together with the other Apostles, invited those whom he addressed to enter into a voluntary adoption of the new religious commitment. Presuming the freedom of conversion — to change one's own spiritual allegiance and to seek one's salvation, not merely as a member of the civic order but as a voluntarily committed individual member of a new 'blessed community' — they effectively declared a universal birthright. St. Paul, assuring his adherents that "where the Spirit of the Lord is, there is freedom," admonished them to remember that "For freedom Christ has set us free," together with the consequent obligation: "stand fast therefore, and do not submit again to a yoke of slavery." He reminded them, "For you were called to freedom, brethren," and promptly advised them how to use it. St. Peter, urging that it carries the obligation to be wisely used, announced a new commandment: "Live as free men."[12] Freedom seems to have been proclaimed as an obligation to think for oneself, commit oneself to the conclusion of one's thought, and, in the acceptance of consequent new obligations freedom imposes, to accept responsibility accordant with the profundity of one's decision to faithful commitment.

Some three hundred years later, Augustine, bringing together his own Roman upbringing and his conversion to Christianity, provided a large part of the distinctively developing outlook of the western part of Europe (which, after a lapse of influence, came to dominate Reformation thinking and the rise of modern philosophy). His polemic against the Pelagian heresy, translated as *On Free Choice of the Will*, finally raised the question of how to reconcile 'free will' with the presumption of God's foreknowledge of what the future will bear. With this theological concern, he brought the question of the nature of freedom into the arena of metaphysical disputation.

If one thus includes the contribution of the Epicurean-Stoic tradition (which gave the idea of 'natural law' to the developing western tradition), Arendt is probably correct to generalize that only with Paul and Augustine had the metaphysical question of the nature of personal "freedom made its first [explicit] appearance in our philosophic tradition."[13]

In the seventeenth and eighteenth centuries, the question of freedom entered into modern thought as a result of the philosophic attempt to portray natural processes as a mechanical system. The Baron d'Holbach, in a classic essay, universalized the determined mechanism of the physical world, which since Descartes was central to the new science; he insisted that it applies to man as well. He thus dismissed the notion of personal freedom as an illusion and enunciated the new determinism: the thesis that all human activities are predetermined as absolutely predictable out of preceding efficacious causes.

Thomas Hobbes had already translated this emerging mechanism into a new materialism; as we have seen, he saw its social meaning as the appropriate reaction of a distraught people, caught up in civil war, to form an absolute government that would enforce civil peace. Hobbes' presumption that peace was the one criterion for deciding the question of governance, authorized the military imposition of peace upon any degree of disorder. But a 'people' must already have conceived itself as a single community in order to act in this way and, thereby, they had already exhibited a somehow nascent capacity to make the commended free decision enabling them to join together and freely opt for that enforced peace which would foreclose their future freedom.

Whether as a social question of political implication or as one of individual self-control within the social order, questions of freedom had been newly, and effectively, raised. Can freedom be rightfully used to foreclose its further exercise? Is a free society necessarily commensurate with a legal order that constrains individual choices? Can we freely make interpretive decisions without merely mechanically reacting to the stimulating 'causes' of the social environment? Are we capable of freely engaging in the inherent constraints of a social order, while yet retaining some meaningful degree of decisional autonomy? How may we justify the restrictions that inhere in any organized society as requisite to enhance the freedom to live one's own life?

ii. Freedom as a Modern Concern

That freedom is central to the being of man is a claim echoing through modern thought. It comes as one symphony, blending different voices on different levels into one central theme. Descartes exempted the thinking mind from the mechanism he saw in nature and urged that each mind must be free to rationally evaluate evidence and develop new knowledge. Spinoza announced the import of intellectual freedom and described freedom as the power of self-determination. Leibniz saw freedom as essential to the individuality of the varied perspectives each of us contributes to forming the total truth of the whole; Rousseau translated this to mean that each citizen's freedom, as his own essential potentiality, contributes to the mutuality of freedom a free society opens up for development. Montesquieu had developed principles designed to ensure the stability of liberty in a free society. Locke had effectively resurrected the Stoic thesis of 'natural rights' and proclaimed liberty to be a 'natural right' tied to the security of property; following in his wake, Jefferson proclaimed it, in the Declaration of Independence, as a "self-evident" right ordained by "nature and nature's God." The American inaugurators of modern constitutionalism, some thirteen years later, grounded freedom in a contractual body of fundamental law, premised on the promise of a governmental system explicitly dedicated to "promote the general Welfare" as inseparable from the ongoing task to "secure the Blessings of Liberty to ourselves and our Posterity."

England's Glorious Revolution of 1668 had already established the reign of some measure of political liberty and parliamentary government. But that was generally seen as a local accomplishment — setting Englishmen apart from others. Indeed, it was not 'human rights' as such but 'the rights of Englishmen' that provided the initial battlecry of the American Revolution. The American Declaration of Independence raised it above parochial nationality, declared the question of political freedom to be a universal concern, and thereby generated an excitement that contemporary Americans fail to appreciate. Condorcet immediately pronounced its significance:

> For the first time, a great nation was seen to break away from every chain that bound it serenely to give itself the constitution and the laws that it deemed suitable for the attainment of its happiness. This great cause was defended before the court of public opinion, in the

presence of all Europe; the rights of man were fervently upheld and
exposed without reserve or restriction in writings that circulated with
total freedom from the banks of the Neva to those of the
Guadalquivir. ... men who lived there were astounded to hear that
they had rights, learned to know them and learned about other men
who had dared to reconquer and keep them.[14]

Francois Chateaubriand, who lived through the French
Revolution, said, not of his own country's revolution but of America's:
"the most precious of all the treasures that America contained in her
bosom was liberty. ...*The discovery* of the representative republic in the
United States is *one of the greatest political events in the world.*"[15]
German Arciniegas, the contemporary Colombian writer, notes:

... only when the foundations for the world's newest democracy are
laid in Philadelphia, only when the modern republic is thus created,
do these spectral ideas elaborated in the prose of European speculators
finally take shape in the flesh. ... Something that had earlier been
exported to the New World as an imaginative invention produced,
upon its return to Europe, the greatest revolutionary ferment.[16]

What had first been proclaimed in Philadelphia as possible, a
civic dedication to the possibility of individual "life, liberty and the
pursuit of happiness," was then institutionalized, again in Philadelphia,
as the first representative republic, dedicating itself to "secure the
blessings of liberty." First, the message was sent abroad that freedom
was possible; then it was shown that it could be institutionalized as
actual. What happened in Philadelphia was of more than mere national
significance; that it inaugurated a new epoch in man's political development becomes quickly evident when one consults the non-American
writers of the time.

France — which helped win the American War for
Independence — and then Latin America, took inspiration from what
transpired in Philadelphia. And it is, Arciniegas notes, ironic that it
was in response to the insistence of Americans on liberty, that the
European commitment to a new 'imperialism' was born:

Where immigrants sought liberty, those who stayed home and
ruled sought an empire. ... When the most powerful man in
Europe — Napoleon — crowns himself emperor, his counterpart
— Bolivar — who embodies America, is proclaimed Liberatador. ...
In spite of all their anarchies and dictatorships, the Spanish
American republics are older than any of those in Europe, with the
exception of Switzerland.[17]

However the varied nations of the New World may have each enacted their own promised ideals, the Constitution, following on the American Declaration of Independence, first realized the possibility of a republican government designed to serve a democratic society; it was taken as a clarion call first in France and then in Latin America. What had been seen by a few as a dream, was finally rendered actual; what happened in Philadelphia was as revolutionary a change in world history as the concomitant Industrial Revolution would yet prove to be. As Karl Jaspers noted, it was only after taking up the gradual development of the "fundamental determinants of the idea of political freedom" in the evolution of England, that it was from there "and America, from whence [ideas of institutionalized liberty] were taken over by France and other States after the French Revolution; they were elaborated philosophically during the period of the [German] Enlightenment, for instance by Kant."[18]

Kant's import for this discussion can be summed up in two theses which figure prominently in this essay: first, that however freedom is explained or explained away, we still must necessarily presume our experienced volitional freedom for our exercise of moral reason; and, second (following Rousseau), the consequence: the only justifiable form of government is a 'republican government' of free citizens, not only as a matter of justice or right, but also as a necessary condition for world peace.[19] The justification of morality (as an individual matter) and of republican government (which opens the opportunity for individual moral conscience to function freely) are reciprocal concepts; they require each other.

Hegel originally tied the question of freedom, which America and France had already made central, to the question of time, and then read human history as having been centrally concerned with developing the idea of freedom as the logical structure of concrete institutions. The American pragmatists — James, Peirce, Royce, and Dewey — building on Emerson's adaptation of the philosophy of German Idealism, found that the experience of true individuality is always in community; that both the individual and the community are constituted by the experience of freedom as the capacity to decide how to use what became known. Working in unison, individuals as such and as community members provide the freedom to forge ahead into the unknown future and thereby develop together new insights useful for resolving the problems of men.

Taking up these themes of the interrelation of individual and community, the existential thinkers of the twentieth century — Heidegger, Sartre, Jaspers, Berdyaev, Merleau-Ponty — developed the idea of freedom with utmost seriousness. They argued that freedom is experienced as much more than the ability to choose between what is already given out of the past. Recognizing freedom as a fundamental human way of existing, they built — and Heidegger first among them — on what they saw as Kant's essential thesis that freedom is presumed as the enabling possibility of human experience. The capacity for freedom enables us to build our knowledge of the world by interpreting what our senses report as carrying meaning; to discern options proposed by that knowledge; and to exercise the ability, and thereby the responsibility, for utilizing that developed knowledge to construct what yet can-be. The exercise of freedom, intrinsically tied to the capacity for a forward-looking temporality, integrates visions of alternative possible futures into the living present, while deciding among them and thereby forging that one future that yet shall be.

Freedom, Heidegger explicitly argued, is itself the foundational 'principle of sufficient reason', the root capacity necessarily presumed in any specific human action, and thereby the ground upon which any rational explanation of specific human actions must stand: To rationally explain any human deliberate act, we must not only explain its 'mechanics' but also *the reason* why-and-how it, instead of some alternative, was done. If the human ability to evaluate, choose, and decide is inherent in human experience, then our human experience of freedom is an essential part of the explanation of what we each do in any specific circumstance.

Freedom, as an experiential fact, has then come to be seen as something more than just an ability to make choices; rather, it is understood as the fundamental enabling capacity of human beings to be creative, to project imaginative ideas into the future and prudently proceed to attain them, to act on the basis of foresight into what can-be instead of merely reacting to forces from the past; to respond to newly emerging possibilities by evaluating them, by making binding thoughtful decisions and to act on the basis of those decisions. The capacity to look ahead and deliberate, to plan, to commit oneself to a course of action, and the freedom to act — regardless of whether explained in theological, metaphysical, mechanical, biological, or sociological terms — are perceived as the fundamental presupposition of human experience. For our actual human experiencing depends, as we have already seen, on delineating possibilities of the situations in which we find ourselves responding to the question 'what should be done about this?'. Our continual immersion into the temporal flow, and our capacity to integrate our continual handling of it in terms of what the horizon of the future seems to present as viable, is necessarily employed in all that we think and all that we decide and do.

☙❦❧

This quick sketch of the development of the idea of freedom may be regarded by some as perhaps interesting but essentially unimportant. However, no human thinking, including our own today, starts from zero. Human thinking is rooted in its history. The concepts we use, as the thinking in which they appear, come out of the historical heritage and the questions which that heritage urges upon us concerning the meaningful possibilities we are enabled to see in the present situation.

iii. The Intellectual Problem

We each experience ourselves as having to face options, to make many decisions every day, as being free. Yet the question of freedom — its reality, its meaning, and its import for the ways in which we may manage our experiences of it — comes forcefully into current discussion because of at least three prominent features of our contemporary world.

On the most metaphysical level, the question is raised by the generally mechanistic view of nature that has dominated the rise of modern thought. Insofar as we explain physical events in mechanically causal terms, the question has been raised as to how we could possibly function as truly free beings within a mechanistically conceived physical world. For, if we are truly part of the natural world, how could we possibly be exempt from its pervasive causal laws? Consequently, shouldn't our own behavior on all levels be reduced to mechanistic explanation?

Those who accept this kind of rigorous determinism have yet to explain the pervasiveness of the *experience* of freedom in such a presumably determinist world. On the other hand, those who take our experience of freedom as authentic have yet to explain how this experiential freedom is theoretically possible *within* the world of physical nature as science seems to understand it. Pursuit of this highly speculative question would take us deep into schools of thought, developing from such varied thinkers as Descartes, Spinoza, Leibniz, Kant, and James. We would then find ourselves concerned with ground questions of metaphysics and be far beyond the purview of this present essay.

More to the point here are two considerations that are rooted in our society membership. Contemporary societies increasingly seem to entangle us into situations that are not of our own choosing, while calling upon us to 'freely decide' what to do about them. We find ourselves, as technology progresses, in a new world that is emerging from the rapid advances of imaginative human invention; beyond all the marvels placed at our disposal over the past hundred years — railroads and radios, automobiles and airplanes — which have transformed all human societies beyond the conceivable imagination of earlier generations, it rapidly accustoms us to using machines — computers, cash machines, push button telephones, and micro-wave ovens — we do not understand but which we learn to use as means to ends we freely seek. This increasingly technological culture has not only been a liberating force by radically reducing the need for drudgery; while opening new undreamed-of possibilities, it has also called us to the discipline of functioning within the complex of interrelated political and economic associations that permit it to function. Many among us — revolutionaries and reactionaries — voice nostalgia for a simpler time by romantic idealizations of earlier and simpler societies; but how many would volunteer to surrender all the advantages of modern complexity and technological instrumentation?

The same twentieth century, in starkest terms for some, has forced us all to face unprecedented ideological attacks by totalitarian powers on the very notion of a free society. These have managed to muster the collective strength of millions in support of mass murder, murderous wars, and suppression of individual freedoms to an extent beyond all historical precedent, unimaginable to previous generations. Faced with threats of frontal assault, free nations have had to wage, and remain prepared to wage, defensive wars of threatening magnitude. The consequent allocation of human and material resources has required social decisions we are called upon to formulate or ratify; they reach, in their import, beyond the present into a future which too often seems threatening instead of reassuring. The ideological assault on the very idea of a free society demands our rethinking its foundations and the alternate policies commensurate with its health. And the particular problems which arise from the development of our complex social order, even if no outside forces were threatening, requires us to think through our priorities in evaluating alternative policies commended to us in a world in which we are not alone.

The justification of a free society ultimately depends upon the thesis that as it prospers, it enhances the freely directed lives of its members more confidently and assuredly than any alternative has so far demonstrated a capacity to do. The lives of free citizens are experienced as being-free (no matter how that experience be explained); and a free society thereby seeks to enhance *the experienced freedom* of its members.

The question of freedom, in its social ramifications, builds on the meaningfulness of the experiential freedom we each prize. On this level, at least, we must then face the legitimacy of the 'problem of freedom': each of us necessarily faces the *experience* of freedom — even the stalwart advocate who seeks to convince us that it is an illusion.[20]

The 'problem' is really intellectual, not practical: to square our continual experience of freely evaluating what appears before us with an attempt to explain how we actually do so. Determinists, ignoring the fundamental difference between the closed nature of the past and the openness of the future, generally root the present in the past which, as already unchangeable, is seen as offering no opportunity for novelty or unforeseeable alternatives to emerge: what *is* is then merely the outcome of what was already factually determinate. This intellectual procedure, Ricoeur noted, is "a vicious circle only for analytic understanding, not for practical reason;" it is animated by the intellectual desire to piece together the rudiments of what has been; it is not guided by a forward-looking reason concerned to forge ahead into new activity.[21]

In view of our pervasive experience of freedom, we may well ask why some people are so persistently set to prove that none of us — always including the questioner — really enjoys this experienced freedom.[22] Significantly, authoritarian doctrines generally dismiss free agency and assure us, in the name of biology, social conditioning, psychological drives, or chosen 'laws of history', that there are no real interpretive choices to make, that all is predestined to the speaker's chosen outcome.

Rather than see such findings, when rigorously justified, as but limiting conditions within which we will still face alternatives and decisions, authoritarian attacks on the authenticity of experiential freedom call upon us to acquiesce before the inevitable as it is being revealed to us.

An elitism often seems implicit: we should do what the self-anointed prophets of whatever is proposed as inevitable tell us to do. Rather than adhere to what has been condemned as the outmoded ideals of 'the freedom and dignity' of free men, we should happily and quietly reconcile ourselves to accept what *must*, in any event, come to pass. To the contrary, most advocates of freedom have effectively accepted Leibniz' admonition: "Instead of saying that we are free only in appearance in a way sufficient for practical life, we should rather say that *we are determined only in appearance* but that in strict metaphysical language we are perfectly independent relatively to the influence of all other creatures."[23] What we think and say should always be tested by the way it 'squares' *with the ways in which we experience it*. No matter how explained or 'explained away', we must come to terms with the experiential freedom which is central to the way in which life is experienced.

In any event, our concern here is not with the speculative question of how our continuing experience can be theoretically justified. Our concern must be with the question of how *experiential freedom* is to be socially acknowledged. For this experiential freedom is bound up with every sociopolitical decision we are called upon to make. How shall, how may, our experiential freedom be preserved and secured, as we build an increasingly complex and uncertain future?

Freedom, *as experienced*, is not itself an option; it is the continuing necessity to face options and to make hard decisions. Much as we may often bemoan this necessity, we somehow continue to place a high value on our freedom to do so; we want its future secured. Why is it so important to us? We must be clear about the import of freedom before we can intelligently consider the varied imperatives urged upon us in its name.

iv. Experiential Freedom

Why is experiential freedom so deeply desired? One reason is, as already suggested, that it functions in virtually every aspect of conscious life. Pervasive in lived experience, it is identified with personal identity and the meaning found in the experience of living.

Two basic kinds of everyday experience point out their common temporal structure. They join to exhibit the reason why freedom is regarded as fundamental.

iv. a. Freedom and Morality

It is a cliché to say that without freedom of choice there can be neither morality nor moral responsibility. To advise me that I should or should not do something rings hollow unless I believe that I am able to decide whether or not to act as advised. And, surely, if I truly have no decisional options but am merely acting out a preordained role dictated by my inexorable past (of genetic inheritance or sociological conditioning), it is hard to see why I should be held responsible for my act.

Of the innumerable decisions made in the daily round, many are habitual and without any conscious thought. But each of us also faces conscious dilemmas every day. Each — trivial or important — is experienced as one that cannot be avoided. Not to decide and let come what may, as already suggested, is itself a decision. And decision cannot be avoided, just because the continuity of temporal becoming does not permit abstention. Oncoming time continually forces a succession of decisions upon me. A continuing array of specific options seems built into that temporally defined activity I regard as *my* life.

These options are always limited: which of these two or three viable alternatives do I prefer? They are limited by the situation in which I find myself, which always includes the capabilities I bring along. The array of real options before me is limited in advance of any decision by the conjunction of (a) the possibilities for development of a particular context, and (b) the capacities which I bring with me as part of the 'I' who I am. Within such limits, I experience myself as compelled to decide just what to do.

Many of these options are set by my own socially-developed preferences, my likes and dislikes, hopes, fear, and aspirations. and usually I justify them by merely voicing my preference. But some decisions — those I specifically regard as moral — seem to be based on something more. Despite my preferences — sometimes in accord with them, sometimes in opposition to them — I find myself saying to myself: 'I ought to do x instead of y'. Both possibilities appear open to me but my conscience, for whatever reason, tells me that I 'should' do one to the exclusion of the other: not which I want to do, but which I should obligate myself to do, make myself do, regardless of whether I want to do it.

I find myself *having to decide*, to respond to the demand of my moral conscience. In any concrete situation, I find myself compelled to act *as if I am free to decide* regardless of what I might believe about the ultimate nature of my experienced freedom. Existentially, I face my own self as necessarily required to act as a free being — I must decide what I ought to do within this specific concrete circumstance I did not choose to face. Such a decision is an experienced act of freedom which I cannot bypass.

Perhaps needless to add — except that it is too often ignored — is the fact that my moral judgments invariably involve my relations with others. As an inherently social being, most of the moral demands I find myself placing upon myself manifest my social membership. And this carries with it an added responsibility not only for my own moral integrity, but also for the impact of my decision(s) upon others. My decisions rarely are mine alone; they are usually decisions that bind others.

Such decisional acts, let us remember, are always decisions about the future, about what in the moment of decision is-not-yet but is judged to be within the realm of what-may-be. Because any decision of mine shapes a future situation that will involve others as well as myself, the morality of my decision requires some sense of prudential reason, intelligent evaluation of possibilities, and foresight into what may come out of what I prepare to do. Moral reason thus includes a responsibility for my use of intelligence in assessing the possible outcomes of my action and the new decisional situations it will create; responsible use of my moral conscience in deciding among the limited options before me requires exercise of my ability to reason.

iv. b. Freedom and Reason

Does the ability to reason, to use intelligence, involve any notion of freedom? Traditionally, freedom was largely relegated to the sphere of moral judgment while the quest for knowledge above freedom, as above individual idiosyncrasy, was elevated to a passive acknowledgement of presumably independent facts. The cognitive role was portrayed as that of a spectator, a mere onlooker whose cognitions are to have no bearing on what the facts themselves might be. Like a casual museum visitor whose judgment of a painting does not affect the painting, one's attainment of knowledge was judged irrelevant to that at which one was gazing.

Whatever else may be said about Descartes' mechanistic view of nature and the spectator notion of knowledge with which he worked, he had indeed exempted human thinking from the mechanically causal explanations that were to be used in understanding nature. Indeed, his entire explanation of scientific objectivity presumes that human thinking is free, that it is able to sort out and evaluate evidence and to judge for itself when adequate evidence for a given hypothesis has been found. This presumption implies that human cognition is an active process, the outcome of which depends upon the intellectual effort and volitional discipline of the investigator.[24] Scientific understanding of nature depends upon the kinds of questions the investigator pursues (in Descartes' view, those that are mathematically constituted and dependent upon efficacious causal relations), *and* doing so presumes the efficacy of free will — the will to withhold judgment until reason confirms that all the relevant factual information is in. Only then, on his account, can one rightfully decide to conclude an investigation and proceed to a decision of cognitive judgment.

The systematic use of reason depends on the disciplined use of freedom to direct any rational inquiry, to make interpretive decisions concerning the relevance of the data uncovered, to determine how this body of information is to be correlated by means of the interpretive categories employed. Our growing body of scientific knowledge and the continuing refinements of their interpretive reports exhibit the discipline of freedom in the use of systematic intelligence or reason.

The morality of knowledge, as of morality itself, requires the free use of reason.[25] The function of reason is to seek out goals for our actions, including the activity of dispassionate investigation; to impose principles by which to evaluate alternatives; and to commit the reasoner to an expeditious manner of deciding among those alternatives. Reason and will, like two horses in tandem, can only function as they depend upon their mutual cooperation. Rational activity is willful purposive behavior and depends upon a disciplined freedom which selects questions to explore, seeks out specific answers to its specific questions, and commits itself to pursue rational procedures in order to attain what its foresight suggests.

The scientist in his laboratory, as the ordinary person in the area of his immediate concerns, faces one question: What should I do? That 'should' points to the future, to what is yet undone but available to prudential human reason. What should I do in order to verify this hypothesis, find the cause(s) for this phenomenon, discover a way to produce this effect? Each activity is guided by a concern for a future result; each retrieves what seems pertinent out of past experience; each evaluates what seem to be genuine possibilities; and each resolves upon a course of action which — however trivial or profound — is only explicable by the foresight which animates its undertaking.

The experiential use of reason is not the mere working out of a preordained deductive chain of correct inferences. Any computer, properly programmed in the light of human purposes, could do that. The experiential use of reason exemplifies the continuing necessity to interpret, by chosen standards and criteria, the meaning of information — in terms of an end result that is judged as the validation of what will then have been done. The actual use of reason in any act of living means reaching out beyond the present to the may-be that can, by a personal decision, be transformed into the will-be; it exhibits our ability to reach beyond what is given to what is rationally anticipated and to bring that anticipation into the present situation as the spur to interpretive decision and action.[26]

The experiential use of reason, as inherently interpretive and decisional, manifests the use of freedom. It is an activity that is not itself a free option — because we have no option except to interpret what the present field appears to offer and to decide about the developmental options available. It is an activity that must necessarily be pursued whether that pursuit, that necessary invocation of judgmental freedom, is done in a way that might be considered shortsighted, grudging, or marked by the careful employment of rational intelligence.

On either an individual or social level, the temporality of freedom represents selective decision about what is not-to-be. As Aron observed, we "cannot choose to achieve one task without giving up others....In this sense, all existence is choice, and choice requires more noes than yesses."[27] Necessarily, as James once suggested, 'we include in only by excluding out'. Temporally framed decisions are exclusionary: they essentially determine what shall not be while narrowing the focus to what shall be.

The freedom incarnate in reason becomes most decisive when it does not merely content itself with choosing from what appears as a set 'menu' for the future; at its fullest, it imaginatively projects itself ahead of itself into an act of deliberate creativity in which fuller dimensions of the can-be are discovered in the process of bringing it to pass. The creative use of freedom reveals the outreach of an imaginative understanding that projects itself into the future and brings a vision of what-can-be back into the structure of the living present. This projection forward of the imaginative intellect takes us beyond present knowledge and known frontiers; it brings the sense of adventure into intellectual activity. It permits us to open up new ground while wrenching out from the past, which we always carry with us, new meanings that serve as an enervating and sustaining resource.

This kind of imaginative projection produces the 'breakthroughs' in the sciences, industry, and in the arts, as well as in the moral art and moral practice of human organization. Often labelled 'intuitions', 'intuitive insights', or 'intimations', imaginative foresight leaps beyond the bounds of the familiar; through the courage of committed freedom, it reaches forward into the unknown. Those who most notably exercise it are those whom we anoint with the title of 'genius'. But imaginative foresight is exhibited in every act of inventiveness, every experiment with a new form, every creative act — be it in one of the recognized arts or in the moral art of creatively responding to the needs of others. It is exercised by those who create the institutions we use and also by those who rescue them and us from their proclivity to swallow us up.

This kind of creative advance, this projection of foresight into the possibilities which the future is seen as holding forth, most often comes from some sense of dissatisfaction with the surrounding present, some kind of alienation from the common mold. This alienation might well reflect some state of 'oppression or repression'; more often, in a society that regards itself as free, it is "a more nuanced estrangement seen as a road to self-discovery."[28]

Creative alienation often manifests itself in youthful cynicism, in questioning the ultimacy of the present state of affairs, in heretical forays, and critical evaluations. Critical questioning, when seeking to improve the present context, saves us from stagnating in the institutionalism of acquired habit and inherited custom; when creatively assimilated, such constructive criticism helps us to use institutions and customs as a buttress for a new advance. The continual challenging of the finality of any specific temporal arrangement is itself "the source of the historical movement"[29] of human society. These challenges are themselves challenged and thereby refined; when taken up into the continuity of temporal development they tie the past into a stream of ongoing orderly change.

Hopefully, youthful cynicism will mature into a creative adaptation of the heritage of the past to the new possibilities beginning to be seen; criticism will not be content to carp, but will look ahead to ways in which specific grievances can be ameliorated without creating new problems that will dwarf those being corrected. Hopefully, those who proclaim and advocate new proposals will acknowledge that their ability to do so ensues from their protected freedom to dissent from accepted views. And hopefully, whatever the proposals may be, their advocates will be careful to see that they contain within themselves a continued protection for the freedom of those who might disagree or find the new reform to be, not the final word, but merely another stage on life's way. Hopefully, the society will be responsive to the criticisms offered, the grievances protested, the deficiencies that creative alienations voice.

The possibility for creative visions of genius, for criticisms to be tempered and be constructively assimilated, for the continual re-formation of the present without upheaval, requires a high degree of social protection for dissent, for the expression of unpopular views and creative alienation. But this protection needs to be contained as the enabling condition of free criticism: those who disagree with strident critics or advocates of reform are equally enabled to voice their views and participate in public debate.

An individual's thinking is his interpretation of the information to which he has access. This freedom to interpret what I see about me depends not only upon the protection of my socially given 'right' to do so, it also depends upon the spread of information that I may find available to me. The protected freedom to think for myself and to express the conclusions of my thinking depends upon the access that my society permits to information for my inspection, upon my access to the thinking of others, and my ability to engage in discussion with others.[30]

Indeed, this is really the prime argument for freedom of speech and expression. Most of us do not speak through the media, take part in political debates, and generally proclaim our various views far and wide. But the protection of the right to do so makes it possible *for us* to be exposed to the various sides of current controversies and come to terms with the issues of our time. Free exposure to the thinking of others is necessary for our own. This is no mere indulgence of individuals comprising a society. The experience of freedom is educative: the more informed a citizenry is, the more sophisticated can be its level of thought. Citizens encouraged to independent thought are enabled to be more creative in their own distinctive specialties and thus to make greater contributions to the common good of the whole. Consequently,

the widest possible freedom of thought has a doubly pragmatic outcome quite aside from any presumed public 'right' to resolve political
debates: it benefits the individual as a person and also the economic or
professional areas in which he serves, thereby raising the level of these
activities for the society as a whole.

As a rationally moral being, each of us exercises a freedom of
thought and decision in every step along the way. When responding to
the question 'what should I do in this situation *in which* I find myself?'
each of us responds to demands of the future by an evaluative judgment that each must be enabled to make. However we may seek to
explain this on a speculative level, we each find ourselves continually
compelled to make decisions which we are not only able to make but
find ourselves actually making.

iv. c. The Temporality of Freedom

My intelligent use of my freedom is tested by the intelligent use
of my time. Whether my freedom be used in thought or action, for
moral, esthetic, or cognitive purposes, its exercise obviously involves
the use of time. How fruitfully I use my time depends on how I assim-
ilate my past into the present, how I delineate the future in terms of
the possibilities it appears to promise.

Whatever time itself may prove to be, it does not appear in our
temporal perspective as an evenly paced straight line, each 'moment'
of which is like any other. And time does not appear to us as resolutely
marching from past to future. Our pasts may have yielded us as we are
and we generally explain ourselves, to ourselves or to others, in terms
of past experiences. But somehow we do not seem to be wafted along
on a smoothly flowing stream. We always seem to be facing the future
coming at us rather than just being pushed along by the past.

So 'past' and 'future' appear to us as very different in kind. The
past is a vast reservoir of experience and knowledge on which, if we
are wise, we readily draw. But the past is over and done with and cannot be done again. In itself it is unchangeable and must be accepted as
solid fact; for that reason it can be known and that knowledge can be
used — for similar, never identical — new situations. But these situations open us into the unknown, onto a future that appears as mal-
leable, indeterminate, undecided; still to be wrought, it suggests possibilities not yet reduced to fact. We proceed into the future by *creating*
it in accord with our guesses and anticipations, but as we build it we

can never be confident about what will emerge from our efforts. The past is reduced to fact beyond repair, although we may, in the future discover new aspects of it; the future is yet to be created and yet to be reduced to fact — it blooms before us as literally unknown and unknowable as we plow our way into making it.

Although we cannot change the past we are continually changing our interpretations of it. And we generally do so in the light of problems we discern in present situations concerning their, as yet, unresolved outcomes. The American Civil War, while it was being fought, was interpreted as a struggle to save the Federal Union; we generally take its meaning for us today, some hundred and twenty-five years later, as having irrevocably foreclosed the possibility of chattel-slavery from the future of the American dream. Present meanings of past events are taken anew by each generation in terms of its own problems and prospects.

However enhanced our freedoms may be, these freedoms are concerned not to change the past, but to take it up anew in facing the future which we are presently forging. Any free act, of cognitive or moral reason, of impulse or desire, is a commitment to project oneself forward into what is not-yet but decided upon as what should-be.

If all free activity is inherently social, it draws upon a heritage while thrusting ahead with others. The common social freedoms, within which each seeks to find his own, is the 'social temporality' that members of a community share together. As individuals and as society members, a foreward-looking freedom is the only freedom we may have, a 'freedom for the future'.

v. Liberty and Freedom

After all that has been said about the pervasiveness of freedom in human experience, we still face an ambiguity of meaning as two rather different concepts are wrapt into colloquial use. The English language fortunately provides two distinct ways of expressing the kinds of experience each sets out.[31] Using them interchangeably, as we often do, no longer makes political sense. For the concepts of 'liberty' and 'freedom' — though often used synonymously — have taken on two somewhat different meanings which are important to distinguish.

The cry of liberty came in political terms; it arose as a protest against despotism, against arbitrary restrictions, confiscations, prohibitions, and compulsions. Serfs and slaves and merchants were to be liberated from arbitrary decrees; the chains were to be removed. This 'negative liberty' was for many a historical first step of emancipation, a "liberty *from*" arbitrariness and oppression.[32] To make sure that the chains were not to be replaced, the immediate focus was on political and legal questions of "how much authority should be placed in any set of [governmental] hands."[33] But what was left open was the question, not of what one is no longer forbidden to do, but what is one enabled, if not encouraged, to do.

Whatever else may be encompassed in the word 'liberty', Locke was already clear that it does not mean "license"; it does not authorize anyone "to harm another in his life, health, liberty, or possessions."[34] Understood as that absence of restraints permitting one 'to do what one wishes' as long as one does not interfere with the like liberty of others, was essentially the position advocated by the nineteenth-century libertarian, John Stuart Mill:

> ... the sole end for which mankind are warranted, individually or collectively, in interfering with the liberty of action of any of their number is *self-protection* ... to prevent harm to others.[35]

Just what "harm," except in a narrowly physical sense, covers — such as deprivation of opportunity? — is not made clear. By restructuring my wants, I restrict the area in which I can be 'harmed'. In any event, as Berlin saw, when left at that, this "will not do. If I find that I am able to do little or nothing of what I wish, I need only contract or extinguish my wishes, and I am made free."[36] Essentially, this 'negative liberty' is but a Stoic's sense of freedom — even a slave protected by law against physical harm could accept it: restrict my wishes to what my society or government permits and, within those self-imposed limits, I shall be happily free. This quickly becomes a very private kind of condition, without mandating the possibility of a public face.

But, as society members, we live publicly as well as privately. We want chains removed so that we able *to do*, to elect new possibilities, to augment future experience. The concern with freedom, in a non-servile society, is not so much with what is not permitted, but with opportunities now opened, allowed, and publicly encouraged. Liberating chattel slaves, who were forbidden to read, did not in itself change their illiterate condition until teachers and books made it possible for them to learn to read, thus opening them to new opportunities. The crucial point for society members is what they are socially enabled to do just because such authorized individual activities are conceived as being in the societal interest.

When we speak of freedom today, Green pointed out,

> We do not mean merely freedom from restraint or compulsion. We do not mean merely freedom to do as we like irrespectively of what it is that we like. We do not mean a freedom that can be enjoyed by one man or one set of men at the cost of a loss of freedom to others. When we speak of freedom as something to be so highly prized, we mean a positive power or capacity of doing or enjoying something worth doing or enjoying, and that, too, something that we do or enjoy in common with others. We mean by it a power which each man exercises through the help or security given him by his fellow-men, and which he in turn helps to secure for them.[37]

My interest in freedom is, indeed, concerned not so much with an absence of restraints as with the opportunities, the 'positive freedoms' for action, I see myself as being socially offered: the social authorizations to undertake specific kinds of acts. My concern for freedom is inherently social; it almost always is phrased in terms of what 'we' are able to do; and it is pervasively temporal: it concerns itself with what can be yet done with oncoming time.

Depending upon the specific social context, the necessary first step to freedom, as the power to do, may often have been the negation of prohibitions — liberty as the removal of constraints or compulsions. But, as Ricoeur noted, "someone who remains at the level of negation remains in the adolescence of freedom. The passage to maturity is the passage to affirmation."[38] One's 'positive freedoms' define the kinds of actions allowed, permitted, encouraged, promoted, protected. They are found in the social milieu which allows one to act "in accordance with a plan of projected behavior."[39] Positive freedoms are found in a quality of life which permits one to plan ahead, to guide a life, to project oneself into the possibilities one seeks; they are just "this power to act with consistency, to bring about a lasting change, a new course of [personal] existence."[40]

Freedom, as the positive quality of social life, is found in those social conditions which enable, authorize, and encourage societal members not only to make separate decisions along the way; more crucially, it enables them to direct their own lives qualitatively vitalized by the ability to plan ahead, as intrinsic to the life one leads, as a 'natural' matter of course. As such it looks beyond arbitrary choices to the temporal continuity of 'being free'.[41]

No philosophic concept arises in an intellectual vacuum. The notion of 'negative liberty' emerged as a conceptual instrument against despotism. The notion of 'positive freedom', was brought into the English-speaking world by Thomas Hill Green (who derived it from Kant), when the new laissez faire system, along with its positive outcome, was seen as having brought about an anarchic state of affairs and a new kind of oppression. The concept of 'positive freedom' was to guide a broad program of social reform, the ingredients of which are today taken for granted in every free industrial nation.

The concept of 'positive freedom' spells out the social authorizations and opportunities whose exercise is to be protected by the force of the organized community for its members. Especially concerned to protect the use of time for each that each is not equipped to protect for himself, it sets out parameters within which individual initiatives are to be enabled and encouraged by the strength of the organized polity. The force of Green's concept of 'positive freedom', as we will see in the next chapter, was to transform mere 'membership' into the notion of full 'citizenship' for each societal member.[42]

Liberty is not license to do as one wishes regardless of its impact on others; a lack of prohibitions needs to be specified. Each denial of prohibition leads to new permitted actions, not all of which may be socially welcome. Neither can be justly handled in abstraction; a responsible society, for its own self-protection and the protection of its citizens, must demand that they both be finitized and specified. An organized society, no matter how free, necessarily proclaims what may not be done (generally enumerated in a criminal code); it enunciates coercive commands as to what must be done (such as, for example, paying taxes); it guarantees societal protection for certain kinds of permitted activities, (generally enumerated in a 'bill of rights'); and it facilitates, by specified procedures and legal protections, certain kinds of activities (such as pursuit of education or commercial transactions). Just as restraints and coercions need to be specified, so must specific liberties be proclaimed.

Even so, the particular positive freedoms a society commits itself to develop, enhance, or defend need specification: (i) some of these inhere in the historic ethos of the society, are borne by the traditions and customs of the culture, and are presumed as 'natural' by its members; (ii) some evolve from older traditions as new situations are faced and new conditions develop or are forced by social confrontations; they may either emerge as modifications of older customs or by reinterpretation of older laws; (iii) some will be enacted by legislative action to correct perceived injustices, to protect individuals without the power to protect themselves, or, in response to new social wealth, to deliberately open new opportunities for the members of the society to pursue as they wish.[43]

However these positive freedoms, or protected social opportunities, come into being, they are soon acclaimed by individual citizens as their 'rights'. It is often a mystery as to how some newly discovered rights derive their authority. If they were truly 'innate' or 'inherent' one can only wonder why they are so newly discovered. If, however, we see 'rights' as the specific 'positive freedoms' with which a society endows its members as citizens, whether by custom or by law, then rights become socially recognized justifiable claims upon the protection of governmental authority for expending personal time on the kinds of activities they authorize.

These claims, as they come into the area of general acceptance, should not be seen as arbitrary. Arising out of the historical development of the society itself they will, as generally accepted, be seen by succeeding generations not as arbitrary impositions, but as 'natural'. Newly recognized but generally acknowledged claims soon come to be recognized as rooted in societal history, as emerging from past development in order to meet new challenges and opportunities as the society continually faces its own oncoming future. The essential function of evolving positive freedoms, as the specific rights a society prescribes for its citizens, is not to provoke conflicts but to harmonize developmental differences — in recognition that the common good must include all within its scope.

A society, then, effectively *pre*scribes 'rights', 'positive freedoms', or justifiable claims for protection of specific kinds of activities, for its members. An organized society may be described in terms of the specific privileges and obligations it prescribes for its membership, the prescriptive rights and duties with which its members endow themselves. These positive freedoms or prescriptive rights are, be it noted, future oriented; they open up an area of futurity for exploration and development by individual members who may wish to do so, in the belief that such individual activity contributes to the common good of all. Their protection, as they become generally accepted, is taken by the community as its obligation. Whether 'written out' by legislation or by changing custom they are socially commended 'as henceforth'. The specific positive freedoms or prescriptive rights that characterize the members of a particular society are their specified authorizations to plan on a future opening before them; these positive freedoms or specified rights open up the vistas, as protected opportunities, their members, as a socially constituted body, authorize or encourage each other to pursue.

Beyond this specificity, the concept of positive freedom illuminates the temporal dimension of human life. Freedom is the freedom to be human and to be human is to be free. Specific freedoms are socially granted opportunities to be self-directive so far as societal procedures permit. In a free society, social policy options are directed, by general consent, by the criterion of the enhancement of freedom.

The concept of 'freedom' was first manifested in voluntary activities. The notion of 'liberty' added prohibitions against social interferences with specified voluntary activities. As society develops, it affords its members increasing opportunities for individual activities that depend for their exercise upon the framework provided by social institutions. As specified positive freedoms constitute a widening range of socially grounded opportunities, the society enriches itself by a general state of freedom which, perhaps paradoxically, renders it increasingly dependent on the widening range of *voluntary* activities afforded to its members. The evolution just traced from the classical notion of 'voluntary' to the contemporary principle of 'positive freedom' is not then one of supercedence but of developmental enrichment.

The state of 'being free' is the enabling condition for voluntary activities to be undertaken. A free society is one in which most activities are deemed, within the necessary constraints of being-together, essentially voluntary — as being given life by the particular temporal decisions of free citizens. The meaning of a free society is that it is one in which citizens are authorized and expected to live their lives as 'being free'. And 'being free' means being able to live with an open future that beckons each one on into new possibilities.

vi. The Import of Procedure

As social beings who live in organized society, our living activities invariably involve activities with others. At virtually every level of life, we are involved in and presume a multitude of communities. This notion of 'community' needs to be clarified.

Any community, Royce pointed out, is not a random collection of individuals at a particular time or place: each is a 'community of interpretation'. What binds individuals into a specific community, whether of deep commitment, joyful camaraderie, or tacit identification with the current social order, is a shared way of evaluating aspects of their common experience. Those who belong to a particular community of interest and concern, share a general outlook, a set of aspirations that draw them together, and a way of assimilating a commonly perceived past that cements the temporal bond between them.

We each participate in a number of such interpretational communities, organized and functioning on many levels. The most apparent is the political community to which we will, in the next chapters, direct prime attention.[44] Organized interpretational communities may be political, economic, or social. They may be organized in a formal fashion or may be informally gathered around social interests. But every identifiable grouping within a society manifests itself as one — and every individual belongs to several. Fellow workers or colleagues comprise one. So do those who share a church, golf club, political-action group, or any other voluntary organization. One's companions, 'drinking buddies', family, special individual friendships — any association in which one manifests some special common concerns, conversational areas, and references; shared ideas, memories, and aspirations. Within each particular circle, one finds oneself discoursing somewhat differently, presuming certain kinds of experiences, sharing particular concerns, hopes and fears, and expectations.

Each interpretive community provides a means to express some aspect of the person one takes oneself to be. Each of these communities imposes its own limits of common concern upon its members and opens up specified areas of mutual exchange. Each such community has its own 'being', not as something separate from its members but as a particular kind of 'togetherness', built by the way in which they together value a particular usage of their time. Within such groupings each participant experiences a recognition of some particular aspect of his own person, certain freedoms to express oneself as well as certain limitations on what may be anticipated or even talked about together.

My personal experience of my freedom to control aspects of my future is bound within these varied interpretational communities with which, in their totality, I somehow identify the person I am. For I am just this center of experience, reaching out in multitudinous relationships — each concerned with some aspect of temporal concern and the freedom to exercise that concern within its chosen area.

Because any community is a time-process, concerned with *doing* something together, the bond of common interest that holds the group together includes a process, informal as it may be, for making particular decisions along the way. A certain 'way of doing things', a certain procedure, prevails in each of these communities. Each functions by a tacitly enunciated set of rules, a usually unspoken set of limits to acceptable behavior, and a narrower area in which 'anything goes'. What almost always is more important to the integrity of the group than any specific decision it makes is *the way* it makes it. Regardless of what particular decisions its members might make together — whether by communal consensus, majority decision, or hierarchical directive — the unity of the group depends upon a working agreement on *how* to *proceed*. When that procedure is fractured, the integrity of the group faces a crisis of its own continuity: feelings are ruffled and need be soothed; tempers must be reconciled. A group 'hangs together' in fidelity to its stated or implicitly accepted *prescriptive ways* of handling its problems far more than to any specific resolution of them.

The primary bond holding a particular group together is its center of a common concern and a shared evaluative outlook concerning it. That shared interpretive outlook includes as the core of its elements, as the cement that binds its members together, its own implicitly understood way to make whatever decisions it is joined to make. When these ways are flouted, members feel betrayed. An interpretive community holds together primarily by the ways it proceeds to resolve disagreements within its common bond while accommodating those who disagree.

One usually comes to acquiesce in decisions with which one disagrees. But only anger or alienation ensues when one feels that either the proper procedures for decision have been violated (including its understanding of how to handle emergency situations) or that the decision goes beyond the legitimate bounds of the common concern. Within the group each member finds a certain area for free self-expression and development; this group-centered freedom is regarded as betrayed when the specific opportunities for social activity which the group affords are seen as violated by the errant way in which the group behaves. What binds a group together is a twofold commitment: to face the future together in terms of its unifying concerns *and also* to an acceptable procedure to decide how to do so. The import of procedure is precisely that it defines the freedom of its members, individually within it and together in future-referring prescriptive terms.

vii. Freedom as Constitutionalism

Every 'community of interpretation' in which I participate explicates some facet of my life and provides opportunities which I could not otherwise enjoy. My positive freedoms become concrete and specific largely in and by means of my participation in my own particularized network of the overlapping communities constituting my society. In them, I find the continuity of my living as a free person.

As with each subcommunity within a comprehensively organized society, no society is merely a collection of disparate individuals. It is an overarching organization of its members which, as Plato had already suggested, serves as the cultural parent of each of its children. The time of each is largely engaged in, or at least is nominally loyal to, particular groups of citizens within it. Each of these groups — described by de Tocqueville as 'intermediate societies' — brings into the common whole its own perspective on free opportunities for its temporally defined concerns. The common whole integrates those concerns into a procedure for acknowledging and resolving conflicts between them within it.

These procedural understandings comprise its functioning constitutional arrangement, specifying which areas of decision it reserves to its governors and which it disperses among its citizens. An organized society may then be described in terms of its decisional procedures: who has the state-protected authority to decide what? As in any group, so in the larger organized society, the process for decision making is, in the social logic of the case, prior to the particular policies decided upon.

When a society is organized as a 'command' society, vesting all decision-making authority in its own hierarchical structure, it 'feeds down from the top'. It reserves the 'right' of free interpretive decisions within announced limits to the subordinate officials of its own hierarchy. A society that engages the free interpretative decisions of its citizens disperses decision-making authority, within whatever limits it conceives as necessary for its common good.

A free society encourages the free interpretive 'input' of its members, in accord with the decision-making procedures it has prescribed. These prescriptive procedures, whether embodied in tradition, custom, a written document, or their dynamic synthesis, comprise its mode of social harmony, its governing constitution: the procedures to be followed in determining regulations and statutes, the limited decisional authorities to be institutionalized, and the ways in which they shall be selected. Regulations and statutory laws are rules which specify *pre*scriptions for the future. A constitutional state is founded upon an agreed-upon set of procedures for resolving future debates concerning them. It prescribes, or sets out *in advance* of any particular decision, the rules by which that decision shall be made, the rules governing those who are charged to make them, and the specified freedoms or opportunities for citizens to 'input' those decisions — by choosing and charging their chosen officials.

A constitutional order is one in which the social agreement that binds the society together is on procedures for making policy rather than policies themselves. Policy decisions, generally enunciated in specific laws and regulations, focus on 'outcome' of decision, rather than the procedure by which the decision is to be made. Procedural, or constitutional, agreements may indeed incorporate policy questions, but they focus not on any particular 'outcome', not on any specific set of regulations, but on the procedure by which policies are to be determined and the limited parameters within which decisions may be made.

A society based on mutually given free consent sustains itself not by its policy agreements but by its agreements as to how to reach them. The freedom to debate, to choose officials, to define their limited authority, to change decisions and choices — these are decisional procedures which embody the agreement on 'how to proceed'. This 'how to proceed' is an agreement on *how* to face the future together, the procedures by which to do it. An organized free society is a society that has agreed upon *the ways* in which it will, as a common community, enlist its membership, face its future possibilities, decide which ones to adopt and which to avoid, in terms of evaluative norms that bind it together — upon a procedure to resolve internal differences which will emerge as specific problematic situations arise. Should this procedure be violated, a crisis of the community — historically, in the American case, a civil war — threatens its future.[45]

In facing this common open future that is literally unknown, a free or constitutional society places a premium on its procedure for resolving policy disputes. And if it is authentically loyal to its own principle of being, it sets one absolute bar to any conceivable policy decision: part of the 'outcome' *must be* the continuing vitality of the procedure that enabled the policy to emerge.

A free society places a premium on keeping its freedoms open — freedom to disagree, to agree, to handle varying interpretations of factual situations, to judge policies enacted and policies yet to be advanced — for further interpretive refinement, and judgment and decision. Its critical limit on any policy resolution must then be that it not abort the free discussional procedure that brought it forth. Any policy proposal that threatens an 'outcome' subversive of the free procedure that produced it is to be viewed with suspicion. Within a constitutional state, the 'outcome' is rightfully denied in advance to any policy that would foreclose the continuity of the free procedures that animate it. The acceptable 'outcome' of any decisional conflict — if it is to accord with the continuity of a free constitutional order — can only be such as does not foreclose the future continuity of the open decisional procedure itself.

In a free society, all decisions come out of a free debate within the procedures enunciated for resolution of differences. Its first priority is not any specific policy decision but the henceforth-freedom to change its mind. A free society is predicated upon the proposition that no decision is final, that the future must somehow be kept open, even if within situational limits. Its freedom is freedom for its future; the assurance of its members that this principle of social union is being maintained is that its procedures for doing so are faithfully observed. That continued openness to the contingencies of the future must be defended as prior in importance to any specific decision it may resolve to take.

viii. The Centrality of Freedom

Everyone wants coercions on one's own actions to be constrained, the exercise of voluntary activity to be socially protected, and the widened areas of its exercise to be sustained by the social order. Everyone claims to want liberty and freedom, even when the meanings are vague and specifications are disputed. Why, we have asked, is this cry for freedom so universal? Why does this notion so often encapsulate our protests and aspirations?

The reason may well be this: the whole notion of self-identity is largely woven into our consciousness of making evaluational and decisional judgments. To be able to express and act upon likes, preferences, chosen obligations, and desires, to be able to determine the activities to which we devote our time, to be able to face and decide the either/or's of temporal existence, and the temporal price for alternatives that must be faced — in such power over our own selves and our own time, the hardly enunciated but nevertheless presupposed notion of temporal freedom is intimately identified with our activity of seeking and trying, beyond any present grievance. This yearning to be masters of our own time may well be why we 'wrap up' our remonstrances and ambitions, against the experienced frustrations and unpleasant requirements of any current condition, by demanding that in which the identity of the self is to be found. The cry "freedom now," is no call for any particular new 'right', nor for complete licentiousness; it voices thirst of each for the power over oneself to become what one feels one can yet be, the positive opportunity to develop potentials for the future that are perceived as being held back. In the cry "freedom now," each seeks the opportunity to realize one's 'real me', the potentials regarded as 'mine'; what is demanded is the social offering of possibilities to be developed so that each may become the person he inwardly seeks to be. What one really asks for is no specific 'thing'; what is asked for is what someone once named as 'the freedom to be free'.

Freedom is basic and generally valued beyond any particular content — because it is one's own opening into the future — to be defined by each for oneself in largely personal ways. Whatever other values are cherished, they are cherished as a means to this kind of personal freedom in which the idea of happiness is generally rooted. Hobbes, for example, seems to have placed the desire for civil peace above all. But why do people desire the stability of peace except to be able to live out their lives as free beings who can spend their time on those kinds of activities they value? Peace, stability, sovereignty, property, equality, prosperity — each has at some time been proclaimed as *the* supreme social-individual need. The basic justification offered for each is generally similar, if only rarely voiced: each is demanded *in time* as a prerequisite to enable each person's varied value-loyalties incorporated in his aspirations to flourish.

My freedom to be myself, to be able to pursue happiness in my own peculiar way, is that ultimate good for the sake of which other social goods are regarded as necessary instruments. The freedom for which one clamors is the freedom, the opportunity, to be oneself — not as fulfilled fact but as a nest of possibilities for temporal development which thrusts one on. Freedom *is* foundational, just because it opens possibilities for the future and the commitments that flow from them. Through the enhancement of individual freedom we find ourselves as self-directive persons in our world with others. What we really desire is not this particular freedom or that one, but the 'freedom to be free', to be the authors of our own biographies.

ix. The Three Principles

Three foundational principles characterize our lives as socially grounded individuals in any organized polity. Each of these principles emerges from considering the nature of lived experience rather than from any theoretical derivation. These three principles are not truly independent; in any one individual, as in any polity, they are only to be found functioning together.

A society is a membership organization into which we are born and in which we remain, or into which we immigrate and thus choose to join; when membership is itself a voluntarily accepted bond, it is a free society even if the voluntary nature of the social bond is thrust upon us as something to be tacitly accepted if not overtly rejected by deciding to remain rather than to leave; a free society functions by the principle that members are citizens who are to participate by their voluntary activity in developing the common good their society seeks to develop.

A society, as the lives of the individuals who constitute its membership, is temporally organized by acknowledging a past while creating a future; when, under the authority of officials selected under public procedures for open debate and evaluative discussion by its citizenry, it disperses the power of decision among its members, it is a free society; a free society functions by the principle of limited governmental authority aimed at opening up the temporality of its citizens who are encouraged to structure it for themselves.

A society delineates areas for governmental directives and individual decisions; when a society seeks to maximize the dependence of its general welfare on the coalescence of voluntarily active decisions of its members, it is a free society; a free society, to the greatest extent possible, entrusts the way in which its members are to spend their time earning a livelihood and enjoying their leisure to the decisions of its citizens.

On one level or another, all organized societies exhibit these three principles of social life.[46] Of the three, the principle of freedom undergirds the other two — even in the most tyrannical societies, by virtue of how it is distributed — because it denotes the sources of public authority. Its generalization distinguishes those societies composed of free citizens from those which are not. Freedom is the ground out of which our social individualities and our individual temporalities emerge as a multitude of unique contributions to the common good. When generally distributed among the citizenry, it undergirds the other two because the way societal membership and temporality function depends upon how freedom is dispersed and shared. Without integrating membership and temporality, freedom would remain an abstraction.[47]

If free members are to function together as a social whole that binds its members together, a concept of freedom must be pervasive. This freedom, this capacity to be included into organization with others who harmonize their temporalities, recognizes the common past out of which we are emerging while we are building a future which we are to share; this mutuality of freedom, socially organized and temporally structured, is what enables humans to be human.

For this primordial human capacity for freedom to be realized, these three principles need to be taken as integral to each other. Only as they function together does their full potential open up. Distinguished in focus while functioning together, they need to be translated into, and reexamined in terms of, the temporally prescriptive dynamic of a free polity.

Part II

The Dynamic of a Free Polity

Three principles structure our relations with each other in an organized society. Each of these three principles itself developed in the historical dynamic of implementation. Each sets out a particular focus to
be pursued in developing the norms of a free society, even while continually incorporating reference to the other two. Taken separately
and together they provide criteria by which a free society may measure its own allegiance to its members who share its ongoing history:

1. Each person finds himself as a member of a social order that
nurtures the individualities it brings forth. A free society considers
itself bound to transform the principle of societal membership into
that of citizenship, affording to each member the power to seek one's
own good as a fully recognized participant in the good of the whole.

2. Each citizen lives out a temporally structured biographical
experience within a politically organized society. Insofar as its overarching organization, the political structure, defines the parameters
within which the free temporality of its citizens may be exercised, the
central concern of a free people is for a mode of governance that max-
imizes the temporal possibilities of free decision for its citizens. A free
society develops a governmental system sufficiently empowered to
maintain the stability required for the exercise of freedom without suffocating the freedom it is designed to enhance — so that it can transform the historic heritage of the whole into the open temporality each
citizen is encouraged to employ.

3. Free citizens generally devote socially allowed time to private
concerns. First among these is the task of earning a livelihood and the

consequent enjoyment of the leisure time it provides. For a free society, the principle of freedom necessarily requires the socially protected opportunity for each to seek his livelihood in the most personally efficacious way and to enjoy the leisure it is able to support, so that these individual efforts contribute to the greater good of the whole.

If we are to bring these three theses together, we may conclude that the common good is developed by maximizing the freedom of citizens to seek their own good insofar as doing so does not conflict with, but contributes to, the mutual advantage. A free society identifies its common good with the possibilities of the future for its citizenry; it defines its common good as the shared freedom to build the future, a good which each of us as a member of a free citizenry is encouraged to develop as our own.

This deliberate openness to an ordered freedom for the future marks a free society. It provides the standard of what is right or wrong, permissible, encouraged, or forbidden, and the standard of justice. This openness, developed on every level of social activity, depends for its continuance upon the rules, procedures, and modes of organization animating it. Such rules Aristotle had already termed "legislative enactments," which spell out procedures to be followed by all so that internal conflicts can be harmonized. Dependent on the "legislative art," the common good depends upon faithful adherence to the principle that ". . . enactments on all subjects aim at the common advantage . . ." and thereby define the principles of justice as the acknowledged social virtue guiding the ways in which one may relate to one's neighbors (1129b–1130a).

The "legislative art" prescribes the authorized procedures of a free society, in both generally constitutional terms and by specific statutes. It thus provides ways to resolve its decisional conflicts and to integrate each as a citizen into the society's good — so as to ensure that the individual freedoms of each feed into, and are nourished by, the common good of the society.

Chapter 4

Citizenship

All individuals are members of some society. Members of a free society have the dignity of full membership or citizenship. By the strength of the whole they are enabled, and often encouraged, to seek out the full measure of 'belonging' by actively utilizing the rights, privileges, and obligations with which a free society vests its members.

When, in contemporary debates, we seek to encompass the protections and privileges due each citizen by virtue of 'belonging', two issues usually arise. One concerns the nature and extent of equality, a notion that has often been paired with freedom even though they are in many ways in mutual conflict and "among democratic nations two unequal things."[1] The second is the way in which 'rights' and 'obligations', justifiable claims for social protection of particular kinds of activities, may be specified — for this specification defines the ways in which members are integrated as citizens.

Freedom and equality, rights and obligations, are central to the nature of a free polity, yet each is more complex than popular slogans suggest. Equality and freedom when left unmoderated, are inherently in conflict. Somehow they must be harmonized — for each, when enjoyed without limitation, not only becomes self-destructive but also destroys the other.

Yet each is somehow crucial to what may be meant by a 'free citizenry'. And each requires not only societal recognition of justifiable claims by individual citizens upon the social whole, but also their recognition of the rights and obligations of the polis or organized society itself. The meaning of citizenship depends upon the clarification of these notions.

i. Freedom and Equality

The notions of freedom and equality have somehow traveled together since the Athenian experience. Conceptually they are antithetical and in concrete practice often adversaries; their balance yet remains central to any theory of popular government. If they are both to prove meaningful, their conjunction requires careful moderation so that they can prosper together.

The conflict between freedom and equality is at the root of the disarray in contemporary liberalism. While confidently proclaiming their conjunction, liberalism has not faced the essential conflict between them. It thus finds itself, because of its confused notion of human nature, caught in the tangle of their conflicting demands.

When faced separately, they are dialectically opposed. For example, if three of us, free to pursue educational paths, decide to go in different directions, we will have differentiated ourselves from each other and no one of us will be equal in any academic regard to the others. If we are each free to pursue private economic advantage and only one does so successfully, we will not be economically equal. On the other hand, if we are subjected to an enforced equality of education or income, none of us is free to pursue those different goals we each may prefer.

Freedom depends upon a spontaneous kind of order which functions by a continuity of individual adjustments to a changing social scene. Encouraged in intellectual life and scientific endeavors, it has proven to be "an efficient form of organization," that employs a "logic of self-coordination."[2] Yet, when pursued without the discipline of regard for the actions of others, it can produce an anarchic chaos which subverts its continuing activity. Equality, which pulls against individuating tendencies, more largely depends upon a directive order by the force of custom or of governmental sanction. Requisite on some levels for the social cohesiveness that permits a mutuality of citizenship, it can bring about a stifling conformity of taste and opinion and lends itself just as easily "to servitude or freedom, to knowledge or barbarism, to prosperity or wretchedness."[3] If each must be moderated so as to balance the need of the other, the *kinds* of freedoms and equalities a free society requires need to be spelled out.

Freedom encourages inventiveness and initiative; as such it immediately individuates disparities among contemporaries. It needs to be reconciled not only with the political idea of civic equality upon which free government depends, but also with equality of 'opportunity' which transforms all members into citizens who share a common endeavor. But the current tendency to insist on equality of 'outcome' denies the equal freedom for each to be as inventive as he or she can be, and forestalls individual initiatives and the freedom of 'pursuit' upon which the health of all of us depends.

An enforced equality of 'outcome' is deadly, especially for a modern society, which cannot afford to submerge potential leadership — whether political, economic, scientific, or cultural — into the mediocrity of the average: for "it is on the recruitment of leaders that [a society's] success for failure invariably depends."[4] The outstanding individuals a modern society requires can only surface through particular kinds of encouragements that are socially offered. A society that educates its children to a conformity of thought denies itself the promise of their imaginative creativity, from which all ultimately benefit. The great advances in human civilizations have only come from those who broke out of the common mold by exploiting opportunities to think ahead: one need only think back to the long periods when society was stagnant, seemingly embalmed in encrusted habit and uniformity of thought.[5] The heroes of cultural advance are those who declined to accept an equality of thought as they pioneered new ways of meeting common problems, thereby raising the general level for all.

When a society deliberately pursues a standard of excellence to which it invites each individual citizen, it encourages the development of particular talents and capabilities which immediately distinguish each one. By the policies it pursues, a society determines whether it seeks to recruit excellence from its new generational recruits, or conform all to a preordained standard of essentially mediocre performance. To enhance excellence on each conceivable level of achievement is to forestall any equality of outcome while recruiting the best future leadership.

Paradoxically, then, a society seriously dedicated to augmenting the equal right of each citizen to participate in its common good needs to encourage that differentiation and individuation in their use of the specific freedoms it is able to protect for them. To educate its children to develop their individual potentials is not to thrust equality upon them, but to encourage a natural de-equalization, for the greater good of the whole.

Inherent in the notion of a social order is the differentiation of labor and function. No modern society, no matter how egalitarian its rhetoric, can fail to do this.[6] For the complexity of any modern society requires a degree of differentiation undreamed of in the past. By time, talent, intelligence, education, and training no individual could be qualified to perform more than a few tasks. My simplest activities depend upon multitudinous specialized efforts in innumerable organized chains of activity by thousands of people I could never come to know. Collectively dependent upon the whole historic heritage that ushered in the present, each of us depends, in pursuing individual ends and goals, upon the thinking and labor of contemporary specialists whose functions and modes of thought can, at best, be only dimly appreciated by the rest of us. The skilled craftsman in a factory does not claim ability to handle most other jobs in his plant, much less the intricacies of invention, finance, or investment that created the function he fulfills; neither could those who distribute the product to the ultimate consumers who thus sustain his activity. The manager who can organize aspects of employee activities may well be incapable of performing any of their specific jobs, and may not even understand the technology of the manufactured product or the sociological implications of its use. Each of us performs a role within a limited horizon of understanding that yet depends upon a wider circle of functioning relationships to make it viable. And each is engaged, like a child tossing a pebble into a quiet pond, in enervating effects that ripple on beyond any individual line of sight.

Each society members plays many roles. Each factory worker, each supervisor, as the investor in the enterprise, also consumes material goods; by the ways in which they exercise their consumer functions, they provide the demand which nourishes the production activities of others like themselves. They are both, also, patrons of leisure-time activities — cultural and sporting events, newspapers, books and magazines, movies and tv programs. In these varied roles, they shape their own lives while their diverse patronage influences the ebb and flow of the economic activities of their society. Each individual plays many roles within an integrated society and thereby exerts an influence, beyond any personal horizon, on what prospers and what fails.

A successful society finds itself integrating diverse functions that bring complex differentiation into fullsome harmony. As in a rich symphony, each separate note contributes to its melody, with concurrent themes and sequential changes of pace and sound contributing to the richness of the whole. Each participant must do 'his own thing', while depending on each of the others to do theirs.

But unlike the performance of the symphony, this harmonic unity does not depend upon a composer. In contrast to the musical performance which plays out what *has already been written*, the social 'symphony' is *being written while it is being played*. An occasional disharmony may indeed embellish the dominant themes, but a complete disintegration of mutual responsiveness can only produce a rising dissonance and final anarchy. One may wonder that countless functions, even when well-performed, harmonize at all. A 'spontaneous kind of order', continually meshing mutual readjustment, ensues. For the next movement is open-ended, and depends upon continuing improvisation by its participants and continual adjustment to what others are perceived to be doing.[7] To progress from one movement to the next requires a continuity of freedom, freedom to interpret what is going on, to evaluate the alternatives looming ahead, to act by improvising beyond any command. And this continuity of open-ended responsiveness must be generally presumed and encouraged if the 'social symphony' is to continue being played.

The vast degree of functional specialization requisite to a modern technological society entails wide differentiations of competence, expertise, and responsibility. Most of us are totally unqualified to make most necessary decisions, and none of us is qualified to make them all. This wide dispersal of the freedom-to-decide through the social order manifests the wide encouragement of individual initiatives that maintain the constraints of mutual responsiveness and social harmony.

This general perception often evokes two rather different kinds of response. One bemoans its conceptual 'disorderliness', its harboring of differing developmental tendencies, its open-endedness and lack of deductive determination; it thus calls for centralized or collectivized direction under the slogans of 'a rational' or 'planned' society. The other, perceiving gross injustices in the intrinsic inequalities that differences of function and responsibility entail, demands the imposition of equality of status and outcome. Different in impetus as they may be, each effectively proposes radical abridgments of freedom under a directive elite, so in practice they tend to coalesce.

i. a. Planning

All rational activity involves planning, the taking up of the past in the light of possibilities inviting realization, the determination of a course of action and the appropriation of the temporal path to pursue it. The question is not whether to plan, but what kind of planning is consonant with the nature of a free society.

Two radically different kinds of planning are proposed. One seeks to vest in the society's 'directorate' full responsibility for comprehensive planning — coordinating all activities into an integrated plan that allocates specific tasks to each citizen or segment of the society; the society's future is then dependent not only on the judgmental intelligence of its rulers, but also on the willing compliance of their subjects. The other sets out broad procedural policies and inducements while dispersing decisional authority concerning specific actions within those rules to its citizens; minimizing comprehensive planning, the planning of individuals and groups is autonomous, and any over-all integration ensues from their mutual responsiveness and harmonization; the society thus renders its future dependent on the free initiatives of citizens.

The first is the old call for a completely planned society — which the young Plato had already issued by demanding the rule of the 'wisest', a society ruled by those most competent to make directive judgments for the rest of us. Rather than leave things to idiosyncrasy or chance, to the hopefully happy coalescing of individual perspectives and judgments, it might seem sensible to plan all things out in advance, to work out the coordination of all individual efforts, so that all work cohesively to the same goal. Rather than leave each major segment to work out its own problems in the hopes that they will ultimately mesh, those who call for a 'rational' or comprehensively 'planned' society seek the economy of avoiding wasted effort and conflicting goals by setting out, in advance, one plan of activity to which *all* elements of the society are required to contribute their allotted share. Rather than encouraging the free interpretive judgments of every discernible sector, they seek to bring all into an imposed order by setting out the particular tasks of each in advance.

Intellectually 'clean' as this may at first appear to be, what is really proposed is a hierarchically organized society in which all decisions come down from central coordinators at 'the top'. Comprehensive planning reserves all freedom to those who are in the decision-making echelons of the ruling hierarchy. Because it forecloses individual inventiveness and initiative, it is not only bad theory; one need merely consult the history of such efforts to see that it does not work.[8] One reason may well be that it cannot remove its ultimate dependence upon the individualized judgments of its subjects — necessarily constrained while necessarily invoked — for its success.

Just how to choose the coordinating directors is one question that begs the proposal. They might be chosen in hierarchical fashion by those on each level selecting those on the next lower level to join them. If those at the 'top' are self-chosen, even by virtue of their conviction of their own competence, their directive role is based upon their seizure of power and not on a demonstration of their wisdom — and no principle of public accountability is operative. If, however, 'the people' may freely choose their rulers, that popular wisdom is the justification of the position which then claims to supercede it, without providing them any procedure but alienated disengagement by which to change their minds.

Dependent as the proposal is on the ability of some to attain a comprehensive insight, it is doubtful that any individuals can attain it, just because every individual has a finite perspective from within his society and cannot possibly observe it in god-like fashion from the outside. Even such a revolutionary collectivist as Leon Trotsky finally came to declare that it would "require a Universal Mind as conceived by Laplace to make a success of such a system."[9] Moreover, each individual, however brilliant, has his own valuational judgments, point of view, and sense of self-interest which necessarily feed into the judgments he imposes upon those he is called upon to coordinate.

A judgement about what is to be done feeds on a prognosis, an evaluational judgment of what is deemed to be deficient, a goal to be achieved, and operating principles to be employed. No prognosis can be evaluatively neutral by abjuring judgment of what is important or unimportant, good or bad. No prognosis can be truly interest- or value-free. And no action is temporally neutral: it carries some possibilities into actuality and consigns others to oblivion. Without debating just which past experiences are relevant to presently presented options, it is difficult to see how any objectively binding judgment could be made. Without infinite foresight, any prescribed action may be counted on to produce at least some effects that were not intended, some effects that will not have been foreseen.

However a directorate is chosen, however wise or foolish its decisions, it clearly forecloses initiative, judgment, and the freedom to decide and to act, by any individual or group of individuals that it takes under its wing — while it yet depends upon their doing so within the constraints of their 'marching orders'. A totally planned society is a 'command society' and "it is the essence of the planned economy to . . . [proceed by] official orders and to transfer the decision of the production capacity of the national economy [that] is to be used from the market to the government."[10] Its whole point is to pre-empt the freedom to decide to the pinnacle of its hierarchy. Whatever the rhetoric, it is clearly incompatible with a society of citizens who prize the freedom of their autonomy, and who see their common good in diversification of autonomous decisions.

Advocates of comprehensive planning invariably think in terms of production, as Marxists do when they claim that changing 'control of the means of production' can solve all social problems. Planning officials themselves are dependent on the products of others, which they seek to distribute; producing nothing, they can only re-allocate the materials and resources of others. The problem of production is a problem 'solved' by the Industrial Revolution: it is *not* the problem of a modern society. Modern production capabilities historically developed in response to market systems which allocated resources in the light of consumption demand, and it is this demand that drives productive energies. Except in times of scarcity, consumption demand depends on freely selected priorities and cannot be commanded. When adequate products are available, demand emerges from countless individual decisions that are freely preferential and inherently not subject to planned control. Since directive planning can only function when consumer goods are scarce, one is tempted to wonder whether the consumer scarcities produced by collectivist societies are not intrinsic.

A comprehensively planned society is inherently misdirected to production because it conceives of a 'rationally organized society' as the rationality of a machine, a production mechanism which processes what is fed into it. As a machine goes through its repeatable paces, the observer sees what it is doing and perhaps understands how and why. But standing outside of it, he is not directly involved *in* its functioning, except as he may modify his own directive orders in responding to its reactions to his initial miscalculations.

But a human society is not a machine; it depends on individually made preferential choices. And its directors are always, no matter how they may seek to disengage, part and parcel of it. Unlike a machine, a society never does the same thing twice. It may repeat similar, but not identical, actions; but, as a historic process, the exact results are never precisely the same. And its director(s) — self-styled 'social engineers': the term is telling of their view of the nature of human society — are continually enmeshed in its operations, and affected by its performance. The rationality of a human society is that of a living being which responds, as a whole and in its members, to the problems it faces in perhaps similar but never identical ways.

As any living organism, a living society depends for its vitality upon the free healthy functioning of its members and their ability to interrelate, adjust to each other's aberrations, and harmoniously readjust. A comprehensively planned society cannot be a free society, in any meaningful sense, because it directs, from above, what each component of that society shall do. In everything deemed important by those in control, it must function as a 'command structure' akin to a military hierarchy.

The planning that is commensurate with a free society depends upon the wishes of the citizenry and gears itself to their judgments and preferences. It prioritizes consumption demands, not production commands. By setting out procedural rules, providing market incentives and even occasional subsidies, it seeks to enhance the value-consensus or general will of the citizenry by leaving them free to proceed in accord with them. In classical terms, its confines itself to setting out the 'forms' of social activities and calls upon free citizen initiatives to fill out the 'content'.

One reason for the widespread contemporary failure of most command-society programs of comprehensive planning is that they cannot avoid their ultimate dependence upon the free cooperation of the societal members. A free society recognizes this dependence at the outset and forthrightly places responsibility, not only for filling out the 'content' of activity on free citizen judgments, but also gears its 'forms' or procedures to fulfilling what they require. Advocates of comprehensive planning are rarely happy with such open approaches because these depend on variegated individual desires and responses which are not always cleanly predictable, thus leaving the future open to new judgments and decisions. These constitute a general 'market' approach which calls for gearing production to what is desired by those constituting the society, and not to the higher visions of a directive elite.

The key issue is not merely whether to plan, but how comprehensively. Any decision is, in a real sense, a plan. The more comprehensive the social plan is, the more fundamental are rarely acknowledged questions: Whose plan is to be imposed? How is this to be selected? By what tests will its effectiveness be gauged? What corrective procedures will be built into it? How is it prepared to rectify the inevitable mistaken calculations made along the way? How will an opportunity be provided to change a particular decision if it does not live up to its promises?

Any plan, whether highly directive or merely procedural, is a social experiment — and these should not be lightly undertaken.

Too many glibly speak of social 'experiments'. These experiments, be it noted, are always conducted with 'others'; they are not conducted in the isolation of a laboratory, where the virtue of failure but augments the knowledge of the investigator. The language of the physical sciences has been so thoughtlessly taken over into the social arena that the social cost of error in 'social experiments' is rarely acknowledged. A scientific experiment proceeds in a laboratory-condition and always involves a 'control' group. If it fails, we merely 'sweep it' from the laboratory table, without any untoward result. But a social experiment usually results from 'we have a problem; let us see if this works'. There is no control group. And, whether it works or does not work, it cannot be 'swept from the table'; it has already entered into human history and irretrievably changed the lives of particular people.

The only comprehensive 'social experiments' truly available for dispassionate study are comparative historical developments of what-has-already-transpired among different people under similar sets of circumstances. Recent history provides us abundant examples to which we will, in due course, repair.[11] But such historical 'experiments' are conceptual: they consist of our re-examining actual experiences in alternative courses of development. They do not manipulate living people, changing their historical development by bureaucratic fiat. In contrast, deliberate social manipulations affect living people, create new sequences of events stretching beyond the particular area of concern into the society at large, new problems as they unfold — and they *cannot be undone*.[12] If plans do not work out as hoped, one cannot simply unpack the situation; a new situation has been created to rectify. Proposals for deliberate social experiments need be broached with humility, 'tried out' in limited areas, and implemented with escape clauses and with caution.

A society may determine that certain problems need some kind of unified direction, and employs officials to make particular kinds of social decisions to meet them. But then it is crucial to distinguish between policies which set parameters for, and even encourage, certain kinds of individual decisions, and those which preempt large areas of individual decision to official directives.

Any decision deliberately excludes certain options from the impending future while it opens others. The more comprehensive any such decision may be, the more demanding are special prudence and measures for quick correctability — they constitute a sign of wisdom. For no one can foresee all contingencies, and the wisest among us are those who arm themselves against those eventualities which might appear unannounced.

After all is said and done, planners are members of their society and so are those who will administer their plans. Yet, by virtue of advocating or administering a particular policy or plan, they have a vested interest in its continuance (which they share with the 'constituency' it creates, those particular individuals who most directly benefit from it). As de Tocqueville remarked, such officials comprise "a nation within each nation; and as they share the stability of the government they more and more fill up the place of an aristocracy."[13] How then are these vested interests to be reconciled with or checked by that of the society itself? This question, which addresses every bureaucracy and directive 'policy' imposition, is the question of how to organize social time. It will lead us, in the next chapter, back to the oldest distinction in political science, one which Aristotle had already made central: the conflict between governance for the benefit of the governors and governance for the benefit of the governed.

i. b. Equalization

The call for equality, although it has rung together with that for freedom in calls for democratizing reform, pulls in an opposite direction. As de Tocqueville observed, "in proportion as equality was more established by the aid of freedom, freedom itself was thereby rendered more difficult of attainment."[14] In some sense, still intrinsic to any free society, its continuing tension with freedom provides the political dynamic a free society enjoys. Aristotle's descriptions of the self-governing states of his time already provided the classic example.

The American Declaration of Independence and the subsequent French Revolution paired freedom and equality in their calls for civic equality, equality in citizenship. Free societies have generally translated equality in the right to freedom to require degrees of equalization. In view of the contemporary resurgence of egalitarian doctrines, which demand specific equalities at the cost of freedom, it is important to underline this distinction.

Civic equality does not mean an absolute equality of position and status. The call for equality must, for the sake of freedom, be severely moderated. As de Tocqueville repeatedly warned, social equality, when pushed too far, destroys the freedom which brought it into being; for equality, once attained, is more secure than liberty which is always in danger:

> If a people could ever succeed in destroying, or even in diminishing, the equality that prevails in its own body, they could do so only by long and laborious efforts. . . . But political liberty is more easily lost; to neglect to hold it fast is to allow it to escape.[15]

The egalitarian call, ever pressing onward to "reducing all conditions of society" to a common level, must always remain frustrated because "the inequality of mind would still remain."[16] As one central lesson from his study of the early American Republic, de Tocqueville sought "to point out the dangers to which the principle of equality exposes the independence of man . . . [for] these dangers are the most formidable as well as the least foreseen of all those which futurity holds in store."[17] Freedom is crucial because, as he warned, "To combat the evils which equality may produce, there is only one effectual remedy: namely, political freedom."[18]

The notion of equality is inherently ambiguous, especially in a society that involves minute diversifications of function and thereby inherent inequalities — of competence, decisional authority and responsibility, and consequent import to the common good of the whole. Few want to abdicate such diversifications in exchange for any absolute equality of all. As the common good of a free society is to maximize freedom, those kinds of equality which are presupposed by, or compatible with, a free society are reinforcing; but, thereby, proposals for those kinds of equality that conflict with the priority of freedom are suspect.

Because the condition of the society as a whole provides the context within which each citizen may seek his own good, the common good must always be the first consideration. For the good of the whole, many kinds of equality are neither equally beneficial nor useful. Especially in our technological age, most of us are wholly incompetent to make the myriad decisions required — to gauge what possibilities are truly viable, which proposals for development are most promising, which are to be spurned. As in technological matters, so in the intricacies of managing what is already committed and in the creativity of invention and initiative, within fiscal parameters and market conditions, we ideally accord responsibility, and thereby remuneration, in proportion to the criteria of expertise and experienced judgment we have come to recognize.

Ideally, educational opportunity should be in accord with demonstrated intelligence, talent, and individual motivation, as opportunities for career and advancement should accord with appropriate preparation, requisite abilities, and skills. And ideally, the distribution of rewards is made to maintain the society's perceptions of its own needs and the contribution of individual citizens to fulfill them.[19] Recognition of educational achievement, employment, and responsibility in the various segments of social organization — all necessitated by the intricate division of labor and function — necessarily leads to inequalities of power of decision, of responsibility, and of income. The necessary result is an institutionalized 'inequality of outcome'.

This 'inequality of outcome' is necessary to even the most ideally developed 'equality of opportunity'; for when the opportunity for advancement for each is maximized, different individuals will pursue different talents and interests — fully aware of unequal monetary reward. Income then becomes a sign of the socially recognized import of what one is doing for the community as a whole. Each level in claiming income, insists on the import of its contribution to the common good; the result manifests the way the social order effectively evaluates, by negotiation, the import of the contribution of each. However fair one may deem any negotiated outcome to be, the diversification of function and responsibility coupled to the freedom of individuals to pursue their own life paths, justifies the principle that the social distribution of wealth and power in unequal amounts is in accord with the socially perceived value of each activity to the common good.

This 'inequality of outcome' coupled to a maximized 'freedom of pursuit' has been ingredient to the development of even the most populist form of democratic theory from the beginning. As Rousseau, described by Mosca as "the real parent of the doctrine of popular sovereignty and hence of modern representative democracy,"[20] clearly argued: "with regard to equality, it is necessary not to understand by this word that every degree of power and wealth should be absolutely the same."

What is of import to a free society is *civic* equality — not any absolute equality of position and station, but opportunities for *equalization*: "No citizen should be so opulent as to be able to buy another, and none so poor as to be constrained to sell himself." A society concerned with its freedom should "allow neither excess opulence nor beggars. These two conditions, naturally inseparable, are equally fatal to the common good; from one spring the fomenters of tyranny, from the other the tyrant."[21]

What was clearly called for — in Aristotle's 'polity' and Rousseau's democratic republic — is a predominantly middle-class society in which "all [citizens have] something and none of them too much."[22] A society deeply divided between rich and poor is really a Hobbesian state that maintains peace at the expense of liberty by repressive force[23] The equality a free society seeks is the *civic* equality of each member; its mutuality of liberty seeks an *equalization* of opportunity, of elemental conditions, so that each citizen is enabled to participate in the common good — in accord with individual interests and talents, with the responsibilities one is freely able to accept, and in the ways in which one is able and willing to spend one's time.

From society's viewpoint this free diversification is crucial. A society's harmonious functioning depends on the continuing good will and loyalty of its members. By encouraging free career choices of its citizens, by fostering the accrual of personal wealth and property ownership, the society ensures that its citizens have a vested interest in the community's ongoing health and welfare. By identifying individual interest with the common interest, the future of their common interest is secured.

As modern technological societies bring their members into a stretch of middle-class status, they broaden general concern for wide access to educational institutions — thereby opening new channels for individual advancement, or the freedom of 'pursuit', and thereby encouraging greater degrees of social mobility. By thus foreclosing the development of rigid class lies and keeping social movement fluid, an open society integrates its varied individual members into a democratized whole. By generalizing education, providing 'floors' under income, and generally opening opportunity to the economically deprived while assessing those who are able to afford larger contributions to the public purse, they have progressively achieved a compression of extremes while raising the general quality of life. Such equalization of opportunity has served to invite free contributions to the common good while encouraging the aspirations its prosperity invites and requires.

Yet a strident cry has been not for progressive equalization but, in a new kind of egalitarian doctrine, for some kind of absolute equality, usually specified as 'equality of outcome'. This is fearsome. An 'equality of outcome' cannot be legislated with destroying 'equality of opportunity', *the* one social equality that is the inherent and sustaining promise of a free society. By opening opportunities to be freely taken up, individual freedom is expanded and allowed to function. By encouraging innovation, the society's growth is enhanced.

A guarantee of result is not only inimical to freedom: it requires a vast army of social managers — a new directive elite — to direct it, by pre-empting the freedom of decision from individual citizens to those who are charged to administer those decisions. This is why the call for comprehensive directive planning and the call for enforced resultant equality so often ring out together. In principle and practice, they each call for an elite class charged to plan the future for others. Too many, given such tasks, rather than dispassionately evaluating the effects of what they are doing, can be expected to exploit their clients to enhance their own vested interests by continuing their projects. Cogent criticisms and individual initiatives are too often resented as interfering with both the foreseen plan and the equality of their 'clients', which are invariably identified as one.[24] Most administrators are sincerely convinced that they do know what is best for their charges; and few administrators are able to differentiate what is best for their charges from their own continued authority to make decisions for them.

These dangers are already with us. For "modern societies push the egalitarian ideal much farther than any society in the past."[25] We need to alert ourselves to the dangers of pushing it too far. Egalitarianism, as de Tocqueville warned, inherently threatens personal liberty and promises despotism, something "peculiarly to be dreaded in democratic times."[26]

Whatever its merits might be, egalitarianism has emerged as the clarion call of those who claim their roots to be in the liberalist tradition. This is doubly ironic. First, because liberalism arose as a protest, in the name of liberty, against the centralized power of absolute directive governments; yet today liberalist spokesmen increasingly champion the power of directive government — to the point of commending a command society — as the cure for every discerned social ill. Second, because the liberalist call never included a demand for a resultant equality as a substitute for an opening of opportunity; yet today the programmatic priorities of those who claim to carry that tradition forward generally seem to value absolute equalities as more important than liberties and freedom.

That this development involves a complex of conceptual confusions is rarely noted; yet these confusions go far to explain the disarray of contemporary liberalism and the arbitrary nature of its specific demands and proposals. The state-ist nature of its contemporary stance has forsaken the conceptual ground from which it sprung, without any rethinking of its animating rationale.

ii. Rights

When we seek to bring societal members into citizenship, another call which beclouds the issue is that of individual 'rights'. Whether these are 'absolute' or contextually related to a society's specific condition is a question which needs to be faced. However conceived, individual 'rights' are specific claims for social protection which a society is called upon to recognize.

Two irreconcilable ways of thinking underlie most contemporary discussion; irreconcilable because they each use a different 'logic' to assess social norms. One stems from classical liberalist doctrine. Nurtured in English experience, it voices an individualism which most of us cherish, but it tends to absolutize individual rights without any rationale for defining the prior right of the community itself to act as a unit; and because it finds it impossible to translate these claimed rights into concrete terms it ends by calls for enforced equalities, which already harbor the seeds of a new elitism. The other stems from what might be called a 'progressive conservatism' that draws on European thought; inherently democratic in its suspicion of any directive elite, it insists on encompassing the whole people within its concerns as it seeks to maximize opportunities for individual autonomy for each. And it is suspicious of radical proposals because it sees specific rights and obligations as evolving out of a cherished historical consensual continuity it seeks to carry forward. Each received fullest expression in Britain, where they came into open conflict, because it was there that industrialization ushered in core problems of the modern age.

ii. a. Locke and Mill

Liberalist doctrine traces its development back to Locke and Mill. The tradition tying them together into a course of coherent development reveals the logic that gave liberalism the coherence and power it once had.

In order to secure life and property against governmental seizures and controls, John Locke had invoked a version of 'natural law' theory (coming down from the Roman Stoics through medieval development); he enunciated a thesis that out of a pre-civil 'state of nature' each person presumably carried a set of 'natural rights' into a civil society whose sole function was to protect them. Individuals chose to place themselves, Locke claimed, under the bonds of political organization only "for the mutual *preservation* of their lives, liberties, and estates, which I call by the general name, *property*."[27] Accordingly, the proper limited function of legitimate government was declared to be, to enact appropriate laws to preserve and extend liberty which is:

> to be free from restraint and violence from others; which cannot be, where there is no law: but freedom is not, as we are told, *liberty for every man to do what he lists*: ...[it is] a liberty to dispose, and order as he lists, his person, actions, possessions, and his whole property, within the allowance of those laws under which he is, and therein not to be subject to the arbitrary will of another, but freely follow his own.[28]

In joining into an organized community for this purpose, all persons

> must be understood to give up all power, necessary to the ends for which they unite into society, to the *majority* of the community. ... And thus that, which begins and actually *constitutes any political society*, is nothing but the consent of any number of free men capable of a majority to unite and incorporate into such a society.[29]

This principle of majority rule was to be focused in a representative legislature or Parliament as "the supreme power," to which the executive power, and presumably a judicial power not mentioned here, are subject.[30]

Governments and societies exist, Locke insisted, as mere instruments to defend those natural rights belonging to each individual as a birthright. Presumably, socially capable individuals already developed in a presocietal state; presumably they had already developed the essentially social notion of agreement or contract, as they were able to enter into one to form a state to protect their inherent rights. And somehow, in a way never acknowledged — much less explained — these inherent rights can be subjected to unmitigated majority rule, which carries with it the consequence that the rights of those who offend the rights the majority proclaims as its own are left without recourse.

In Locke's political teaching, we find no mention of rights to think for oneself, to free speech, to the 'right' of trial-by-jury, to free association. Most remarkable, we find no explication of what the traditionally vaunted 'rights of Englishmen' truly are. We can only read these in from a later stance by implication. The rights of the society seem to be merely those delegated to the society from the presumably 'inherent' rights of its individual members; society as such creates none of its own, and seemingly has no real rights as a corporate entity. The sole legitimate function of an organized society, then, is but to act as a policeman and fireman for the protection of individual life and property. For these are the *only* particular rights that Locke specified in any way: "Every man is born with a double right: *first, a right of freedom to his person . . . Secondly, a right* before any other man, *to inherit* with his brethren his *father's goods.*[31]

John Stuart Mill carried this mode of thought forward in his classic *On Liberty*, first published in 1859. In his Introduction to this eloquent defense of individual liberty, he made this clear. The purpose of his essay, he explicitly stated, was to set out "the nature and limits of the power which can be legitimately exercised by society over the individual."[32] Its clearly stated object was to enunciate:

> one very simple principle...that *the sole end* for which mankind are warranted, individually or collectively, in interfering with the liberty of any of their number, is *self-protection.* That the only purpose for which power can be rightfully exercised over any member of a civilized community, against his will, is to prevent *harm to others.* ...The only part of the conduct of any one, for which he is amenable to society, is that which concerns others. In the part which merely *concerns himself,* his independence is, of right, *absolute.*"[33]

Both Locke and Mill expressed a concept of 'social atomism' — they worked with an atomistic model of man that sees society as but an aggregate of individuals, each somehow endowed with really unspecified rights somehow inborn; society is then but a convenience with the sole legitimate function to protect those inherent rights, and to adjust possible conflicts between them.[34] Neither acknowledged the politically organized state as natural or necessary to man; both ignored the inherent social relations that constitute any individual; both ignored the role of one's society — as the cultural parent to the individual — which provides the historical communal framework within which one's inherent humanity may flower. Neither seems to have developed any real notion of an inherently social common good upon which the good of its members depends; nor any notion of a 'corporate' community interest as the framework sustaining individual interests, and which therefore must take precedence over particular individual wishes because its well-being is crucial to the individuals composing it. Each was so focused on the rights of individuals against a potentially (or actually) tyrannical government that each ignored any notion of individual obligations, as well as any concept of the rights and obligations of the community itself as an organized body, the health of which is prerequisite to that of its members.

Mill's writings reflect an admirable individual who was open-minded, dedicated, and committed; they commend often sensible and often wise admonitions that are still germane to many problems we still face. But they redound with conceptual confusions — largely because his own new insights tried to look beyond the atomistic model he still carried forward from Locke, the elder Mill, and Bentham.[35] His primary concern seems to have been not the social issues emerging in his time, but the importance of individual intellectual thought, the ability to advance heretical ideas and viewpoints, and a general freedom of discussion, which his own forebears may have presumed and which Locke (aside from a plea for a limited religious toleration) never brought into his political thought.

Mill also worried about a conceivable "tyranny of the majority", a problem which Locke apparently never considered. Mill's inexplicable handling of this but reiterated the import "of the power of government over individuals."[36] Although Mill took neither Locke's notion of an original state-of-nature nor the idea of a historic social contract seriously, he effectively carried forward the Lockean notion of society as composed of irreducible elements, individuals whose rights are paramount before any notion of a communal social good. Rejecting the doctrine of 'natural rights' he nevertheless seems to have presumed it.

Mill accepted the Lockean principle of parliamentary supremacy based on majoritarian right. His corrective amendment was to urge that Parliament be composed by a system of proportional representation so that all major social *groupings* have a voice in its never-questioned sovereign deliberations.[37] This proposal is already, in principle — beyond the pragmatic question of the efficacy of a proportional representational system — an incipient betrayal of the *democratic* principle just because it regards citizens not as individual members each with a diversity of interests and concerns, but only as members of particular ideological or vested-interest 'factions', as Madison had already termed it.[38] In the light of history, if not of prior principle, we can now say that whatever else a free society may be, it cannot be constituted by representing group interests (though it must deal with them); it must represent citizens who are individual human beings, each one with an individuated *diversity* of interests.

Beyond this notion of coagulating groups, Mill took Locke's majoritarianism further: for the utilitarian tradition, of which Mill came to be the prime spokesman, built on Bentham, who took his inspiration from Locke; Bentham's central principle was "this sacred truth: — that the greatest happiness of the greatest number is the foundation of morals and legislation."[39] Application of this principle can only produce what Aristotle had already termed a perverse form of government: majoritarian democracy which rules for the interest of the majority, not for the interest of the whole society as one body of individual citizens — upon the health of which the majority, too, ultimately depends. As a convenience, a properly constituted polity may use majority voting as a mode of settling electoral questions and specific disputes (within its constitutional framework); but its function is to coalesce the interests of the society into one whole — and the whole must always include whatever minority voices participate in it.

Locke could not have conceivably seen beyond the agrarian-mercantile society of his time and thus he could not have foreseen the social problems that began to emerge at the end of the eighteenth century as the Industrial Revolution took hold. Having brought the inheritance of widespread rural poverty into the public purview of urban centers, it provoked the mid-nineteenth-century crisis of liberalism.

But Mill lived through its rise, and should have been able to address the miseries of early industrialization which his contemporaries, Charles Dickens and Emile Zola, so forcefully portrayed. Rather, Mill was confused by the new issues of his time and offered but superficial remedies for the miseries at hand. His biographer has noted that "He thought payment by the day would be immoral, and that piecework, coupled with fixed working hours and an increased rate for overtime, was the perfect system. The intricacies of mass-production never occurred to him."[40] Nor did his outlook permit him to envision the temporal opportunity of increasing production by time- and thereby labor-saving cost.

Most unfortunately, Mill seems to have built into liberalist doctrine a pervasive notion of elitism. Claiming to espouse the 'greatest happiness' principle of the utilitarian school, he explained in a famous statement that "It is better to be a human being dissatisfied than a pig satisfied; better to be Socrates dissatisfied than a fool satisfied." But how are we to discriminate between those who are wise and those who are fools? Mill clearly brought the issue to the fore:

> Whoever supposes . . . that the superior being, in anything like equal circumstances, is not happier than the inferior — confounds the two very different ideas, of happiness and content. It is indisputable that the being whose capacities of enjoyment are low, has the greatest chance of having them fully satisfied; and a highly endowed being will always feel that any happiness which he can look for, as the world is constituted is imperfect. . . . On a question which is the best worth, having two pleasures, or which of two modes of existence is the most grateful to the feelings, apart from its moral attributes and from its consequences, *the judgment of those who are qualified by knowledge of both, or, if they differ, that of the majority among them, must be admitted as final.*[41]

Those "highly endowed" who have the widest experience are to judge what is best for the rest. This appreciative or esthetic elitism feeds directly into a liberalist doctrine that seeks to develop bureaucratic governors to direct social freedoms — in contrast a genuinely democratic doctrine insists that all citizens be admitted into an equality of opportunity to use their own judgmental freedom. Reserving ultimate decision for those 'superior' individuals to set standards for the rest, Mill's liberalism coupled its incongruous call for equality to the elitism of "those who are qualified," by their own selective majoritarianism to judge, to direct others to their own tastes. A more genuinely democratic doctrine asks only for an equality *in freedom* — and declines the arrogance of directing its individual development which it leaves to the, perhaps erroneous, judgments of the free citizens it nurtures.

Many of these conceptual ingredients feed into some of our contemporary disarray. Without an overriding sense of a common good which sets out normative standards for free development, we are left with the reduction of atomistically conceived individuals to factional alignments, together with the justification of a directive bureaucratic elite. A group- or single-issue politics results: each group gathered around a particular issue stridently seeks to force its own perceived interest into the decision of a majority coalition of diverse groups enjoined to rule without limit. When coupled with a utilitarian standard of the 'greatest happiness for the greatest number', which only a directive elite can judge, the only practical way one can proceed is to conjoin nonconflicting groups into majority coalitions that can create directive bureaucracies to impose their conjoined will.

Locke and Mill can perhaps be counted as modern 'libertarians', despite their invitations to effective majoritarianism, in that they each personally believed in the irreducible liberty of individual citizens and of minimal government. Neither provided any real guidance as to *how* their evaluative standards are to be ensured. Neither demonstrated any notion that a prime function of free government is to serve as a positive guardian of the freedom of the citizenry; neither seemed to recognize that the community itself has needs, important to its citizens, and that citizens need a positive government that is simultaneously curbed in its potential excesses while being empowered to do for the community as a whole what its members, as individuals, want done but cannot do by themselves.

Little is to be learned from them about the importance of proper procedures for decision, procedures which must invariably take precedence over any specific proposal if the public's business is to be conducted in a context of free discussion. And little is to be learned about the dynamics of political power. We receive no guidance to sorting out conflicting social values and how these value conflicts may be resolved. The 'right' of every 'faction' to seek its own happiness in a negotiated majority decision, and the lack of any standard by which specific claims are to be measured, naturally leads to the contemporary 'special issue' politics which in turn endangers any priority of both individual right and a common good.[42]

The liberalist call may have been effective as a call for rebellion; as we have received it, it offers few guidelines for progressive consolidation. Indeed, Locke's central import for the American experiment faded with the Revolution which drew its inspiration from his work. Notably, no edition of his *Two Treatises* was published in the U.S. between 1773 and 1937.[43] New influences were already evident in Jefferson's replacement of Locke's emphasis on "property" with "the pursuit of happiness" in the Declaration of Independence.[44]

Although the Lockean "life, liberty, and property" entered into the American consciousness, the Constitution itself clearly substituted for the Lockean notion of parliamentary supremacy a tripartite governmental system of 'checks and balances', clearly designed to limit the reach of majority rule by confining the powers of government to specific authorizations. And its acceptance was conditioned by the Bill of Rights amendments, which are further explicit limitations on majority power. Notably, the new Constitution's authoritative defense, *The Federalist*, repeatedly invoked the authority of Montesquieu as we shall see, while ignoring Locke completely. A doctrine of absolute and irreducible rights remains a seductive abstraction while citizens quarrel over how to specify them by a procedure of unmitigated majority rule which, on its face, seems to set them aside.

ii. b. Burke and Green

What brought the liberalist tradition to crisis in Britain, where it was conceived, was neither the American departure from its imperial rule nor any political development at all. On its own home ground, it provoked the moral crisis of societal responsibility: it proved incapable of facing the challenge provoked by the Industrial Revolution. Liberalism provided no rationale by which to bring the benefits of citizenship to the vast number of the British people, so that they could share in the revolutionary promise of their new industrialization.

Building on the earlier commercial revolution which had begun some two centuries earlier and the consequent rise of a commercial middle class, industrialization began in England in the 1700s — roughly between Newcomen's invention of the steam engine in 1712, and Watt's improvement of that engine (patented in 1769 and initially manufactured in 1774). In due course, the commercial revolution's invention of the factory system[45] rapidly developed — with large concentrations of poor and overworked workers, drawn out of a poverty-stricken peasantry and clustered in newly aggravated urban slums.

The Industrial Revolution was revolutionary because, for the first time in human history, it brought forth the possibility of eliminating poverty by creating new wealth rather than merely dividing present possessions. But few signs of this promise were readily apparent as the new industrialization, in all earnest, initially began. The new industrial installations, freely operating under general laissez-faire principles — drawn from the Lockean teaching that the sole function of government, beyond providing for the national defense, was to protect private property, no matter how it might be used — had, indeed, resulted in a state, not of ordered economic liberty but one of economic license. Liberalism, in the context of the time, had little to say to the rampant poverty or to guide any improvement of the widespread degrading living conditions. Rather, it appeared to sponsor a somewhat anarchic economic order — in which investors in the new machines and the distribution of their products prospered, while the rest, left out of its new distribution markets, were reduced to continued penury.

The reigning philosophy sorely needed to be rethought — in order to enable the citizenry to join the new advance; Thomas Hill Green, a philosopher of a different stripe, framed a new outlook. Turning from the atomistic liberalism of the Lockean tradition, Green brought into the English-speaking world a very different understanding of what membership in a free polity truly means. Although he has sometimes been described as the creator of a 'new liberalism', his developed concept of democratic citizenship explicitly built upon prime insights of Edmund Burke, the great conservative thinker of the preceding century.[46]

Green's appropriation of Burke's thinking becomes crucial when we face contemporary questions about just which 'rights' are to be specified or justified. Proclamations of 'human rights' are good rhetoric but rarely provide specificity or rational justification. Different cultures accord different 'rights' to their participants — and each of us, coming out of a specific historic culture, regards certain 'rights' as 'natural'. Our political rhetoric abounds with strident claims to newly discovered 'rights' — and each is initially proclaimed as 'inherent' or 'innate'. But if so, why are they so newly discovered and how may they each be validated?

Green took up Burke's thesis that traditional citizen-rights are 'social prescriptions' and developed this view into a powerful instrument for democratizing reform. Any society does 'prescribe' specific 'rights' for its citizens. These are regarded as rightful claims on social protection for their exercise: protecting them is generally seen as one prime obligation of government. They are generally tied to social obligations and evolve as the society develops. Their explication provides something of an 'objective' portrait of the degree of a society's development at a given time.

Green's point was to propose guidelines for social reform to carry his developed society forward; recognizing the new possibilities industrialization had produced, he called for a pervasive democratic commitment that would open the benefits of citizenship to all societal members. Useful as Burke's concept of historically grounded prescriptive rights promised to be, it required augmentation with creative principles of a new republicanism to meet the new circumstances. Turning to the work of Rousseau and Kant, he subjected their teaching to a critical redevelopment that proposed a new way of perceiving the relationship between citizen and government. Green took from them, and added to his acknowledged Burkean heritage, the thesis that the idea of freedom provides a standard by which to selectively evaluate the heritage from the past for enriched development in order to form continuity into the future. Designed to meet the crisis for a free polity which the Industrial Revolution presented, Green developed the idea of the free positive state whose prime function is to serve as the guardian of the freedoms of its citizens.

Green thus joined Burke's repudiation of liberalist atomism, a view of society as but a convenient aggregate of individuals without any real understanding of its essential nature as a continuity of historically evolving process. Burke, repudiating the notion of unspecified 'natural rights' which Locke had proclaimed,[47] asked for *the origin* of those *specific* individual rightful claims that the tradition of his own society had already recognized as its obligation to protect for each of its members. As Green explained:

> Before the trumpet-blast of natural right . . . Burke pleaded the ancient rights . . . with a power which has made all subsequent conservative writing superfluous and tedious. Notwithstanding his violence and onesidedness, he had so much of the true philosophic insight that he almost alone among the men of his time caught the intellectual essence of the system which provoked him. He saw that it rested on a metaphysical mistake, on an attempt to abstract the individual from his universal essence, i.e., from the relations embodied in habitudes and institutions which make him what he is. . . . Whatever might be the case practically, [England] had not learnt speculatively that freedom means something else than doing what one likes.

Continuing, Green condemned the irrelevance of the inherited liberalist creed while making clear the need to take up and develop Burke's teaching:

> Burke was not a prophet. . . . He saw the rottenness in which the [atomistic] 'metaphysics' of the eighteenth century resulted, but had nothing with which to replace them. The practical reconstruction of moral ideas in England was to come, not directly from a sounder philosophy, but from the deeper views of life which the contemplative poets originated, from the revival of evangelic religion, and from the conception of freedom and right, which Rousseau himself popularised . . .[48]

Burke had insisted, albeit in an unsystematic way, that 'rights' are not abstract, and that political institutions are not created *ex nihilo.* A 'right' is always a *specific* claim upon one's organized society which the society has accepted as its obligation to protect. The historical development of a people embodies a living history of "prescriptive rights" — those rights which the social order specifies for its citizens and accepts as its future or 'henceforth' responsibility to protect; they are its ways of handling affairs, dictated by custom or embodied in legislation, and have evolved out of the continuity of its historical experience.

While disparaging abstract, ungrounded, and thereby arbitrary proclamations of individual rights, Burke had looked rather to the vitality of the social order in which specifically enumerated rights are generally protected for the sake of the perceived good of the whole. The moral quality of human beings derives from membership in a particular society with its own tradition of specific liberties and concurrent obligations. A society that is civilized protects specific rights for its members, and its being civilized is the work of communities, not of isolated individuals. Perhaps unwittingly, Burke echoed both Aristotle and Rousseau — in his insistence that to truly be a human being one must already be a fully acknowledged member, a citizen of one's specific social order with rightful claims ensuing from that recognized belonging. Ironic because of his antipathy to Rousseau (or at least the way Rousseau was used by the French Jacobins), Burke effectively joined Rousseau in insisting that society is not merely a convenient aggregate of sovereign individuals; a society is a living historical process within which citizens are enabled to develop their own individualities. Burke clearly expressed this outlook within specifically British terms:

> Our [British] Constitution is *a prescriptive constitution*; it is a constitution whose sole authority is, that it has existed time out of mind. ...Prescription is the most solid of all titles, not only to property, but, [that] which is to secure that property, to government. ... It is a better presumption even than of the *choice* of a nation — far better than any sudden and temporary arrangement by actual election. Because *a nation is not an idea only of local extent and individual momentary aggregation, but it is an idea of continuity which extends in time* as well as in numbers and in space. And this is a choice not of one day... *it is a deliberate election of ages and of generations*...it is made by the peculiar circumstances, occasions, tempers, dispositions, and moral, civil, and social habitudes of the people, *which disclose themselves only in a long space of time.*[49]

In view of Burke's expressed antipathy to the Jacobin uses of Rousseau, it may seem strange to weld them, as Green did.[50] But as Sabine had observed, "In Burke . . . [Rousseau's notion of] the general will was released from [its] temporary bondage to Jacobinism."[51] To Burke's concept of the developmental nature of society and of the rights and obligations that together constitute the relations of its members, Green wedded Kant's original delineation of two concepts of freedom — negative liberty and positive freedom — which Kant, working from Rousseau, had forged in highly theoretical terms.[52] Focusing this delineation — of both the negative and positive aspects of freedom — onto the social problems ensuing from the Industrial Revolution, Green tied them to Burke's concept of 'prescriptive' rights to forge a powerful conceptual instrument carrying the social past into the prescriptions for reforms needed for its continuity into the future.

The more elemental notion of freedom is negative liberty — that freedom *from* external restraint or compulsion within which we are allowed to discover options and the possibilities for decisions. Much of this area, however, may be of no real interest to me. If I am told that I am not forbidden to fly to the moon, this newly announced liberty does not do much for me. To remove a prohibition, enlarging the area of the permissible, is only of interest if I both *want and can do* what is permitted. When I am told that I may smoke in this area, it does not move me if I neither want nor have access to tobacco. To say I am no longer compelled to go to school leaves me unaffected if I really want to continue doing so.

I am only concerned about a negative liberty when it removes prohibitions on activities that I desire, and am able, to undertake. A lack of prohibitions is meaningful only when it correlates with specific positive freedoms or abilities to do what is now permitted. Freedom, in any existentially meaningful sense, is open opportunity to act in accord with individual desires, abilities, and concrete opportunities severally available. To tell an illiterate person that he is allowed to read is a rather empty liberty; to teach him how to read is to provide a positive freedom or opportunity enabling him to do so.

Only negative liberties were proposed by the Lockean tradition. In its view, the only business of government is to prevent interference with the liberty of the individual.[53] And, indeed, in a period of enslavement or oppression, the attainment of liberty-from has often been a necessary way station to full freedom. As civilizations have developed and societies become more complex, the expanding network of justifiable demands, obligations, and rights creates new burdens which a just society will seek to share among citizens as openly protected opportunities in the essentially cooperative endeavor that a society incarnates. Against despotism, the first task has often been to establish a set of negative liberties. But these are not really wanted as self-sustaining ends; they are desired primarily because they open the doors to positive opportunities for individually desired development.

"Having done its work," Green observed, "the [Lockean] theory now tends to become obstructive."[54] To tell me that I am permitted to use my property as I see fit may be pernicious if my use creates a social hazard for others; and if I have no property, it is empty and meaningless. To tell me that I am permitted to develop my potentials is not meaningful if I lack the education, sustenance, or means to do so.

> If there are such things as rights at all, then, there must be a right to life and liberty, or, to put it more properly to free life. No distinction can be made between the right to life and the right to liberty, for there can be no right to mere life, no right to life on the part of a being that has not also the right to use the life according to the notions of its own will. What is the foundation of this right? The answer is, capacity on the part of the subject for membership in a society for determination of the will, and through it of the bodily organization, by the conception of a well-being as common to self with others. ... the qualities which enable him to act as a member of any one society having the general well-being of its members for its object...[55]

An organized society is based upon the principle of the *moral equality* of its citizens. Arbitrary pre-emptive claims to special rights or status are to be abjured simply because all individuals who belong to a society properly dedicated to "general well-being," by virtue of this belonging, have a claim to some share in what their "general well-being" is generally understood to comprise. An organized free society devoted to the well-being, or common good, of its members need be concerned with their 'general welfare'. "Society is made for man, not man for society; it is humanity, as Kant said, that must always be treated as an end and not a means."[56] A society is an organization of positive opportunity for each member to pursue individual development as far as personal potentials can be developed within the context of the common good. The common good is the sustaining fullness of freedom of opportunity, enabling each member the maximal freedom 'of pursuit'. What is then proposed is an opening of opportunity to pursue what is individually intended within the context of the 'general welfare' or the common good. It is an *equality in freedom*, not an 'equality of outcome'. And this must be so, just because the latter removes all freedom and imposes the equality of subjection to paternalistic direction.

The virtue of social organization is that it opens up opportunities for development that would otherwise be foreclosed. As Rousseau had pointed out, by virtue of being in an organized society one is transformed "from a stupid and ignorant animal into an intelligent being and a man."[57] A free society transforms its members into citizens. Society as such opens up new opportunities for development, for self-determination of the course of individual life, for the development of moral consciousness — and, most crucially, it invites each citizen to join into this common endeavor. As Green added:

> *The real function of government being to maintain conditions of life* in which morality shall be possible, and morality consisting in the disinterested performance of self-imposed duties, 'paternal government' does its best to make it impossible by narrowing the room for the self-imposition of duties and for the play of disinterested motives.[58]

To the extent that a society respects the humanity of its members, it will not direct their use of their freedom; rather, it will try to outfit them all to use it.

Green's theoretical reconstruction was worked out in his *Lectures on the Principles of Political Obligation*.[59] Finally, he explicated its direct import for the new social conditions induced by industrialization in a lecture delivered in 1880, two years before his death, which brought the import of his theoretical reconstruction to justify the general reforms Disraeli had sponsored. These social reforms of Britain's factory laws, Green noted, enacted

> a great system of restriction, which yet hardly any impartial person wishes to see reversed; which many of us wish to see made more complete. Perhaps, however, we have never thoroughly considered the principles on which we approve it. It may be well, therefore, to spend a short time in ascertaining those principles. We shall then be on surer ground in approaching those more difficult questions of legislation which must shortly be dealt with, and of which the settlement is sure to be resisted in the name of individual liberty.[60]

Merely abstract liberties, Green argued, are not good enough. Needed are socially protected *concrete freedoms*. The state, as the organ of the organized society, has a duty in the name of the common good to interfere with the abstract liberties of some for the sake of concrete freedoms for all. Just as each citizen has an obligation to his society, so the organized society has a reciprocal obligation to equalize opportunities to participate in those freedoms the society defines as its common good. Justifying reforms already made, to mitigate the social Darwinism ('let the fittest survive and the rest perish') that marked the rise of economic license, Green set out some basic principles to guide the ongoing integration of members as citizens.

Focusing on the 'freedom to contract', he pointed out that contracts between people who are grossly unequal in their ability to negotiate can open new oppressions in the name of law. Society has a consequent obligation to pre-empt the abstract right to agree to work an unreasonable number of hours or under health and safety standards that endanger members of the community.

> We shall probably all agree that freedom, rightly understood, is the greatest of blessings; that its attainment is the end of all our effort as citizens. . . . We do not mean merely freedom from restraint or compulsion. We do not mean merely freedom to do as we like irrespectively of what it is that we like. We do not mean a freedom that can be enjoyed by one man or one set of men at the cost of a loss of freedom to others. When we speak of freedom as something to be so highly prized, we mean a *positive power or capacity* of doing or enjoying something worth doing or enjoying, and that, too, something that we do or enjoy in common with others. We mean by it a power which each man exercises *through the help or security given by his fellow-men*, and which he in turn helps to secure for them.

> ...Thus, though of course there can be no freedom among men who act not willingly but under compulsion, the mere enabling a man to do as he likes, is in itself no contribution to true freedom.[61]

Any particular freedom, including the freedom to enter into a contract for one's labor, is like any other particular freedom. It "is valuable only as a means to an end. That end which I call *freedom in the positive sense . . . the liberation of the powers of all men equally for contributions to a common good.*"[62] It is this reasoning that justifies enactments of minimum wage and hour laws; safety, fire, and health standards for conditions of employment — flagrant interferences with *abstract* liberties of property and of the right to contract what is recognized as one's own, yet social protections of individual right to participate in the common good. In the same vein, we have, more recently, generally come to accept the principle that the priority of the social good authorizes the social body to pre-empt other abstract liberties: the 'right' to negotiate one's own employment conditions by protecting the right to oganize unions for collective bargaining; by requiring contributions to social security and unemployment insurance programs; by fire and health regulations for residences and zoning rules for neighborhoods; and, more recently and more generally, by environmental and pollution controls.

Indeed, such restrictions on abstract individual rights have been wedded to more ancient limiting authorizations: the limitation of free speech by laws concerning libel, slander, incitement to riot or treason, and endangering the public safety; the participation by the state in commercial transactions and employment income by virtue of taxation, its enforcement of contracts and maintaining the currency; and, by imposing the priority of a community interest even over personal affairs by legislation controlling marriage, divorce, abortion, military service, and compulsory education.

Most of us today regard the authorization of such powers by government, as the agency of the society, to be fully legitimate, and, perhaps, necessary — even when we might not agree with the prudential wisdom of the way each authorization might be exercised in particular instances. Yet it is difficult to see how any of these *social* intrusions could be justified by a simple principle of 'negative liberty', or embodied in an abstract right to "life, liberty, and property," without torturing their initial meanings.

In point of historic fact, the conception of a positive state as the protector of positive freedoms, and therefore as mandating basic social reforms of liberalism's early industrial state, was developed — be it noted under the 'Tory' leadership of men like Disraeli and Bismarck[63] — by utilizing democratizing principles originally enunciated by Rousseau and Kant. These principles were concretely brought into practice by conservatives, not liberals. Green brought them to Britain and the English-speaking world by uniting them to the concept of prescriptive rights he had learned from Burke.[64]

Having judged Burke's analysis as essentially correct, Green recast it in the light of the totally unprecedented conditions engendered by industrialization. Prescriptive rights due all citizens provide the means by which a society takes its members in as citizens. As social conditions evolve, specific rights must also. Taking up this theme, Green developed the concept of positive freedoms, which a society obligates itself to protect, as the means to integrate its whole citizenry into its construction of a future which they are to share together. If a society is to prescribe the rights of its citizens, which its government is then bound to protect for them in their exercise, it follows that that society has an obligation, through changing customs and laws, to pre-empt certain liberties, as conditions change, in order to prescribe new enabling protections, positive freedoms, or new opportunities.

The government of a free society may rightfully 'intrude' on the lives of its citizens, as new situations develop, beyond customary procedures and criminal laws. For example, it is expected to set out the rules that govern economic activity in much the same way as it is expected to control traffic on its highways.[65] Green notably did not address such questions (which we will address shortly). His prime focus was on the nature of the social freedom which citizenship entails. The concern of 'Greenian reform' is that of the responsibility of the society to its individual members *qua* citizens. And his essential argument was that a prime social responsibility is to interfere with those abstract liberties that foreclose the possibility for each societal member to enjoy the full fruits of citizenship by exploring, each for himself, the opportunities, prescriptive rights or positive freedoms which the society can provide for all.

The essential lesson conveyed is that organized society is not an unfortunate burden which each must bear as a mode of personal protection. Society opens up new opportunities for its members, opportunities they could not otherwise have. When properly conducted in accord with its true nature, a society continually expands its protections as conditions permit in order to enable the lives of its citizens to flower.

To this end — once a society has displaced despotism, and enshrined into its constitutional structures forward-looking defenses against the recurrence of tyranny — its function is no longer to be defined in the merely negative terms of what it 'cannot do'. An organized society has a positive function to perform — as a communal effort to do cooperatively what each cannot do separately[66] — to provide a basis for the fulfillment of the individualizing lives of its members. It is to serve as the guardian for the freedom of its citizens — not only by specifying their liberties, but, more so, by securing their opportunities to enjoy those positive freedoms which a common prosperity enables it to hold out to its citizens as fully acknowledged members. As social conditions radically change, a society alert to the responsibilities it bears for its citizens may, indeed, restrict or enhance the "prescriptive rights" which it pledges to support for its members, but always to enhance their positive freedoms.

By bringing its citizens into active participation in the dynamic of their society, a society itself thereby enriches itself. The first security for a free society is to ensure that every citizen sees a vested interest in the healthy development of its future — by equalizing the opportunities for each to see his own future as dependent on its. By opening up the possibilities for individual development within its scope, by equipping each of its citizens to appropriate that common future as his own, a society gives each a vested interest in its future and thereby ensures itself of their loyalty to its social common good, the mutuality of their shared freedom.

As Green warned, to extend this positive function to paternalistic control, or as he once charmingly put it, "grandmotherly government,"[67] is to defeat the purpose of a free society which has for its prime mission the enhancement of the freedom of its citizens. Just how to draw the line between directive paternalism, to which governmental power tends, and the maintenance of minimal support without encroaching on the freedoms it makes possible, is not an easy one to delineate in abstract terms. Social concern to open opportunities (which necessarily includes the possibility of failure) and to provide 'cushions' (against such failures), must be balanced if true freedom is not to be foresworn. No one who demands clear-cut directives for handling every situation can be satisfied with a neat formula. Perhaps the best advice on this score was already offered by Montesquieu's admonition "that even the excess of reason is not always desirable, and that mankind generally find their account better in mediums than in extremes."[68] The "excess of reason" leads to the imposition of utopian schemes, to be imposed by the reason of some upon the freedom of others. A steady readiness to balance programs and demands, by moderating each in the light of the others, seems to provide the best course for preserving options for rectification while seeking to meet immediate needs.

Opening freedom means opening up avenues for self-development; it does not mean enforcing a predetermined result. Freedom means ensuring a 'fair chance' — but the individual freedom to make the most out of the opportunities one has is negated when the ways in which these are to be used are dictated at every stage along the way. Freedom-to-achieve is meaningless without the freedom to fail — and a responsible society will ensure that failure may be experienced, while nevertheless cushioned so that a new start may yet be made. Freedom means the freedom to decide what, in the social offering, is important to the individual by the individual himself. If I choose to pursue a life of scholarship instead of one of entrepreneurship, or prefer to focus my attention on my hobbies instead of advancement in my employment, I recognize that the fiscal rewards will be grossly different — but the choice is mine; having exercised my option, instead of having it imposed upon me, I have no moral right to complain.

The essential difference — between 'negative liberty' and 'positive freedom', between the 'equalization of opportunity' and the often demanded 'equality of outcome' — is epitomized in the contemporary demand that all society members be educated to citizenship. This is an old idea which was only resurrected with the emergence of the modern age. It is the paradigmatic example of the difference between classical liberalism and the kind of essentially democratic commitment that emerges from the classical heritage brought into the modern world by thinkers such as Burke and Green.

The requirement that *all* children be provided an education is a common feature of a modern society. It is difficult to see how this intrusion into the privacy of family life could be justified by any theory of abstract 'negative' liberty. This societal demand traces itself back to Plato who had boasted of the Athenian requirement that "regulat[ed] the nurture and education of children" with laws regarding "the charge of education . . . *commanding*" each father to have his children properly educated.[69] It was brought into modern times by Rousseau who, having objected to Locke's plan for the education of 'gentlemen', invoked the Greek thesis that society is both prior to and responsible for its own citizenry, and, on this principle, issued one of the first calls for *universal, free, and compulsory education* for citizenship as requisite for a free and, thereby, legitimate society.[70]

Yet the demand for universal compulsory education is a gross social interference with any notion of parental rights and family prerogatives. Its justification is really twofold. First, the interest of society is always prior to any individual preference: society's interest is to rear an educated membership qualified to participate in its life and to contribute to its decisions. Second, society obligates itself to serve as the guardian of the concrete freedoms of its citizens, and thereby is required to guard the open futural opportunities of its junior members so that they may enjoy to the fullest their oncoming participation in its freedom, by insisting that they be enabled to do so.

iii. The Priority of Freedom

Even before the advent of universal compulsory education, de Tocqueville saw the democratizing genius of the new American republic in its 'equality of condition', its rejection of that inherited status which in European societies marked out the particular opportunities an individual was free to pursue. Now, one was newly authorized to enjoy the privileges of social belonging, not because of inheritance but because of the way one managed one's equality of citizenship.

This general equality of condition is to serve freedom, not replace it. Some inequalities are contributory to general social betterment and necessary for freedom to function. The freest governmental system necessarily entrusts some individuals to make decisions, in specified areas, for the rest and thereby invests some with an inequality of decisional authority. Any notion of representation, any social dispersal of authority, rests on an agreement to inequality of decisional power.

Quite aside from the political structure, we readily find such inequalities strewn across the societal landscape. The owner of a store makes decisions about merchandise, inventory, and pricing; we do not question his right to make them, even though we might occasionally protest the decision by taking our patronage elsewhere. In technical fields, we expect experts to be endowed, not only with a special knowledge, but also with special authority to employ that knowledge in making decisions for which they are to be held accountable. We may decide to sit in judgment upon the social implications of those decisions — shall we permit a nuclear energy plant to be operated here? — but we are then judging not the expertise but the wider effects of that expert judgment as we see it bearing on us.

Most gradations of organized life, in any complex society, involve a multitude of complex hierarchies of decision-making authority — a pluralization of decisional authority which is, as we shall see, requisite to the functioning of a free society. We find workers in some factories deliberately taken by management into the decision-making process in their own realms of expertise; generally it seems prudentially wise to invite those involved in a process to participate in decisions concerning its most efficacious implementation. But it is a very different question whether that participation, as an element of an over-all process, itself qualifies its members to evaluate the broadest aspects of that process insofar as its social utility is concerned. And just how the managerial oversight, however controlled, of that particular process feeds into the general perception of social well-being or social need, usually determines the success or failure of the entire enterprise.

Such questions raise important issues for contemporary democratic politics. How are we to reconcile the civic equality of citizens with the specializations and expertise needed for the proper functioning of a modern social order? These questions raise issues of principle, of evaluative priorities, of the lines along which the social future is to be formed.

In the light of social reality, we must remember that whatever be the individual function in the economic or political structure, each citizen is engaged in a variety of decisional communities — which further complicates such questions. As consumers, they effectively determine which products shall continue to be offered and which shall be withdrawn from the marketplace. As members of religious bodies, they bring their perceptions of their accepted value-loyalties into their personal lives and their judgments on social issues. As voting citizens, they each bring a complex of varied perspectives to bear in a consensual judgment on which candidates, and which policies, are to be authorized to govern their future.

The animating principle on which this social cohesion depends, and therefore the end to be achieved in order to secure it, is the ability of human freedom to function. It is this idea of freedom that enables the exercise of intelligence in action. Such a state of freedom itself rests upon the notion of the *moral* equality of man, the right of each to participate in the freedom open to all. As Kant had insisted, each person has a dignity and is, as such, to be honored as a being of intrinsic worth; although we necessarily 'use' each other functionally in any integrated society, no person is to be reduced to merely instrumental value. A person's birthright, as Locke should have said it, a person's essential potentiality, as Rousseau argued, is the ability to participate in a free community. However persons differ and whatever similarities they share, the first principle of a free society is that its members — its citizens — each have a vested stake in the exercise of the freedom they share.

This 'equality of membership' — the 'equality of right' of each to participate in the common good, of education as the enabling qualification to do so, and thereby of open opportunity for the future — is the only kind of social equality a free society can rightfully nurture without betraying its own basic commitment. Each citizen capable of participating in a free society, contributes to it by using the opportunities it offers to enhance his own life and thereby the life of the whole;

to the extent that a person exercises this capability he is acting as a free citizen within it. Civic equality is an equality *in* freedom — to respond to the social invitation to become an individual, which a free society holds open as its promise to its members. In fidelity to its own nature, a free society treats its citizens as individuals and seeks to represent and reconcile their varied interests in its decisional dynamic.

Freedom means the ability to make one's own commitments in the face of individual assessments of possibilities, to act upon them and accept responsibility for what they produce. To transmute this civic *equality in freedom* into specific equalities of status and outcome is to interfere with the most important equality that citizens can share — the equal right to make one's own evaluative decisions and to act upon them, the 'freedom to be free'.

Whatever claims a citizen may make upon the social whole, a state of freedom is their foundation. Any use of this freedom to subvert the condition that makes it possible is self-destructive. Participation in freedom is the goal of a responsible society. A free society prescribes procedures by which to sort out the multitude of conflicting personal claims and to set policies which permit them to be voiced. The first priority of social decision in a free society is to keep the avenues for free social decisions open, to maintain the freedom for individual decisionmaking as a positive contribution to the social whole. Whatever forms of 'liberation' may be sought, as a recent Vatican statement urged, "there can be no liberation if from the beginning, the rights of freedom are not respected."[71]

Societal membership is transformed into citizenship when members are invited to participate in the processes of a free society; availing themselves of the opportunities offered, accepting the possibilities of disappointment that are concomitant with its freedom, they contribute out of individual experiences to the processes of the society itself. A free society prides itself on the opportunities it opens for its citizens; its first priority must always be, within any conflict of values and demands and decisions, to keep open the channels and procedures within which the processes of free decision may continue to function.

iv. Freedom and Power

The self-interest of a person entering into a society's membership is to be admitted into the fullness of belonging as a citizen. The self-interest of a free society is to encourage the contributions of the citizenry to its own mutually perceived common good, to be open to the contributions its free citizens build into it. The self-interest of the citizen is to appropriate the opportunities for free development the society offers. The interest of citizens is really the interest of the society, for a society only realizes its own potential, its common good, insofar as its citizens utilize their freedom to develop their own talents as responsible members of the social whole. This social whole — whether loosely or tightly organized — nurtures its constituents: individuals can only find personal goods, happiness, or fulfillment insofar as the society itself provides the stability and the freedoms for their individual pursuits as private citizens.

But freedom is power. Any positive freedom is the power to take up an opportunity that is offered. The freedom of citizenship is the power to make a difference — on some level of contribution — whether it be in the form of discussion, new endeavor, participation in a common concern, or the autonomous ability to experiment with an idea or a project. The obligation of the society's governmental agencies is to use the power of the whole to enhance the freedoms, the opportunities, of its citizens. They exercise this responsibility by prescribing rights and exacting payment for them in terms of obligations; these socially bestowed rights are activated by maintaining social institutions that facilitate their exercise: equitable courts, high educational standards, and legislation that addresses general needs and wants — conditions enabling its citizens to freely function. As social conditions evolve, the balance between individual and community interest must prove itself flexibly dynamic if the social order is to prosper. This may require the government of a free people to pre-empt certain liberties, certain powers, that may prove nugatory in particular circumstances in order to enlarge the area of prescriptive rights, positive freedoms, or grants of social powers which it undertakes to protect. Freedoms need to be specified, just as equalities need be defined; as positive opportunities, they must be explicated and thereby limited in order to be made real.

The self-interest of a free people is to be free. The self-interest of a free people is to be able to forge individual destinies that contribute to the good of the whole. The power to do this is found in a dynamic social order that uses the opening of opportunity — the power to make a difference — by its citizens as its prime criterion for its policy decisions. A free society is one that effectively disperses the *power to be free*, to make decisions, among the citizenry. It enhances their operational freedom by protecting its exercise. By dispersing the power of decision among its citizens, it enables the differences between them to enrich their society by bringing a plurality of intelligence and perspective to function together in loyalty to the common endeavor: a society of free citizens.

Freedom is power. A mutuality of freedom requires a diversification of power. Free citizens accept limits on their own individual power by ordaining a government with powers to handle what they conceive to be the needs of the community as such, while limiting the freedom and power of their selected governors to this concern. The self-interest of the governed is, however, not always perceived as being in the best interest of the governors. For the nature of power is such that those entrusted with some power invariably demand more. The interest of a free people is to empower their governors to govern in the perceived common interest of the organized community while yet restraining their governors from pre-empting any power beyond this end. For the power taken up by their governors pre-empts, while it defines, those areas of free activity to be reserved to the citizenry.

This problem — how to reconcile the requisite of governmental power adequate to what needs to be done, with the power of citizens to pursue their own lives — poses the central question of how a free people may allow themselves to be governed. They need to carefully balance the freedom of the organized community to act into the future as one unit with the freedom of its citizens to face their own futures as individuals. As responsible citizens of a free society, the interest of citizens in the health of their society impels them to want a government powerful enough to do what they believe needs to be done, to anticipate, in the light of their continuing freedom, those future needs which the ongoing continuity of their mutual freedom may require. But responsible citizens of a free society jealously reserve all other freedom of decision to themselves. In ordaining a governing system, a citizenry sets out the way it disperses and limits authority by the specific requirements, stipulations, and announced freedoms, it prescribes and permits; by the way it disperses authority and power, it determines to what extent the time of free citizens is to remain free.

A free people's political problem is to empower their governors to fulfill their charge, while keeping the public's future options as open as possible by foreclosing the governors from doing more. This is essentially a temporal problem: how are citizens to ordain their chosen governors with the authority to do what present possibilities require while retaining the authority to determine the nature of the specific kind of free future they seek to build? To simultaneously empower and limit their governors, to empower decision-making authority for present needs while keeping the future as open as possible? The problem of free governance is to reconcile the conflict between adequate delegated authority to handle the problems of the present while reserving for the citizenry itself adequate control over their own freedom for the future.

Chapter **5**

Governance

Whatever else particular governments do or do not do, however they are organized, they control — by laws, regulations, institutions, and procedures — the time of their citizens. A command society systematically regiments their temporality for those ends deemed important by its governors. A free society strives to keep the temporality of private citizens as open as possible.

When we evaluate different governmental systems, the first question must be how well it defends its territory against intruders. Once that territory is effectively secured, however, we ask about the condition of the society it governs. As the over-all coordinating agency of the entire society, a system of governance can be gauged by the degree of prosperity and opportunities for advancement the populace enjoys in the light of their resources, historical condition, and the level of their educational and cultural attainments.

The simplest criterion is the general satisfaction of its people. If their complaints are minor and they are generally content; if they do not consider emigrating, but rather fear being overwhelmed by new immigrants from other lands, one can surmise that generally speaking 'something is being done right', that their system is functioning well.

In a free society, what the average citizen wants most is to be left alone to the fullest extent possible, while the government operates without scandal or crisis and does what it has been charged to do. What the average citizen values above all is a rising level of general prosperity, the security of person and possessions, and these, in large measure, because they open the freedom to control individual time.

The government of a free society, as the general coordinating agency of that society, by its laws and rules, engages or disengages the possibilities for individual temporal self-control. In contrast to command societies, for example, it does not assign each citizen to a particular job but leaves each free to find one's own; it does not assign leisure-time activities but leaves each free to choose them for oneself. The 'freedom to be free' is the freedom to pursue one's own temporal course.

One prime political obstacle to the development of freedom has been the intrusive tendency of governmental power. "Power," Lord Acton warned, "corrupts and absolute power corrupts absolutely." Those with some power, even in good conscience, usually see virtue in gaining more. One can safely say that a general tendency of those entrusted with government is to aggrandize their own authority.

Governmental power has always been requisite to building a free society. The paradox of a free society has always been that it needs a government powerful enough to do what needs to be done and yet under such popular controls as enable the populace to retain ultimate control over its policies. Citizens of free societies live under some of the most powerful governments in human history — largely because of the resources available and the complex tasks that need to be undertaken. And yet they have succeeded in developing governmental procedures that permit this concentration of social power to function for the defense of freedom by being kept under due restraint.

This accomplishment represents the struggles of a long history to which we are deeply indebted. The accommodation of political power to political freedom that has been achieved brings to bear lessons spreading over two millenia.

The thinking that this development brought into force evolved in at least four decisive stages, each predicated on the understanding of man as an inherently social being concerned for a measure of free citizenship. At each step the lessons perceived in earlier stages were taken up and refined so as to commend specific principles for the future. Taken together they present a continuity of thought that speaks to us today as we continue to face the necessity of integrating freedom and power.

The problem of power largely 'boils down' to one twofold question: 'who has the authority to decide what?'. The problem is most acutely faced whenever we seek to square the need for focused authority that expresses the freedom of the community to act as one entity while yet enhancing the power of individual freedom to serve the common good. This essentially political problem is not confined to the political arena; it pervades every aspect of social life, our economic and cultural institutions, our organized activities. The problem of power is the core problem for the organization of freedom.

Yet it was in political terms that principles were worked out by which to reconcile and harmonize the freedom of the whole with the freedom of the members. Lessons learned from political development speak forcefully to any area of concern in which the problem of power and freedom appears. The central theme of this development is that the continuity of freedom depends on fragmenting power so that freedom may function,while yet pluralizing centers of authority so that the use of power might be effectively utilized while being held accountable to popular control. Embodied to some degree in the government of every free people, this theme comes into clearest light as we briefly review the four chief stages of its development, each of which developed the thesis that power must be pluralized if it is to serve freedom.

Once we are clear about the political ramifications of this principle, its ramifications for extension to other areas of social concern will readily appear.

i. The Legacy of 'Polity'

The first encounter between the forces of freedom and power, as far as we can tell, took place in ancient Greece. Aristotle's *Politics*, an empirical examination of the principles exemplified in the governments of his time, can still be read as a comprehensive attempt to face this issue, even if in the simpler terms of his own society.

In an incisive if perhaps oversimplified way, Aristotle had spelled out a distinction of governmental types — which still speaks to us. His distinction of six types of government asked first about how many persons share supreme authority and then, more crucially, whether that authority is used for a partial or general benefit.

Governmental types represent 'perverse' and 'true' forms of political authority; they are to be distinguished by the principle of justice operative among free citizens:

> governments which have a regard to the common interest are consti-
> tuted in accordance with strict principles of justice and are therefore
> true forms; but those which regard only the interest of the rulers are

all defective and perverted forms, for they are despotic, where as a [polity] is a community of freemen (1279a).

'True', or we might now say 'legitimate', types of government are to be composed of free citizens whose authority is used for the good of the governed, for the good of the governed society-as-a-whole. 'Perverse', or 'illegitimate' types of government use their power for the good of the rulers, whoever they happen to be: A government headed by one supreme power is a tyranny when run for the benefit of the ruler, but a true monarchy when run for the benefit of the society; an oligarchy when run by the wealthy few for their own benefit, but an aristocracy when run by the few who are best qualified to rule for the benefit of the society; and, a democracy when run by the majority of the people for their own benefit, but a 'true polity' when it is rooted in popular rule and conducted for the benefit of the entire society.

The best practical form of government incarnates the idea of 'polity' itself: "when the citizens at large administer the state for the common interest, the government is called by the generic name, — a constitution" (1279a). Pure democracy, or direct self-rule by the majority for its own benefit, is 'perverse' because its principle — rule for the benefit of the ruler — is not inherently different from other self-interested modes of governance.

Aristotle's political realism promptly faced the question of how a 'constitutional government' or 'polity' might actually be formed. As a practical matter, he argued that it arises out of the fusion of the two best of the 'perverse' forms, oligarchy and democracy:

> polity or constitutional government may be described generally as a fusion of oligarchy and democracy; but the term is usually applied to those forms of government which incline towards democracy, and the term aristocracy to those which inclined towards oligarchy, because birth and education are commonly the accompaniments of wealth (1293b).

Because this fusion brings into unison the prime divergent forces constituting a society, it compels them to rule together for the good they share in common, the good of the society as a whole.

A state does not need to be governed by its best citizens in order to be well-governed: for good government consists of not only "the actual obedience of citizens to the laws," but also of "the goodness of the laws which they obey"(1294a). Insofar as a merit system applies to the distribution of offices which functions for the common good, the society is an aristocracy, "for the principle of an aristocracy is virtue, as wealth is of an oligarchy, and freedom of a democracy"(1294a).

Three divergent justifications are invoked by men who "claim an equal share in the government, freedom, wealth and virtue." We might settle for a combination of two, but ideally all three would be combined in the best of all practicable states:

> the admixture of the two elements, that is to say, of the rich and poor, is to be called a polity or constitutional government; and the union of the three is to be called aristocracy or the government of the best, and more than any other form of government, except the true and ideal, has a right to this name (1294a).

But a government is always the government *of* a society and the health of government depends upon that of the society it governs: A free and stable society must be based on a strong middle class:

> the best political community is formed by citizens of the middle class, and . . . those states are likely to be well-administered, in which the middle class is large, and stronger if possible than both the other classes, or at any rate than either singly; for the addition of the middle class turns the scale, and prevents either of the extremes from being dominant (1295b).

This is so for several still-pertinent reasons. A predominantly middle-class society permits it to anticipate a lessening of divisive factionalism: a middle class places a premium on social harmony and is not given to fomenting "factions and dissensions"; because it seeks to avoid social divisions, it generally encourages a preference for larger rather than smaller states (1296a).[1]

A middle-class society is a relatively stable society; in contrast, a state divided between the rich and the poor cannot attend to the common good because it is continually preoccupied by their continuing struggle for "political supremacy" (1296a). In contrast to continuing civil strife, sound governmental structure presumes, "as a general principle common to all governments, that the portion of the [polis] which desires the permanence of the constitution ought to be stronger than that which desires the reverse." Thus, "there only can the government be stable where the middle class exceeds one or both of the others"(1296b):"a government which is composed of the middle class" which generally owns property "more nearly approximates to democracy than to oligarchy, and is the safest of the imperfect forms of government" (1302a).

Finally, a middle-class society is better able tó anticipate future problems. Because of its generalized composition, it is able to discern and anticipate streams of discontent and take timely measures to anticipate them: by heading off pending disruption, it can bind the loyalties of all citizens to the common good. A stable polity is not faced with revolutionary challenges; the test of social policy is to *anticipate* grievances likely to ferment into social disruption and to ameliorate them before they ignite.

A strong middle class shares interests with both the poor and the rich, and has a vested interest in mediating conflicts between them so that neither side is disruptive because it feels it is being treated unjustly. "The only stable principle of government is equality according to proportion, and for every man to enjoy his own" (1307a): the health of a free society depends upon justly compensating all contributions to the general good and seeking to ensure that even the most destitute own some property — have some 'relation to things' (1280a) and reasonable expectations of gaining more.[2]

To what he already had said, we might add a fourth: a middle class is schooled by its own commercial preoccupations to function in freedom. It is habituated to assess goods and services, to implement coherent criteria for free evaluation of alternative possibilities, and to engage in private negotiations that are subsequently binding. These customary practices teach its members to negotiate individual judgments and to abide by the compromises they produce. This training in the free use of reason, which a middle-class economy provides at its core, is itself an important contributory factor to its general preference for free governments that function in similar ways.

In setting out the standard of 'polity', in which the well-being of the whole society is taken as the object of governance, Aristotle enunciated what we today take from its Roman development as the principle of 'republican government'. To this must of course be added the Roman Republic's legacy of a concept of law which embodies all social rights and obligations in the concept of citizenship.

Already, Aristotle had pointed out that a 'polity' must be composed of a constituted 'mixture' of the elements composing the body of citizens — the original meaning of the idea of 'mixed government' — so that their common interest could be represented in its decisional councils. In order for an organized society to be well-governed, *all* of its elements need a voice in its councils — only so, can they be reasonably expected to consolidate all divergent interests, attract all loyalties, and rule for the good of the whole.

Without using the phrase, Aristotle had already perceived the danger of 'majority tyranny'. His prescription was not to invite unmitigated majority rule by centering the government in a legislative assembly. Rather, he proposed the division of governmental power between those exercising executive, legislative, and judicial authority (1297a ff.) so that balance and consensus could be achieved. Those citizens who do not participate in a governing majority, nevertheless are societal members; the interest of the whole is that they feel free to voice dissenting opinions and perceive that their interests and perspectives are respected, if not always accepted. A society of free citizens does not 'ram down' decisions; it rather seeks, within the lack of pressing need for decision, to conciliate varieties of opinion into a general consensus of the whole.[3]

Of the three 'perverse' forms, Aristotle clearly saw that "democracy is the most tolerable" (1289b). But he clearly understood democracy as the rule of the 'many', who in his time happened to be the poor. This, however, was not democracy's prime distinction: for "democracy is the form of government in which the free are rulers, and the oligarchy in which the rich; *it is only an accident that the free are the many and the rich are the few*" (1290b, [italics mine]). The essential point is not whether the 'many' are rich or poor, but whether they are free. And the dominance of a middle class is socially salubrious because the ownership of material possessions gives free citizens a vested interest in enhancing the society to which they belong.

In today's industrialized free societies, the borders of poverty have been pushed back beyond any ancient expectation. The poor are no longer the 'many'. Social progress has succeeded in absorbing ever larger portions of population into a growing middle class; the poor have become a minority — and face the dangers of any minority under a majoritarian system of government: that their interests may be ignored.[4]

In any free society, Aristotle admonished, "the citizen is a member" of the community (1276b). He should, as such, be enabled to enjoy the benefits of membership by participating in its common good. A free polity identifies its common good with the freedom of its citizens; to the extent that a polity identifies its own good not merely with the good of its governing majority but with the good of the whole, it is incumbent upon it to ensure all the opportunity to share in its freedoms.

For a society to be free, membership must be voluntary. it is patently contradictory to say that a person is free *within* his society but not free to leave it. This central principle had already been enunciated in Plato's *Crito*. Its concluding passages, as a conversation between Socrates and the Laws of Athens, announce the principle that a free society provides to its citizens the opportunity to leave without penalty; in return, it requires that, should they choose to remain,they agree not only to be bound by the procedures and laws of the society, but also to call to general attention those social defects they think need correction:

> we further proclaim to any Athenian by the liberty which we allow him, that if he does not like us when he has become of age and has seen the ways of the city, and made our acquaintance, he may go where he pleases and take his goods with him. . . . Anyone who does not like us and the city, and who wants to emigrate . . . may go where he likes, retaining his property. But he who has experience of the manner in which we order justice and administer the state, and still remains, has entered into an implied contract that he will do as we command him. And he who disobeys us is, as we maintain,thrice wrong; first, because in disobeying us he is disobeying his parents; secondly, because we are the authors of his education; thirdly, because he has made an agreement with us that he will duly obey our commands; and he neither obeys them nor convinces us that our commands are unjust; and we do not rudely impose them, but give him the alternative of obeying or convincing us . . . (51-52)

This social bestowal of individual rights upon citizens presumes that the relation between an individual and the society is generational; that society membership carries obligations with it; that the right of private ownership is socially recognized; that the society *insists* that no individual shall be required to stay beyond his will to do so; *and* that deciding to remain as a citizen requires not only an obligation to obey the law but also the exercise of a socially protected *obligation* to evaluate specific proposals for reforming the law through free discussion with fellow citizens.

As given, what might well be called the 'right to resign', the right to take one's property and leave without penalty, is spelled out as *the essential socially bestowed freedom* undergirding any subsequent obligation. The socially protected obligatory freedom to constructively criticize if one stays, and the right to *un*punishable emigration if one prefers, become two prime principles a society must exhibit for it to claim political legitimacy.[5] The essentially voluntary nature of a free society grounds the obligations it exacts from its citizens as the price of the freedoms the common strength of the society protects for them.

A just society is a voluntary society that defines itself in terms of freedom. It pursues its own best interest by representing the broad spectrum of its membership within its governing structure; it governs for their general welfare as the common good in which they all are to have a shared vested interest. Recognizing different levels within its citizenry, it depends upon a community of mutual respect. Composed of free citizens, it seeks their general integration by moderating their disparities and affording them the opportunities to seek their own well-being within the context it provides. The common concern is to engage the interests of free citizens to find their social membership advantageous for whatever pursuits they might each select to engage their time.

ii. The Politics of Power

The idea of republican government emerged from the ashes of the classical world during the Renaissance, one thousand years after the end of Roman rule. The rise of city-states together with the rebirth of commercialism produced an urban middle class in northern Italy and Germany, in Holland and Switzerland; the renaissance of learning and the crises of individual conscience induced by the Protestant Reformations led to the assertion of the right to think and speak for oneself. These new forces, passing over the rural countryside characterized by serfdom and feudal hierarchies, found nourishment in resurgent towns where they joined to reawaken ideas of self-government and individual liberty.[6]

Perhaps no one played a greater role in bringing lessons from the ancient world into the modern than Niccolò Machiavelli. His *Discourses*, still a prime textbook for facing the real questions of a free polity, had searched out lessons from Livy's history of the Roman Republic in order to guide the new republics of his time.

Machiavelli's concern was the preservation and enhancement of liberty. He quickly saw that the question of liberty is inseparable from questions of power. "Here we are in the presence of something little short of a revolution in political thinking. . . . The whole drift of his work is toward a political realism, unknown to the formal writing of his time."[7] Developing some themes already enunciated by Aristotle,

Machiavelli's work initiated modern political science and the theory of the free republic.

As Aristotle had seen free polity emerging from the union of the two primarily opposed classes into a unified society, so Machiavelli saw his free republic as unifying the three civic classes of his time. But Machiavelli explicated and brought to the fore a theme which is only hinted at in Aristotle's texts: the thesis that political activity is concerned with a struggle for power. This struggle is not to be lamented; it needs to be strengthened by being ordered if liberty is to be made secure. A state of liberty requires that power is so divided that no one part of the community holds all of it.

Bringing all social elements into the composition of governing authority, into a 'mixed' constitution, precludes any monopoly of power: "when there is combined under the same constitution a prince, a nobility, and the power of the people, then these three powers will watch and keep each other reciprocally in check."[8] Modified in terms which can be directly equated with Aristotle's formulation by substituting the Renaissance term 'nobility' for Aristotle's 'oligarchs', he said, "in every republic there are two parties, that of the nobles and that of the people; and all the laws that are favorable to liberty result from the opposition of these parties to each other."[9]

The enemy of liberty is concentrated power. Insofar as those who wield power can be expected to identify their own good with that of the society as a whole, they will seek to impose their authority as far as lack of resistance permits. Liberty ensues only when each acknowledges a vested interest in forestalling any monopoly of power; fearful of dominance by others, each finds security despite any lack of complete power by insisting on a state of liberty for all (which always includes oneself).

Further, Machiavelli's republic incorporates within itself that degree of equalization that democratization requires. Democratic republics, Machiavelli came close to saying, constitute the best form of government yet devised. Their superiority is manifested by what they are able to accomplish: "cities where the people are the masters make the greatest progress in the lest possible time . . ."[10] And, "only those cities and countries that are free can achieve greatness."[11]

Preeminently, a free state provides unique possibilities for general prosperity because it brings a greater diversity of outlooks to bear upon common problems and it incorporates a greater willingness on the part of its people to contribute to their common interest. Such a republic is generally industrious and neither honors nor calls to power "those who are called gentlemen who live idly upon the proceeds of their extensive possessions . . . [for] such men are pernicious to any country or republic."[12] Because its citizens are industrious and prize their liberty, they have learned to depend upon their own judgments and commitments; being practiced in the art of thinking for themselves in the practical situations upon whose outcome they depend, they generally "are more prudent and stable, and have better judgment than a prince" even "if he be esteemed wise."[13]

Precisely because its social decisions are necessarily responsive to the diverse sources of its authority, such a society places a premium on the public good and grants the general prosperity a priority before that of any one of its members; thus, in contrast to a one-man government, "the general good is regarded nowhere but in republics, because whatever they do is for the common benefit."[14] And this is because the good of the individual citizens, whatever their own efforts may be, ultimately depends upon the general prosperity of the society within which all individual efforts transpire. Because each has a vested interest in the good of the whole, a republic maintains and protects free discussion of public affairs and advocacy of reform so that "every one may propose what he deems for the public good," and thus may feel himself participating in its determination.[15]

The liberty of a republic encourages the expression of diversity, of individual initiatives, the contributions of the divergent perspectives of citizens upon the problems they share together, the diversification of the citizenry a state of liberty encourages: "It is this which assures to republics greater vitality and more enduring success than monarchies have; for the diversity of the genius of her citizens enables the republic better to accommodate herself to the changes of the times than can be done by a prince," who may always be expected to consider his own personal self-interest first.[16]

In order to sustain a stable, prudent, and intelligent people who combine community loyalty with that loyalty to diverse individuality upon which a free society depends, Machiavelli argued that there must be a sound moral fiber, good habits, and a recognition of religion's import for the affairs of life. He thus regarded "religion as the most necessary and assured support of any civil society."[17] Often accused of having attacked religion and its impact, what he criticized was not any particular religious commitment or speculative theology, as such (the import of which he underlined), but specific ecclesiastical actions and dogmas — and always from the vantage point of their effect on the health of a particular society. This is not to be 'anti-religious'; indeed, it is to acknowledge religion's central import for a free civil society.

Sound moral and religious teaching encourage good laws that induce "good habits on the part of the people," a prerequisite for laws to be observed and a free people to prosper.[18] The developed moral fiber of a people is necessary if they are to maintain their liberty. And the quality of the laws, which regulate their affairs and command their obedience, joins their religion to the personal examples of their more prominent citizens, in the educative function of setting out standards for acceptable civic behavior.

It is to be expected, Machiavelli noted, that popular liberty may, at times, lead to some follies and excesses. But what is to be most feared is "not the immediate evil that may result from them . . . but the fact that such general confusion might afford the opportunity for a tyrant to seize the government" by demagogic appeals.[19] As Röpke observed, "Machiavelli was . . . perhaps the first to recognize clearly that the demon of power is not only to be found in despotic rulers but also in the people and can easily be released by any demagogue."[20]

The first task of a free society is to preserve the conditions of its liberty. Doing so depends upon keeping excesses from becoming dominant while maintaining a public balance of social elements and forces continually competing for a greater voice in the public councils. For this reason, it is especially incumbent upon those charged with the governance of a free society to "think in advance what adversities may befall them."[21] Because a free society brings diverse perspectives to bear on any social problem, its practical advantage is that its citizens, trained to build their own futures, are trained to look ahead, to anticipate possibilities, evaluate alternatives, and commit themselves to present courses of action in the light of reasoned expectations.

"Time," Machiavelli said, is "the father of all truth."[22] The practical experience of free citizens is experience in managing their own time-relations. Time is experienced in handling the sequential relations of events, not of theoretical moments of measurable intervals. Managing our own time teaches us to relate particular events and actions in terms of what is presently actual and what is genuinely possible: to evaluate with a practiced intelligence the relation of what is antecedent and what can be rationally anticipated as the consequence of a course of action connecting the two. "The size of an event is its consequences."[23] In such a temporal perspective — and this is one reason why historical experience is so important to evaluating what realistically yet-can-be[24] — the constellation of events, as they focus on the prospects before it, *is* the situation which it discerns as what is now "on our hands," for resolution into the future. A constitution — the accepted set of procedures by which public decisions are to be made — is thus "a temporal device" created to regulate "the [oncoming] sequences of legal and political events." Machiavelli's central thesis is that a constitution that 'mixes' the strata of the society *into* its ruling *pre*scriptive procedural code "has a staying power"[25] superior to any alternative construction.

Each citizen pursuing a personal life path is seeking out the better future which a state of liberty authorizes. He is concerned, not merely to select from a 'cafeteria' choice of proffered possibilities arrayed before him, but to project himself forward into a future that is to be created, and to bring that vision of possibility back into the present situation as a new point of departure. An individual is *"a turner of events,"*[26] who changes the course of development. The efficacy of individual decision is that it makes a difference to the society, in a minute if not a profound way, by altering the details of its course. A rich multitude of individual decisions enriches the society and requires an openness to futurity in the social community — that general ongoing freedom which one identifies with one's own being. This kind of experience, enabling one to feed one's own insights, demands openness for freedom in the social consensus in which one participates. Creative individuality finds no advantage in a pervasively directed social order — seriously curtailing individual foresights and creative appropriation of individually conceived possibilities. Creative individuality requires a social order in which the perspectives of others freely feed into the sustaining consensus that enervates them together.

Exercise of individual initiative, foresight, and creative anticipation, depends upon a social order that not only permits but also encourages individuating activity. The citizen of a free society requires a stability of social processes, which enables one to avoid distracting crises and upheavals along the way. For this reason a free society is a generally conservative society: it is reluctant to change its own basic procedural arrangements and modes of operation.[27] It may generally be expected to prefer to ride out a storm rather than undergo any radical transformation.

In many ways, what Machiavelli had done is remarkable in both prescience and principle. In sharpest contrast to the Greek ideal of an all-wise and benevolent ruler, Machiavelli did not turn to constitutional government as a reluctant 'second best'. Rather he warned against "that unrealistic disregard of the daemonic quality of naked political power"[28] which too many passionate advocates of favored proposals and quick cures for social illnesses too readily ignore. For this reason, he argued that republican government is *the best kind* of government we can envision — because it is the *only* kind in which liberty can be secure.

The patent superiority of republican government is the stability it provides for the exercise of liberty, the kinds of citizens that its liberty produces, and its general devotion to its conception of the common good. This liberty for each to manage one's own life combines the power of each to pursue his own within a community empowered to act for the common good. For the first time, perhaps, he highlighted the import for a free society of the middle-class virtue of industriousness. And, perhaps also for the first time, he directed attention to the significance of temporal considerations for the intelligent formulation and appraisal of proposals for public policy.

His method was to examine historical experience, to presume that unique as any contemporary situation may be it still has antecedents essentially similar, and that any prudential sense of moral obligation requires us to learn from the experiences of previous generations. Knowing which specific kinds of measures 'worked' or did 'not work' can illuminate ways out of present quandries. Because all people seem to be animated by essentially similar desires and passions, "it is easy, by a diligent study of the past, to foresee what is likely to happen in the future in any republic, and [this consideration can enable us to] apply those remedies that were used" in earlier societies to meet our similar problems.[29] Prudential use of historical knowledge is not to merely repeat an intrinsically unrepeatable past but to more intelligently anticipate our possible futures.[30] Foresight and historical knowledge are intertwined; intelligent operational prudence has a responsibility to perceive sequential connections between past experience and what has not yet been rendered into recorded history.

Three of Machiavelli's themes merit particular attention for the light they offer to contemporary political wisdom: First is the strictly pragmatic advice to always look ahead to the practical effects of any program or proposal and judge it accordingly. The evaluation of a course of action or a proposal is not to be judged by how responsive it may be to the problem it claims to address or by what it promises — but by what outcome it is likely to *produce*. The evaluation of any pro-

gram or course of action should be in terms of the actual 'effects' that
can be rationally expected to ensue. Our *retrospective* judgments do just
that. And one consideration which Machiavelli notably did *not* always
take into account (and which will engage our attention at the end)
must be: the precise way in which we pursue a specific outcome, itself
produces all the 'effects' that will come out of the efforts we expend to
achieve it, whatever it may be.

Second is loyalty to the enabling condition: the central criterion
for evaluating any course of action is not any arbitrarily chosen goal
— the course of action must itself prove conducive to the maintenance
of public liberty to be judged as good. Evaluation is to be in terms of
public liberty — precisely because it alone can faithfully promise the
continuing possibility of re-evaluation and re-decision. An essential
criterion of any proposal to ameliorate a particular grievance is that it
does so in a way that carries into the future the stability of that liberty
which is the condition for still further improvement.

Third and crucial is the prescient insight that the stability of the
state of liberty depends upon the legal protection of ordered continuity
of the struggle for power. Any monopoly of power is to be foresworn
— because each 'faction', especially when convinced of its own righ-
teousness, seeks to impose it on all. Each 'faction' may be expected to
read the good of the community in terms of its own self-interest.[31] The
triumph of any particular 'interest' or 'ideological' 'faction' when
placed ahead of the common good can only hold out a promise of its
own tyrannical imposition for the rest of the community.

The possibility of liberty, against the sincerity of all zealots,
depends upon fragmenting political power, dispersing it among the
members of the entire community. To protect that dispersal is the
common interest of the society as a whole, as it maintains the continuing possibility for the struggle for power and influence, *within* the
community's procedural structure. This protection of the diversification of the power of freedom makes a free society free.[32]

An essential criterion for the evaluation of the procedural structure a society accepts, is that it specifies viable procedures by which
dissent from the predominant view may be expressed and be afforded
access to participation in the institutions it ordains. A 'right to revolution' may indeed obtain under a government which forecloses such
procedures for changes in policy or its governors by popular decision,
or that forecloses the public discussion of proposals for change and the
ability for expression of changes in the public will. But when a set of
peaceful procedures is established for such changes, it would seem that

armed uprising by any concerned group is, itself, a gross infringement of the rights of all other citizens. One principle, as Aristotle already pointed out, by which free government is guided is meeting grievances instead of aggravating or encouraging them in order to pre-empt any perceived need for revolution. One reason for representing social diversity in the councils of state is so that grievances may be voiced and become known, and thus, to open up procedures for change in accord with general consensus, and to forestall any justifiable perception of a need for lawless procedures.

The exercise of political activity in a free society is always a struggle for influence and power; the basic freedom a free society bestows on its citizens is the ability to control their own lives to the fullest extent consistent with universalizing that ability for all citizens. This kind of freedom can only be secure when it is generally presumed; this presumption depends upon the society's stable and continuing dedication to the health of its freedom. The stability of freedom depends upon the socially protected opportunity to discuss, advocate, and seek representation for particular views and programs in the decision-making structures of its governing system. Machiavelli's most important insight is that liberty is power: the stability of liberty and the individuated power of decision it entails depends upon its democratization, its dispersal among the citizens of a free republic, whose free dedication of their time to its utilization is regarded as a prime virtue of their common good.

iii. Constitutionalism

The notion of the city-state dominated political thought and provided the criteria for free government — from Aristotle who, writing at the end of Athens' Age of Pericles, died in 322 B.C., to Machiavelli, who died in 1527 at the height of the Italian Renaissance. Even Rousseau, who died two hundred and fifty years later — two years after the American Declaration of Independence — still had thought in terms of the city-state.

It was left to Charles de Secondat, Baron de la Brède et de Montesquieu,[33] to bring their issues and concerns into what was rapidly becoming the novel political form of the developing modern world, the emerging commercial nation-state. His *The Spirit of the Laws* finally explicated the principle of Constitutionalism which has, in one way or another, guided the development of all free republics since its original publication in 1748.[34]

Its political (as distinct from more sociological) sections, took up Machiavelli's concern to secure and enhance public liberty in the struggle for power that characterizes a free society. It thus set out the principles of modern republicanism. Although Montesquieu commended the unique British achievement of having attained the greatest degree of liberty then known, the political parts of his work nevertheless failed in what may have been part of his intent — to urge that democratizing reform of the French monarchy which could well have foreclosed the need for the revolutionary upheaval that would occur in 1789. More immediately, however, it was to have a decisive practical political impact: 34 years after the death of its author, 41 years after its initial publication, its leading principles, embodied in the Constitution of the first democratic republic of the modern world, began to govern the newly created United States.

His prescriptive itemization of the social conditions necessary for a free society has stood the test of time. Despite the fact that British government, by combining executive and legislative functions into one body, violated one of Montesquieu's central principles,[35] his influence was brought to bear on the development of English law by Blackstone in his landmark *Commentaries of the Laws of England*,[36] and as "Burke's inspiration."[37] Montesquieu provided the crucial principles which structured the American Constitution, as *The Federalist* clearly shows. His principles thus contributed to the development of both Britain and America: in a subordinate way, to the former which he had used as his ostensible model, and, most prominently, to the free 'confederate republic' explicitly constituted by the light of his work. These principles would seem to provide needed guidance for any free polity concerned to ensure the stability of its liberty and its own duration.

Montesquieu drew his central lessons out of his portrayal of the government of England, "the one [contemporary] nation that has for the direct end of its constitution political liberty."[38] Just why England was the first major nation to develop enduring institutions of liberty is a complex question rooted in British history. But in the early 1700s, with the possible exception of Holland, it was the only model to which an advocate of liberty could look for any guidance.

Serious questions have been raised as to how accurately Montesquieu had portrayed Britain's governmental structure.[39] Randall noted that Montesquieu had seriously "misinterpreted the British constitution almost as badly as had Voltaire . . . [for] he found in it a calculated system of checks and balances, which in fact parliamentary and cabinet government was in the process of transforming."[40] It is, however, conceivable that this misrepresentation of the British system's actual functioning may have been deliberate in accord with literary practice of the time: to commend reform in one's own country by projecting unpublishable criticisms and proposals onto the description of another, as he had already done in his *Persian Letters*.

However this may be, Montesquieu regarded the principles he was enunciating as more important than their descriptive accuracy.[41] He brought to bear, in his portrayal of the governmental structure that presumably grounded English liberties, an invocation of the lessons to be gleaned from a careful study of the Greek polities and particularly of the Roman Republic, the only previous extended system of legal justice designed to protect the liberties of its citizens. Looking back to the "spirit [of] the classics," as Strauss remarked,[42] Montesquieu brought to the modern nation-state the lessons he had taken from Plato and Aristotle, Cicero and Polybius, and Machiavelli.[43] Above all, his effort was directed "to analyze the constitutional conditions upon which freedom depends."[44] In doing so, he succeeded in bringing the classic tradition of republican government into the modern world, and set forth a standard to which, he claimed, any government dedicated to the freedom of its citizens must adhere.

Montesquieu delineated three types of government — despotism, monarchy, and a republican government that seems to be a combination of democratic and aristocratic elements. Most of his remarks were directed to that kind of moderated monarchy which even today provides the constitutional structure of most free countries, which are, as often observed, truly republics even in the guise of a monarchical form.

Elucidating the nature of republican government, he set out the standard for modern representative government. A governmental system "in which the body or only a part of the people is possessed of the supreme power" he described as a republic; it is a "democracy [when the whole] body of the people in a republic are possessed of the supreme power." By this was not meant the direct-democracy of the Greek city-state or a New England 'town meeting', but rather, the degree to which the right to vote is extended to the full body of the citizenry. Citizens "in whom the supreme power resides, ought to do of themselves whatever conveniently they can; and what they cannot well do, they must commit to the management of ministers." The "fundamental maxim" of popular government is "that the people should chuse their ministers, that is their magistrates," their governing officials charged to represent them.[45]

The reason for preferring representative government as proper for a democratic republic is not merely convenience — imagine the impossibility of convening the whole people of any modern city, much less any modern nation, into one compact meeting. More importantly, the average citizen is simply not qualified to represent his own interests and his own will in the complex affairs to which the government must attend. "The people are extremely well qualified for chusing those whom they are to intrust with part of their authority. . . . But are they able to manage affairs, to find out and make a proper use of places, occasions, moments? No, this is beyond their capacity." Yet: "The public business must however be carried on, with a certain motion neither too quick nor too slow. But the action of the common people is always either too remiss or too violent,"[46] especially in large states where people do not know each other.

Additionally, representative government has a "great advantage" over any kind of direct participatory democracy: representatives are "capable of [freely] discussing affairs. For this the people collectively are extremely unfit." While representatives require only a "general instruction" from their constituents and not detailed consultations on every item of proposed legislation, they are charged, in their deliberations, to effectively voice the "general will" of their constituents. To do otherwise would "throw them into infinite delays, would give each deputy a power of controlling the assembly; and on the must urgent and pressing occasions the springs of the nation might be stopped by a single caprice." After deliberation, because they are acting on general matters rather than dealing with "private subject[s]," they should, as legislators, express "the general will" of the people which it would then be the function of the executive to administer.[47]

The end to which popular government is directed is public liberty, clearly not to be an unrestrained 'license' to do whatever one pleases regardless of social consequences. As any citizen in concerned to destroy or forestall tyranny, the source of liberty is to be found, not in multiplying individual license, but forestalling any license, especially by the rulers. True liberty can only be found in popularly sanctioned law: it "consist[s] only in the power of doing what we ought to will, and in not being constrained to do what we ought not to will." Social liberty means a mutuality of constraints that are generalized by law. And law is necessary for the liberty of all because, "if a citizen could do what [the laws] forbid, he would no longer be possest of liberty, because all his fellow citizens would have the same power."[48]

Political liberty depends, Montesquieu insisted, not upon any metaphysical explanation of the experience of freedom, but on the common *perception* of personal (or, as Montesquieu phrased it, "philosophical") liberty: it "consists in the exercise of our will, or at least (if we must speak agreeably to all systems) *in the opinion we have of exercising our will*."Representative government promises "political liberty," the individual feeling of "security" in the exercise of one's will within the boundaries of laws that are equally applicable to all citizens. This security of individual liberty requires a system of laws governing public accusations and a criminal code.[49]

Representative government needs not only equitable laws, but public virtue to sustain them.

> This virtue may be defined, as the love of the laws and of our country. As this love requires a constant preference of public to private interest, it is the source of all the particular virtues; for they are nothing more than this very preference it self.[50]

The preference for 'the common good' is prior to varied individual goods if the liberty of the society is to be ensured. For it is only within the scope of a system of just laws representing the general will of the populace and their devotion to their society's well-being that private or particular goods can be achieved.[51]

A democratic republic, because it renders all citizens politically equal while depending upon their mutual loyalty to the common endeavor, requires a a general moderation of beliefs, endeavors, and judgments. Just as democracy is "corrupted" when civic equality is obliterated, so it is also "corrupted" when citizens "fall into a spirit of extreme equality, and every citizen wants to be upon a level with those he has chosen to command him." A democratic society has, therefore, "two excesses to avoid, the spirit of inequality which leads to aristocracy or monarchy; and the spirit of extreme equality, which leads to despotic power . . ."[52] Presuming the division of the populace into varied social classes[53], he urged, not their obliteration, but for the sake of their common liberty, their need to bring their variety together in a dynamic harmony: for "peace and moderation is the spirit of a republic."[54]

Neither aristocracy nor democracy can assure a guarantee of freedom without moderation: "political liberty is to be met with only in moderate governments." In order to attain moderate government, constitutional bars to the "abuse of power" are necessary. Enunciating the principle that Lord Acton would later make famous — "all power corrupts and absolute power corrupts absolutely" — Montesquieu noted, "constant experience shews us, that every man invested with power is apt to abuse it; he pushes on till he comes to the utmost limit."[55] Safeguards must be built into the structure to forestall aggrandizements of power. But this cannot be done by denuding the government itself of power.

A government, and each of its subordinate branches, is concerned to exercise political power — ideally for the common good. Public officials are entrusted with power to act for the common good; they are charged to do, in the name of the whole people, what neither the whole people nor their individual members can do themselves.

A government not concerned to exercise power would lose its *raison d'etre*. We endow it with power to make general regulations governing specific areas of behavior just so that we will not, in our individual endeavors, 'bump' into each other. By setting out and enforcing rules and regulations, a government of laws enables each responsible citizen to pursue personal ends within the general rules governing all, while it does for all what cannot be done except by collective action. Without government, and its regulatory role, anarchy would prevail, bringing only the insecurity and instability of chaos. The problem, again, is how we are to 'govern our governors'.

In order to forestall even well-intentioned abuses of power and authority, constitutional limitations on the possibility of abuses of delegated authority by any official are needed. Montesquieu's classic solution is the principle "*that by the very disposition of things power should be a check to power.*"[56] His famous prescription, the separation of the three powers of government — executive, legislative, and judicial — means dispersing their authority and functions among different persons: "When the legislative and executive powers are united in the same person, or in the same body of magistracy, there can be then no liberty." And, again, "there is no liberty, if the power of judging be not separated from the legislative and executive powers."[57]

The first limit was to be placed on executive power, by making the legislature the sole source of the laws it is called upon to administer. But legislative dominance is itself to be feared. The legislature was to be restricted in its enactments by the right of executive veto, thus providing a legislative role for the executive branch. And further, the legislature was itself to be divided into two houses so that "one checks the other, by the mutual privilege of refusing [assent to proposed legislation]. They are both checked by the executive power, as the executive is checked by the legislature."[58]

But no nation lives alone. Any nation, no matter how grand, is but one in a world (then) increasingly composed of many large states. Were a republic determined to speak through its legislature to other states, it would be lost in discussion and debate and unable to handle any foreign crisis. The need to speak promptly with one voice when facing other states is the prime advantage of the monarchical form of government: by virtue of speaking through the single voice of the crown, it is able to speak decisively when dealing with other nations.

But the monarchical principle, necessary for the foreign relations of a free state, borders on despotism and threatens tyranny when applied to domestic affairs. Just as the multitude of voices in a legislature weakens the country in its dealings with others, it is the strength of the republic that its many voices are brought together to express the people's will in managing its domestic affairs. It is this that guarantees what should be their prime concern, their ability as citizens to pursue their private lives within the context of a mutuality of liberty.

Because a legislature can only offer debate and discussion when prompt decisive action is required in foreign relations, monarchical government might well have been necessary in the world composed as it is of different contesting states. Fortunately, a *new* political idea forestalls such necessity. The conception of a "confederate republic" combines the virtues of both: it "has all the internal advantages of a republican, together with the external forces of a monarchical, government."[59]

A "confederate republic," Montesquieu urged, can speak with strength abroad, while it guarantees liberty at home, and accepts the principle of political equality needed for representative government and the personal security of liberty. Such a government grounds its political structure by developing the structure of the society that is to sustain it. The society of a confederate democratic republic necessarily moderates not only the specific powers of its governmental agents but also the demand for equality itself. It does so, not by legislating grants of status, but by opening the doors of opportunity for individual decision, commitment, and advancement.

Such a society conceives itself as a 'commercial republic'. For, it is its commercial base that guarantees its liberty. In such a republic, "democracy is founded on commerce"; citizens have a vested interest in being free to pursue their own activities within orderly rules upon which they can depend; they require a high state of liberty so that each can evaluate courses of action, commitments into the future, and the free advocacy of policies and programs deemed necessary to enhance both individual and general prosperity. Producers must be free to solicit orders for their wares, merchants must be free to argue for the use of their products, and customers, to judge the value offered by competing suppliers. The continuity of freely evaluating alternative commercial exchanges educates a people to freely assess options, argue preferences, and extend this practice of free evaluative discussion to public questions of policy and program. In such a society, "private people may acquire vast riches without a corruption of morals. This is because the spirit of commerce is naturally attended with that of frugality, economy, moderation, labour, prudence, tranquility, order, and rule."[60]

For such a 'commercial republic' to prosper, "the spirit of commerce" needs to be stimulated by popular support; it is necessary

> that all the laws should encourage it; that these very laws, by dividing the fortunes of individuals in proportion to the increase of commerce, should set every poor citizen so far at his ease as to be able to work like the rest, and every rich citizen in such a mediocrity as to be obliged to labour either to preserve or to acquire his wealth.[61]

Such a republic will face the danger that industriousness and frugality may be lost and idleness becomes acceptable. To forestall these dangers, such a republic is advised to make sure that the poor have prospects for improvement, and the rich no excess of wealth. The ideal of the 'commercial republic', as Aristotle had initially proposed and Rousseau was to insist again, is to become and to maintain itself as an essentially middle-class society in which moderation of the disparities of wealth are wedded to moderations of power, of equality, and of liberty itself.[62]

Moderation is so crucial that even these basic principles for organizing human liberty, Montesquieu urged, need to be moderated in practice. No human planning or prescription can be without some conceivable fault and not even a carefully thought out plan should be accepted without serious qualification. Unforeseen circumstances can be expected to require modification of any program as it is implemented; planning that is intelligent keeps itself open to change. Above all other considerations, then, one should subject any belief in even a rationally thought-out scheme to suspicion: "*even the excess of reason is* not always desirable . . . [for] mankind generally find their account better in mediums than in extremes."[63] With quiet foreboding he, perhaps subliminally, anticipated "the potential danger of sweeping change in the name of abstract reason."[64] What he feared, would preeminently come to pass: the French revolutionary upheaval and its Jacobin betrayal, symbolized by their elevation of the goddess of Reason in the temple of a secular religion, culminating in the Terror imposed upon a people who thought they had been freed.[65]

Proposals for reform express grievances that need to be addressed. When reform is repressed, revolution follows. When moderation in power or wealth is brushed aside, gross "disorders of inequality . . . immediately arise."[66] Equality, like power and liberty, must be moderated along with the encompassing sweep of any person's or any group's claim to the prophetic vision of reason itself.

A free commercial republic, to survive and maintain a healthy state of liberty for its citizens (who are both sovereign and subject), must moderate its policies in its distribution of produced wealth, as in its distribution of the authority to make the innumerable decisions for others that marks any integrated social order. While it must plan ahead, in the specific as in the general, its planning too must be conceived in the light of what we would now term 'the essential finitude of human reason': acknowledging its own limited perspective onto the future, it readjusts its programs as new circumstances, unforeseen or unforeseeable, may arise. To tie oneself to an unalterable commitment to a particular development is to bind one's liberty to make differing evaluative decisions as circumstances change and anticipations prove to have been erroneous. The function of a free society is to keep the future open — open to facing new contingencies with a fresh face and a free, forward-looking, evaluating mind.

Montesquieu was, in his concerns, very much a thinker in the traditional mold while he was in fact yet setting out parameters for a new age; thus he took up the old question of cyclical thought — how may a society eventually fade? His answer, directed against the prime thrust of liberalist theory, still speaks to us. The entire burden of liberalism's call to political liberty had been raised against the tyrannical power of the ruler: the limitation of the ruler, the executive, was the first call of liberal reform which sought to establish the power of the representative assembly, the legislative arm of government, so that the voice of the people might speak with ultimate authority.[67] Precisely in this legislative power, Montesquieu saw the root of disintegration of the democratic republic:

> As all human things have an end, the state we are speaking of will lose its liberty, will perish. . . . It will perish when the legislative power shall be more corrupt than the executive.[68]

The alarm has always been sounded over excessive and corrupting power in the executive. On Montesquieu's reasoning, concern for the safety of a republic requires a powerful executive who can focus its vigilance on the integrity of its legislative bodies. One reason for a strong executive is precisely to counter the tendency of the legislature to 'despotic determination' of all governmental power.[69]

The legislature's function is to represent the voice of the people. But when the people's voice is confounded, not with overriding concern for its view of the common good, but with conflicting interest-group demands and single-issue political commitments that seek power by majoritarian coalition, they pre-empt concern for the common good. When what Madison was to call "special factions" drive into control, the concern for the common good, the appointed function of the legislative branch to voice, falls by the wayside. This is, indeed, the highest corruption to which a democratic republic is subject; when this corruption pervades its legislative organ, the society as such faces the danger of its mortality.

Montesquieu lived under absolutist government. Yet, significantly, his fear for the future of liberty was not directed to the idea of a strong government or a strong executive — but to legislative malfeasance.[70] The liberty of a free people requires a strong government operating in the common interest. His fear was directed to the prospect of a legislature that bows in turn to each separately strident interest permitted to exercise delegated power. His essential teaching was that common interest must be empowered to check separate interest, by finitizing political authority so that each separate voice can be checked by those others whose ultimate interest must be the strength of the whole. This insight was most eloquently voiced by an Italian disciple of Montesquieu's who wrote as fascism was about to descend upon Italy:

> if a nation is to be free, in other words, governed according to law and not according to the arbitrary will of its rulers, it must have a political organization in which authority arrests and limits authority,

and in which, therefore, no individual and no assembly has the power to make laws and at the same time the power to apply them. . . .

If, again, we take due account of the individual liberties that protect the citizen from possible arbitrary acts on the part of any or all of the powers of the state, especially of liberty of the press, which, along with liberty of parliamentary debate, serves to call public attention to all possible abuses on the part of those who govern, one readily sees the great superiority of the representative system. That system has permitted the establishment of a strong state, which has been able to canalize immense sums of individual energies toward purposes related to the collective interest. At the same time it has not trampled on those energies or suppressed them. It has left them with sufficient vitality to achieve remarkable results in other fields, notably in the scientific, literary and economic fields. If, therefore, the nations of European civilization have succeeded in maintaining their primacy in the world during the age that is now closing, the fact has been due in large part to the beneficent effects of their political system.[71]

Montesquieu had voluntarily surrendered whatever political power he had been able to exercise as a French jurist under the absolutism of the Bourbon monarchy. He wrote to advocate peaceful change, insisting that the first end of civil government is to ensure liberty and maintain the conditions for its exercise. He saw that civil government must, to this end, anticipate the social upheaval that follows when both gross inequalities and immoderate equalities are permitted to erode the continuance of liberty. His work propounded the principles for a constitution of liberty. Focused on the need to fragment power in order to sustain liberty, it constitutes a set of perceptive advices for those who would, indeed, practice the art of statecraft. In the condition of his time, he was only able to advise. As we know, it was not long before other individuals were able to, and did, seize the opportunity to give Montesquieu's admonitions flesh and structure.

iv. A Compact For the Future

The American Constitution, Alexander Hamilton repeatedly pointed out, was conceived not merely to meet the pressing problems of the moment; it was designed "to look forward to remote futurity."[72] Taking up lessons from the past to face the immediate problems it was designed to meet, it was formulated as a social compact that looked to "posterity" for vindication.

While being self-consciously set on a newly defined course, its authors appropriated for its departure the English development of civil rights and the common law, and a conviction concerning the virtues of republican government that they read out of the work of Aristotle, Cicero, and Montesquieu. Building on but one hundred and fifty years of colonial history, they assimilated into the constitutional system of government set forth, a selective appropriation of the fruit of western political history.

Having "paid a decent regard to the opinions of former times and other nations, [its authors] have not suffered a blind veneration for antiquity, for custom, or for names" but engaged in "the experiment of an extended republic . . . of which an exact model did not present itself." Framing the constitutional structure around principles they developed from Montesquieu, the founders saw themselves as having initiated a "revolution which has no parallel:" they had "reared," as Madison stated it, "the fabrics of governments which have no model on the face of the globe. They formed the design of a great confederacy, which it is incumbent on their successors to improve and perpetuate."[73]

The intent was to secure the stability of what was conceived as a "commercial republic"[74] and the popular liberty it both requires and secures. The prime format for doing so was the new notion of American federalism, an idea drawing "heavily upon Montesquieu's solution to the problem of how small republics can survive."[75] The 'small republics' were the individual states. Federalism was to unite them into a consolidated Republic without destroying their local autonomy. The solution, Hamilton explicitly explained, was borrowed from Montesquieu's concept of a "CONFEDERATE REPUBLIC as the expedient for extending the sphere of popular government and reconciling the advantages of monarchy with those of republicanism."[76] The Constitution was designed to ensure that popular rule could maintain liberty and a diversity of customs at home, while, at the same time, the union of states could speak with one voice in dealing with other nations.

As its Preamble shows, the Constitution was presented in the form of a social contract. It was to be a contract by the people of the several states as irreducible sovereign entities.[77] As Madison said, it was to "be a *federal* and not a *national* Constitution."[78] And its popular base was to be secured by an unprecedented process: ratification was to be, not by state legislatures but by the people themselves, as expressed in separate state conventions specifically elected to pass upon ratification.

Innovative as it was conceived to be, the institution of the new 'Republic' was intended as no radical break with the ordered continuity of history. Seeking to secure the continued exercise of the 'rights of Englishmen' and the health of the several states, it was to enhance the *continuity* of the kind of government to which its citizens had been accustomed — but with elected officials, the end of hereditary status, and the promise of a representative democracy. Taking up teachings from the past and their own accepted practices and customs, the new Republic was built on their reformulation as a prescriptive set of procedures for the future.

Because of Madison's concern to provide succinct definitions of each, it is well to remember that the terms, 'republic' and 'democracy', have a long and often ambiguous history not always accordant with their contemporary usage. The word 'republic' has always had a strictly political meaning, coming from the Latin *res publica* and roughly translatable as the 'public affair' or 'public property', or 'commonwealth'.[79] Generally used to denote a government deriving its authority from its citizens, it had come to mean a 'representative government', whether its chief of state was an elective or hereditary office, although today it generally denotes a government headed by an elected official. The word 'democratic' (hailing from the Greek *demos*, the people) has the broader meaning of a society devoid of any firm sense of class or hierarchy,[80] as well as the classic political meaning of the participatory self-government of free citizens in the Athenian city-state. Today, its most widespread use is to refer to a free state governed by popularly elected representatives, regardless of whether republican or monarchical in form.

Whatever continuity may have been intended, McDonald suggests that Madison, seeking to define these two key terms in their political ramifications, radically sharpened the definitions. "The true [political] distinction" between 'democracy' and 'republic', Madison wrote, is that

> in a democracy, the people meet and exercise the government in person; in a republic they assemble and administer it by their representatives and agents. A democracy consequently will be confined to a small spot. A republic may [therefore] be extended over a large region.[81]

Madison, seeking to explicate "the distinctive characters of the republican form" of government, found no precedent in European history. The new American Republic was then an innovative experiment in government. It was to be, he explained:

> a government which derives all its powers directly or indirectly from the great body of the people; and [to be] administered by persons holding their offices during [their] pleasure, for a limited period, or during good behavior. It is *essential* to such a government that it be derived from the great body of the society, not from an inconsiderable proportion, or a favored class of it. . . . . It is *sufficient* for such a government, that the persons administering it be appointed, either directly or indirectly, by the people."[82]

'Democracy', understood as the direct participatory involvement of a town meeting, was not only impractical on any but the smallest scale; it was also undesirable — and not only because of the general lack of expertise as questions for decisions grow more complex, as Montesquieu explained. Because of the time it requires, a commercial society composed of farmers, mechanics, and merchants would neither be able to afford nor desire to spend time this way. To impose participatory demands instead of free representation would be to impose a new kind of tyranny. The new Republic, again without precedent, was built from the beginning on a middle-class society, on a new kind of general citizenry, "that class of persons, neither rich nor poor, which Franklin celebrated as our 'happy mediocrity'."[83]

As McDonald points out, the idea of a 'republic', as the Constitution defined it, was a distinct innovation in the annals of political history. It "defied categorization by any [then] existing nomenclature: it was not a monarchy, nor an aristocracy, nor a democracy." It could not be described "even as a *representative democracy*, for parts of it represented nobody and other parts did not represent the *demos*."[84]

Madison had effectively appropriated the word 'republic' for what both Locke and Rousseau, in different ways, effectively joined to urge: a political organization composed of officials who derived their authority, directly or otherwise, from the sovereignty of the people. By-passing Locke's transposition of this into parliamentary supremacy and Rousseau's problems with the notion of representation, Madison yet accepted their common principle of popular sovereignty as the only legitimate source of governmental power. Combining this with Montesquieu's principle of dividing governmental powers, he effectively created a new concept that built creatively out of the intellectual heritage. In doing so, however, Madison appears to have justifiably enhanced an old word.

"A concept," as Gadamer pointed out, when brought into precise modern usage "is [necessarily] more artificial and hence more fixed than in the ancient world, which did not have any foreign words and very few artificial ones."[85] Madison had effectively forged a new definition for the old word: if "he was presumptuous in appropriating the word *republic* to describe it, he was also a prophet, for thenceforth 'republic' would mean precisely what Madison had said it meant."[86]

But, the nature of a government is to be seen not only in the source of its authority; as Aristotle had already noted, its legitimacy more crucially depends upon "the supreme object to be pursued," the object for which its power is to be used. This, as the essence of republic government, Madison insisted, is "the public good, the real welfare of the great body of the people."[87]

The goal of this new Republic, Hamilton argued, was to provide that "vigour of government [that] is essential to the security of liberty."[88] This is "the genius of Republican liberty"; it "demand[s] on one side, not only that all power should be derived from the people; but, that those entrusted with it should be kept in dependence on the people . . . [and that the public's] trust should be placed *not in a few, but in a number of hands.*"[89] Central to the constitutional plan was both an ordered delegation of public authority and the *dispersal* of the power of that authority among the various states and through them to the federal government; each of them was, in turn, to disperse its own delegated power to different officials.

Designed to serve 'the general welfare', the Constitution conceives this, as *The Federalist* consistently explains, as "the preservation of liberty." The way to ensure this defining end, as every American schoolchild is taught, is to separate governmental powers into a finely tuned system of checks and balances.[90]

The crucial principle, however is *not* a rigid sequestering of the three governmental powers into three branches, each exercising a stated monopoly of authority. What is crucial and often overlooked in the principle of checks and balances is the ordered *sharing* of these powers so that no one group of officials can monopolize any one of them; even with each specific authority focused in a specific department of government, no one department is to be able to exercise that power alone.

Denying complete control of any one of these powers to the members of one branch had already been tried by the New Hampshire Constitution which Madison took as a model because it had already recognized the practical "impossibility and inexpediency of avoiding any mixture whatever" of the powers of the three governmental branches.[91] Citing the Constitution of Massachusetts, as another example, he explained that it

> goes no further than to prohibit any one of the entire departments from exercising the powers of another department. . . . [however,] a partial mixture of powers has been admitted. The Executive Magistrate has a qualified negative on the Legislative body; and the Senate, which is a part of the Legislature, is a court of impeachment for members both of the executive and judiciary departments. The members of the judiciary department again are appointable by the executive department, and removable by the same authority, on the address of the two legislative branches. Lastly, a number of the officers of government are annually appointed by the legislative department.[92]

This diversification of specified powers among separate departments, officials and branches of government is, indeed, central to the constitutional plan. As Madison explained,

> An *elective despotism*, was not the government we fought for; but one which should not only be founded on free principles, in which the powers of government should be so divided and balanced among several bodies of magistracy, as that no one could transcend their legal limits, without being effectually checked and restrained by the others. . . . [thus] the legislative, executive and judiciary departments should be separate and distinct, so that no person should exercise the powers of more than one of them at the same time. But no barrier was provided between these several powers.[93]

The prime responsibility of each was separated from the others; the powers of the branches are not to be monopolized but shared. The principle of checks and balances is then not an absolute separation of powers but what Hamilton described as "the trite topic of the intermixture of powers."[94]

One central lesson taken out of Montesquieu was that any monopoly of power is not to be trusted. Power is to be fragmented and shared; even as prime responsibility is spelled out, that responsibility is yet always accountable to others by virtue of being shared.

Designed to secure the personal liberty of *all* citizens — even against a majority — one pervasively significant fear is clearly embodied in the constitutional formula: the fear of legislative dominance. In sharpest contrast to the liberalist tradition, which feared executive power and therefore called for parliamentary supremacy, the Constitution rejects the doctrine of legislative primacy[95] — because the

legislature is, as the most directly representative body, the most likely
to abet a dominant majority's thrust for complete power and be the
branch most responsive to demagogic pressures. One prime reason for
strengthening the presidency, as we shall see, was to enable it to represent the *whole* people in standing against any such pressures for majoritarian tyranny. And one prime reason for empowering the judiciary,
beyond anything Montesquieu suggested, as we shall see, is to enable it
to keep legislative enactments within constitutional restraints.

The need for a strong government necessitates a strong executive. And even the constitutional formulation — providing for one
executive as the sole official whose election stemmed from the whole
people — it was feared, might not have succeeded in providing one
strong enough. Facing the fear of the possibility for tyranny that can
come, not only from a "hereditary monarch" but also "in a democracy," — and here is the import of the earlier distinction between
'democracy' and 'republic' — Madison warned:

> But in a representative republic where the executive magistracy is
> carefully limited *both in the extent and duration* of its power; and where
> the legislative power is exercised by an assembly, which is inspired by
> a supposed influence over the people with an intrepid confidence in
> its own strength . . . *it is against the enterprising ambition of this [legisla-
> tive] department*, that the people ought to indulge all their jealousy
> and exhaust all their precautions.[96]

He continued:

> The legislative department derives a superiority in our governments
> from [the fact that] . . . Its constitutional powers being at once more
> extensive and less susceptible of precise limits, it can with the greater
> facility, mask under complicated and indirect measures, the *encroach-
> ments* which it makes on the co-ordinate departments. . . . On the
> other side, the executive power being restrained within a narrower
> compass, and being more simple in its nature; and the judiciary
> being described by land marks still less uncertain, projects of usurpa-
> tion by either of these departments would immediately betray and
> defeat themselves.[97]

Against liberalist doctrine that fears executive power, and dis-
owning British precedent whereby the House of Commons had
already begun to pre-empt unto itself all the powers of government,
Madison warned against "the tendency . . . to an aggrandizement of
the legislative, at the expense of the other departments." A legislature
has a propensity to disturb "the public tranquility by interesting too

strongly the public passions," and by too frequently referring "constitutional questions, to the decision of the whole society." Always urging that we frame our current procedures by anticipating future problems, he warned that we should not count on moderation and virtue to prevail if the public should become unduly excited in "the future situations in which we must expect to be usually placed."[98] We should be especially wary, Hamilton added, when

> The representatives of the people, in a popular assembly, seem sometimes to fancy that they are the people themselves; and betray strong symptoms of impatience and disgust at the least sign of opposition from any other quarter; . . . They often appear disposed to exert an imperious control over the other departments."[99]

Limiting the reach of the nation's legislature is one prime reason for the system of checks and balances. To this end, the Congress was itself divided into two separate branches whose concurrence on any proposed legislation must be complete before it could be submitted for presidential approval. Just "as the weight of the legislative authority requires that it should be thus divided, the weakness of the executive," Madison wrote, "may require, on the other hand, that it should be fortified."[100]

Both the executive and the judiciary are to exercise their power to forestall legislative excesses. The import of each was explicated in turn.

In contrast to members of the two legislative chambers, each of which represents but a fraction of the people, the executive's election derives from the whole people.[101] The executive is to stand against "encroachments" from the legislative body. Especially, Hamilton warned against any "servile pliancy of the executive" to legislative pressures:

> The republican principle demands, that the deliberate sense of the community should govern the conduct of those to whom they entrust the management of their affairs; but it does not require an unqualified complaisance to every sudden breeze of passion, or to every transient impulse which the people may receive from the arts of men, who flatter their prejudices to betray their interests. It is a just observation, that the people commonly *intend* the PUBLIC GOOD. This often applies to their very errors. But their good sense would despise the adulator, who should pretend that they always *reason right* about the *means* of promoting it. . . . When occasions present themselves in which the interests of the people are at variance with their inclinations, it is the duty of the persons whom they have appointed to be the guardians of those interests, to withstand the temporary delusion,

in order to give them time and opportunity for more cool and sedate reflection. Instances might be cited, in which a conduct of this kind has saved the people from very fatal consequences of their own mistakes, and has procured lasting monuments of their gratitude to the men who had courage and magnanimity enough to serve them at the peril of their displeasure.[102]

Using similar language and reasoning, Madison defended "the utility of the Senate" as a separate legislative branch:

such an institution may be sometimes necessary, as a defense to the people against their own temporary errors and delusions. As the cool and deliberate sense of the community ought in all governments, and actually will in all free governments ultimately prevail over the views of its rulers; so there are particular moments in public affairs, when the people stimulated by some irregular passion, or some illicit advantage, or misled by the artful misrepresentations of interested men, may call for measures which they themselves will afterwards be the most ready to lament and condemn. In these critical moments, how salutary will be the interference of some temperate and respectable body of citizens, in order to check the misguided career, and to suspend the blow mediated by the people against themselves, until reason, justice and truth, can regain their authority over the public mind.[103]

Madison and Hamilton joined in hoping that civic leaders would be courageous statesmen, not demagogues or unprincipled servile politicians. But this hope could not be counted on and constitutional precautions had to be available. because "Enlightened statesmen will not always be at the helm,"[104] Madison saw the strength of the Constitutional system of checks and balances to lie in its capability to ride out periods of poor leadership and avoid the pitfalls of demagoguery always to be anticipated.

In order to forestall legislative "encroachment," the judiciary, as well as the executive, needs to be strong. The judiciary may, indeed, be "the weakest of the three departments,"[105] but one of its prime functions is to review and restrict legislative enactments. A common cliché has questioned the constitutional sanction of this principle of judicial review — even eminent historians have been heard to say that judicial review "may not [even] have been intended or imagined by the framers."[106] The cliché is plausible only if one persists, as some do, in reading American constitutional development as but a minor emendation of British liberalism's parliamentary doctrine, rather than its disavowal. Yet, as Boorstin has pointed out:

In Great Britain, the 'constitution' was the whole sum of charters, statutes, declarations, traditions, informal understandings, habits, and attitudes by which the government was actually administered. Technically speaking, then, there was no such thing as a British statute being invalid because it was 'unconstitutional': any British statute could change the constitution. There was no 'constitution' by which a court could test legislation.[107]

The Federalist clearly enunciated the principle of judicial review as inherent to the entire Constitutional enterprise, especially as this "limited constitution [is] one which contains certain specified exceptions to legislative authority."[108] As Hamilton noted,

the laws of the Union are to be the *supreme law* of the land. . . . It will not, I presume have escaped observation that [the Constitution] *expressly* confines this supremacy to laws made *pursuant to the Constitution.*[109]

The Constitutional system thus brought to the fore and institutionalized the cardinal difference between constitutional and statutory law, a new distinction which few philosophers had only begun to suggest.[110] This American innovation in the art of statecraft found its roots in the heart of the Puritan tradition.[111] It had seen its first full embodiment in the Massachusetts Constitution of 1780.[112]

Going far beyond Montesquieu, whose concern for judiciary independence, even as he raised it to status as a coequal power, seems to have been confined to guaranteeing trials by jury instead of by administrators, the Constitution insists that the judiciary must be a fully coequal part of the governmental structure.[113] It has two central functions: the first is to breathe life into laws which "without courts to expound and define their true meaning and operation," would be moribund.[114] The judiciary's second and truly innovative function — which rests on the primacy of Constitutional to statutory law — is to "declare all acts contrary to the manifest temper of the constitution void." The new and crucial task of the judiciary is to protect the integrity of the Constitution itself "against legislative encroachments."[115]

The principle of constitutionalism makes an *absolute* distinction between the "constitution established by the people, and unalterable by the government; and a law established by the government, and alterable by the government." Madison praised this principle and proudly noted its innovative force: it "has been little understood and less observed in any other country."[116] In order to maintain this principle it is crucial that an authorized body be mandated to see that "No legislative act therefore contrary to the constitution can be valid."[117]

Rather than being a superior body, the judiciary is a body "intermediate . . . between the people and the legislature in order, among other things, to keep [it] within the limits assigned to their authority." The function of the courts is "the interpretation of the laws. . . ." whose ground and justification "must be regarded by the judges" within the scope of the Constitution as "fundamental law."[118] On the premise that the Constitution itself is the continuing will of the people, the process of judicial review is not to raise the courts above the other branches but to ensure the *subordination* of all branches to the fundamental law that ordains and empowers them together.

This task of judicial review is to resist not only the legislature's expected attempts to expand its power, but also any popular passion moving the legislature to ignore "the provisions in the existing constitution." For the Constitution is itself a solemn self-limiting pact binding on the people themselves:

> Until the people have by some solemn and authoritative act annulled or changed the established form, it is binding upon themselves collectively, as well as individually; and no presumption, or even knowledge of their sentiments, can warrant their representatives in a departure from it prior to such an act. But it is easy to see that it would require an uncommon portion of fortitude in the judges to do their duty as faithful guardians of the constitution, where legislative invasions of it had been instigated by the major voice of the community.[119]

Why, then, was this power of review not explicitly stated in the Constitution itself? Hamilton's answer is that the doctrine is already encased in its conceptual justification; it is deducible "from the general theory of a limited constitution; and as far as it is true, is equally applicable to most, if not to all the state governments."[120] The principle of judicial review is requisite to the fundamental distinction between *constitutional* and *statutory* law: it is intrinsic to a constitution that sets inherent limits on the power of a government whose sole authority is but to 'administer', not supercede, that constitution.

This answer fully accords with the rationale of the framers for omitting a particular 'bill of rights' from the original document. As a 'limited constitution', a bill of rights was also deemed inherent in it. Vague abstractions which do not spell out just what is meant are troublesome and in themselves do not provide the guarantees they ambiguously promise.[121]

The Preamble to the Constitution was written as a contractual statement, The Constitution is, Hamilton urged, "a better recognition of popular rights than volumes of those aphorisms" found in some of the state constitutions "and which would sound much better in a treatise of ethics than in a constitution of government." The reason is simple: whatever else the rhetoric may suggest, the enforcement of any specific rights will depend, as subsequent history has demonstrated, "on public opinion, and on the general spirit of the people and of the government." Rather than requiring a specification of particular rights which some will regard as incomplete and others as ambiguous, he argued: we should recognize that in and of itself the Constitution "is itself in every rational sense, and to every useful purpose, A BILL OF RIGHTS."[122] The Constitution, as Friedrich has explained, is to be understood "as the process by which political action is limited and at the same time given form . . . [insofar as it] is based upon a self-limiting decision of the people when they adopt it."[123]

A Constitution is not inherently accretionary in its temporal force; it is, by definition, a deliberate attempt to write out procedures for the future. Historically grounded in past experience, tradition, and custom, it is a deliberate 'new beginning' that faces the future. Its essential prescription is always implicitly prefaced by a 'henceforth'. It *pre*scribes a procedure for choosing its officers; provides defined and thereby limited authorization for the powers with which it endows them; and a *pre*scribed method for adjudicating disputes citizens might have with each other or with the governmental authority they endow.

By definition, a Constitution, ratified by popular vote, is the people's agreement to limitations on its own collective authority. These limitations on public delegated offices are not only defined in terms of specific authorizations; they are also defined by temporal, or "durational," limits of that authority.[124] By doing so, they have, for the foreseeable future, denied the omnipotence of majority rule to themselves by *pro*scribing limits on their own legislative power. Insofar as the Constitution protects contest and the right to disagree, it is, in itself, inherently a protection for dissidence and minority proposals. And if one insists, as Americans did, on adding to it a 'bill of rights', that but augments the limitations on what the majority 'henceforth' permits itself to do or authorizes in its name.

Implicitly, this is recognized in the defense of the Constitution itself, and on two different levels. The most widely read papers of *The Federalist*, the Tenth, centers on the problem of 'factions', the aim being to moderate the dimensions within which they may operate. A 'faction', Madison defined as "a number of citizens, whether amounting to a majority or a minority of the whole," who are "adverse to the rights of other citizens, or to the permanent and aggregate interests of the community" as a whole. When a subversive faction is a minority, their frustration is easy: "relief is supplied by the republican principle, which enables the majority to defeat its sinister views by regular vote." The real problem, and the genius of the constitutional arrangement, is to be tested not with a dissident minority but with a passionate majority: the constitutional structure is specifically designed to erect institutional barriers barring such a faction from "concert[ing] and carry[ing] into effect schemes of oppression."

The prime function of constitutional government is to protect "the diversity in the faculties of men" from which arise all the other differences to be found among them — of property, interests, policies, and proposals. A large republic, more than any of the smaller states, brings in "a greater variety of parties and interests [thus making it] less probable that a majority of the whole will have a common motive to invade the rights of other citizens" or to "discover their own strength" in doing so. The requirement for concurrence in the different branches of government provides additional "impediments" to any enactment of majority tyranny.

Designed to balance regional and, we would say today, also 'ideological', 'interest-group' interests against each other, it calls for their pluralization:

> a religious sect, may degenerate into a political faction in a part [of the Union]; but the variety of sects dispersed over the entire face of it, must secure the national Councils against any danger from that source: a rage for paper money, for an abolition of debts, for an equal division of property, or for any other improper or wicked project, will be less apt to pervade the whole body of the Union, than a particular member of it; in the same proportion as such a malady is more likely to taint a particular county or district, than an entire State.[125]

The Constitution's method of controlling power is to fragment it by dispersing it — thereby encouraging each 'faction', in its own self-interest, to be intent on checking the power of the others. The constitutional system is directed, not only to effective government; it is also directed to foreclose the seizure of the governmental mechanism by any particular 'faction' of the people, no matter how strident or how powerful that 'faction' may be.

This diversification of power rests on faithfully acknowledging that the prime function of government is, *not* to preserve men in their possessions, but to protect "the diversity of the faculties of men from which the rights of property originate." Protecting the diverse "faculties of men," Madison insisted, "is the first object of Government." Doing so calls for the pluralization of the society itself; by regarding the citizenry as composing a social system of inherent checks and balances, the public becomes a bulwark of the mandate of the constitutional system to "guard against the oppression" of any by its officials — the initial aim of the checks and balance system. Beyond specific governmental concerns, however, the function of constitutional government is "to guard one part of the society against the injustices of the other part." In order to forestall any possible tyranny of a dedicated minority or an overpowering majority, it is necessary to pluralize the composition of the society itself[126]

> by comprehending in the society so many separate descriptions of citizens, as will render an unjust combination of a majority of the whole, very improbable, if not impracticable. . . . In a free government, the security for civil rights must be the same as for religious rights. It consists in the one case in the multiplicity of interests, and in the other, in the multiplicity of sects.[127]

Whether in government, or in the society that is governed, the stability of liberty depends on pluralizing the affiliations of the participants, 'multiplying' the number of interests and partial allegiances so they can each be vigilant against any quest for dominance. The competition for dominance, for favor of particular interests, the continuing contest with each other for power, is itself a form of inherent cooperation in the preservation of liberty. For each 'faction', interest group, sect, or party requires general liberty for its own 'protection' against the encroachments it may see as threatened by others. The cooperation required by republican government is the cooperative protection of pluralization, the cooperation of a community itself animated by the ordered competition of its members with each other for influence, power, and program.

The purpose of the governmental structure is to give expression on each level, as Hamilton stated it, to "the general will";[128] a government that maintains and enhances the conditions of liberty exhibits continued fidelity "to the public good and to the sense of the people"[129] as to what is required in the way of specific governmental policies. but this generality needs be inclusive. It is not to be the domi-

nance of any one segment to the detriment of the others. Any minority also participates in the life of the nation, and its members, too, must
be allowed to participate in the good of the whole. The "general will,"
"the sense of the people," or "the deliberate sense of the community,"
as Hamilton stated it; or, in Madison's phrasing, the "cool and deliberate sense of the community,"[130] means that the basic purposes of the
community as a whole, and not its most strident or dominant voices,
must be acknowledged as authoritative in the actions of the whole. As
each citizen participates in the society's quest for what is conceived as
its 'common good', that 'common good' itself requires that each be
respected in the measures taken to achieve it. The ultimate protection
of the whole is a set of ordained procedures that effectively frustrates
any attempt to disrupt this mutuality of citizen-membership, *even
against the majority itself.* Only within this compass of the interest of
each in all, and of the 'all' in each, is it possible for discussions, rights,
privileges, and powers to be exercised with the assurance that general
liberty is itself secure.

The new 'confederate republic' was *not* to be an extended participatory democracy. The principle of its republican government is one
of delegated government — with the people as the final judges of how
the trustees they have chosen to exercise specific temporally defined
powers and authorizations do so. The republican principle is not
grounded on a daily referendum of general opinion; it was conceived
as an ordered delegation of specified powers for a specified duration,[131]
to make limited decisions in specifically defined areas, and always
requiring the conjunction of another similar finite authorized delegation of public authority in order for that decision to be determinative.

The power of the people, like that of all other elements in the
constitutional system, is finite. Citizens are, first, to choose, on various
levels, their delegates; and second, to pass judgment on what these delegates do with the responsibilities entrusted to them within the time
period of their authority. The constitutional meaning of 'self-government' is delegated government that is always subject to popular review
and admonition. To the extent that the society recognizes itself as a
unified plurality of minority interests, classes, orientations, and sects
working within prescribed procedures for negotiating their differences,
it can face the future in confidence that its liberty is secure — against
any threat of despotism which would threaten a minority imposition
and against any majority coalition that would impose its oppressive
will. Either attack on the integrity of the society as a whole is to find

itself frustrated by the institutionalized diversification of power, the pluralization of the society itself, and by the finitization of power that can be exercised at each level within the governing structure.

By providing for ordered negotiation of differences, the constitutional system mandates a moderation of demand and expectation from governmental action. And this principle of prudential moderation is itself a key to what was intended. As Hamilton noted, the Constitution itself turned out to be a happy surprise. After the passions arising out of the Revolution, it was

> hardly to be expected, that in a popular revolution the minds of men should stop at that happy mean, which marks the salutary boundary between POWER and PRIVILEGE, and combines the energy of government with the security of private rights.[132]

Not only power, but liberty itself, needs to be governed by a spirit of moderation: for "liberty [itself] may be endangered by the abuses of liberty."[133]

The "good of the whole," Jay — perhaps the most conservative member of the trio — added, "can only be promoted by advancing the good of each of the parts or members which compose the whole." The guide to public policy was set: By accepting the Constitution, the people — in order to retain and expand the stability of their liberty for which they had fought and to which they committed themselves — had pluralized governmental powers and recognized that the society itself needed to nurture its own diversification in order to ensure the liberty of its members. Opening the opportunities for each as being crucial to the health of the whole, they therefore instituted a government that, despite the dispersal of authority among its citizens as well as their chosen officials, could be energetic in its dedication to serve as the active "promote[r] of the general welfare and secure[r] of the blessing of liberty."[134]

Ratification effectively enacted the first institutionalization of the distinction between constitutional and statutory law on any national level; this first 'confederate republic' was the first system of government designed to divide power and to finitize authority. And rarely noticed: ratification instituted the first modern government to open public office to its citizens *without any religious or property test for public service.*

Looking to the future, the test of the constitutional formulation was not to be found in its immediate application. First, problems of

adjustment and harmonization were to be worked out.[135] Explicitly
acknowledging human finitude in the lack of "perfect wisdom and perfect virtue," it eschewed "utopian speculations," and instead sought
the more responsible goal of devising the most practical way of organizing a free society. Trusting that the new governmental system
would, aside from national defence, direct attention "to the internal
encouragement of agriculture and manufactures, (which will comprehend almost all the objects of State expenditure),"[136] they could look
forward to the task of developing the potentials of this new 'commercial republic'. The Constitution's Preamble was a commitment to
"posterity."The closing of *The Federalist* invoked a trust in the efficacy
of Time.[137] As Hamilton concluded,

> we must bear in mind, that we are not to confine our view to the pre-
> sent period, but *to look forward to remote futurity*. . . . Nothing there-
> fore can be more fallacious, than to infer the extent of any power,
> proper to be lodged in the National Government, from an estimate
> of its immediate necessities. There ought to be CAPACITY to *provide
> for future contingencies*, and, as these are illimitable in their nature, it is
> impossible safely to limit that capacity.[138]

It is remarkable, from the vantage at the end of the twentieth century, just how long this Constitution has uniquely served, among governing compacts around the world, as an accepted framework of popular government. Despite the vast changes of geographic extent, the
crisis of civil war, industrialization, the multiplication of population still
drawing from all quarters of the globe, and emergence as a world
power, it has proven itself adaptable to radically changed circumstances
with virtually no fundamental changes in its inherent structure.[139]

What is, perhaps, equally remarkable is the continuity of general
acceptance, with the exception of the Civil War (which de Tocqueville
had anticipated as virtually inevitable).[140] The Constitution stands
today without serious challenge — or any serious proposal to change
its inherent structure. Even during the social upheavals of the sixties
and seventies, none of the contending parties proposed any change in
the constitutional structure; rather, each side, vociferously appealed in
support of its own position to the Constitution itself. In its two-hun-
dredth year, as the oldest operative Constitution in the world, its
accepted authority remains untrammeled.

The framers conceived, in the wrangle and negotiation of debate (conducted in a secrecy hard to imagine being countenanced today), a governing structure that has weathered the test of that time and so far the futurity to which its authors and proponents had appealed. It has largely worked itself out, as Hamilton had hoped, and has, in a country so enlarged and so transformed that its founders would hardly recognize it, found within itself the organic vitality to provide to the framers' "posterity" precisely that for which they had hoped.

What the framers conceived themselves as having proposed was a new order of freedom. Uniquely conscious that their proposal — the Constitution itself as well as the requirement for popular ratification — was without precedent, they offered it to posterity as a new institutional system to guard and guide the future development of human freedom. What they offered was a *novus ordo seclorum*, a new order for the temporal world, a new order for the ages, built on "ideas never before realized in human history,"[141] but providing an incisive lesson in how freedom may be ordered and its power utilized and controlled.

v. Securing Freedom

When we speak today of the modern era, we generally have in mind the world as it has developed since the late 1700s. Three roughly coincident, unprecedented events marked its beginning: the American Revolution, nurtured by growing degrees of self-government, separated thirteen colonies from the British imperium and brought forth the first modern Republic; the French Revolution, sparked by the American, threw Europe into a war which destroyed most vestiges of feudalism, spread republican ideas across the continent, and precipitated the rise of its modern nation-states; the emergence of the Industrial Revolution initiated the new economic order. Each of these was equally unique; together they joined to mark the onset of the modern era.

All three had been nurtured in the rebirth of learning, the diversification of beliefs, and the slow resurgence of the newfound faith in what reason might accomplish. The Industrial Revolution, taking up a long incubation in the rise of European commercial life, finally emerged in the freest of the European nations and was quickly taken up in the overseas nation that emerged from its womb. The two national revolutions brought ideas of the Enlightenment into political play. But differences between them are instructive.

The American Revolution, while truly a war for independence, proclaimed in its Declaration a new standard for all free government. It was fought by a people who had already developed the life and institutions that harbored a free commercial polity. It brought about no social upheaval, and pitted no class against any other. Its leaders, nurtured in the governmental and social institutions which had governed a relatively free colonial life, were, indeed, the more prominent citizens, who sought the continuity of the evolving societies for which they spoke. Continuing most colonial institutions in an essentially evolutionary development, it moderated its expectations in a Montesquieuean constitution emanating from the heart of the French Enlightenment, and sought to have its separation from foreign rule mark a minimal disruption of everyday life, which largely picked up much as it had been lived before.

In sharpest contrast, the French Revolution, which still captures the romantic imagination, was no evolutionary call for self-rule on the part of a developing society, but a disruptive social upsurge directed against rulers who lacked the foresight to try to meet grievances which wisdom would have had them ameliorate. Pushed by social upheaval to utopian hopes and doctrinaire positions, it quickly wrapped itself in romantic exuberance, abjured all moderation of practice or aspiration, and collapsed into a populist terror only to be rescued ten years later by Napoleon's *coup d'etat*. Its ramifications so alarmed the rulers of the other European powers, who were similarly blind to the tenor of the times, that it resulted in a general war only ending in 1814, a quarter of a century later. Undergoing repeated changes of government, it was not until 1953 that De Gaulle's Constitution, ingeniously combining presidential government with the European parliamentary tradition, for the first time seems to have, at least implicitly, invoked some of Montesquieu's teaching and provided the French with a stability of free government. Had the rulers of the French monarchy originally been open to the futurity which hovered before them, they might have acceded to the specific possibilities that the developing conditions of their time opened before them and moved to meet them, instead of permitting their recalcitrance to force their opposition into the self-defeating extremities of doctrinaire utopianism.

The Swiss social thinker, Wilhelm Röpke, writing during the Second World War, remarked that it was "the errors of rationalism . . . [that] caused all the great and promising beginnings of the eighteenth century to end in a gigantic catastrophe of which we can still feel the effects: the French Revolution," while, at the same time, "in the domain of politics it produced a piece of work so mature and enduring as the American Constitution."[142] Rationalism's unalloyed faith in its own deductive conclusions, without regard to the contingencies of human experience, succeeded in imposing the very tyranny that its avowal of freedom was supposed to circumvent. Its moderation, setting out procedures for its free development instead of ordaining one necessary goal, opened the doors to the development of a free society. As Montesquieu had already admonished, the reach of reason itself, as of liberty and equality, needs to be moderated in order to become real.

The year 1789, indeed, provided the dramatic contrast. As the French Revolution, somewhat inspired by the American success (albeit with French imperial assistance) commenced, the American people began to live with moderated expectations as a free nation under their newly inaugurated Constitution, which still provides the framework for their institutional life.

The writers of the American Constitution realized that they were forging a temporal document, which would have to appeal, as Hamilton said, "to remote futurity"; not by determining its specification but by keeping the future open, so that the possibilities laying before it could be developed. They took history seriously, not only by taking up its lessons but also by recognizing that they had but provided procedural channels by which its promising future was to be wrought.

Effectively appropriating Cicero's standard of a government to be ordered by 'laws and not by men', they might well have adopted as their motto Cicero's statement: "We are servants of the law in order to be able to be free."[143]

They seem to have taken from Aristotle the idea of mixing the elements of the society and the three functions of government into one cohesive organic entity, centered around its middle class as the source of stability for the liberty they cherished; the principle that moderation in any pursuit is itself a political virtue; and the insistence that the final test of a governmental system is that it is structured to direct its efforts to the welfare, not of its rulers, but of the whole.

They had learned from Machiavelli that the stability of liberty rests on the protected continuity of the struggle for power and influence which all segments of the society must cooperate to maintain; that wise legislation is framed, not by expecting all men to be virtuous but against the expectation that some will seek to vent evil on the rest; and that the life of the polis, as the substance of history, is to be carried forward with a wisdom that learns from the past while it looks to the future.

From Montesquieu they took up principles for institutionalizing liberty, the fundamental tenet of which is a set of procedures to ensure that no individual, and no group, is to be trusted with unchecked power; that no prophetic vision is to be allowed unallayed play, and that institutional barriers are necessary to moderate its disruptive passion; that a constitution for liberty takes up from the commercial culture on which it rests, the requirement of ordered procedures for negotiation and compromise of differences; that it must enhance that commercial culture by opening opportunity to all, thereby enabling each citizen to pursue his private life and differentiate himself by his own pursuits, while choosing representatives to handle public affairs; and that its priority of loyalty is to be its liberty, which itself may need to be moderated in practice if the spirit of freedom is to animate the common good, if its continuity as a free people is to be secure.

This new order of freedom was not meant to be self-consuming. It founded itself on the principle of responsible representation to ensure popular control. Seeking the freedom of each within the freedom of the whole, they recognized that a tyrannous majority constitutes as great a threat to a free society as a tyrannous ruler; they designed a governmental system to forestall both and thereby set a standard for free government.[144]

Proceeding far beyond traditional democracy in seeking to forestall majority tyranny, they looked to a democratic society under republican government. They forbade right by status — inherited or acquired — and, in the spirit of a 'commercial republic', looked to a fluid social order in which the marketplace of ideas would be as open as the marketplace of commerce, and in which citizens would be free to enjoy their own achievements.

In looking to an open society, dedicated to the liberty of each to pursue his own, they formulated a cardinal lesson in the control of power. Institutionalizing what Polanyi would come to call a system of "polycentric" power — dispersing power among a multitude of competing centers which yet harmonize in their creative functioning[145] — they recognized that a free government requires a free society for its sustenance. Casting this, as their task required, in primarily political terms, they drew on the lessons of political history — because it has been the political arena in which the question of the organization of power had been most explicitly faced — while they clearly recognized that a free government must accord with the society it is charged to govern.

Their call for a pluralization of the society itself thus recognized that government does not stand aloof or alone. A republic, as a representative government, represents the society it governs. If that society is to be free, it needs to diversify the interests, sects, and factions — the 'intermediate' societies which occupy the time and attention of its citizens — so that they may be free to voice the views of their adherents and to compete for public favor. To the extent that government represents the society it governs, its own diversification of power and influence needs to represent and encourage the diversifications of power within the society itself.

Dedicated to a mutual concern for the common good, as the area within which the good of each citizen is to be found they rejected at the outset the liberalist dichotomy between the interests of the free citizen and that of his government. Indeed, that "the private interest of every individual, may be a centinel over the public rights" of the community itself, is requisite for community institutions to function in the spirit of freedom for the public good without getting 'out of hand'.[146] This polycentric handling of the problem of power calls for the continual fragmentation of concentrations of power as they continually tend to coalesce, so that communal power can be effective while it maintains and protects the competition of powers to preserve the stability of liberty.

This diversification of power, representing an increasingly pluralized society, enables freedom to prosper. At times the conflicts it ensures bring on vigorous debates and at other times develop a harmonious consensus. Their ebb and flow mark the dynamic of a free society. One vibrant sign of a free society is the continuing cooperation of the citizenry in maintaining the continuity of competition for influence as the varied powers within the community are exercised.

And the government ordained is not expected to stand as an idle observer. It is charged to express the common voice of the community, to attend to the common concern for the common good. The function of a free government is to serve as the "guarantor of the general interest." This "general interest" is the common prosperity of the society as a whole. In a commercial society that functions by means of a market economy, this necessarily means that its role, as a prime defender of a market economy argues, "is to fill the gaps left by the market economy and to act so that the social efficiency of decisions made by the various economic agents is greater than if the state had not intervened."[147]

The proper governmental role of a free commercial republic, as Hamilton had originally pointed out, is to concern itself with the commercial life of its citizens. Speaking in official capacity as the first Secretary of the Treasury (in Washington's administration), he simultaneously repudiated the notions of a government that either stands aloof from, or else directs the economic life of the citizenry. Its task is not to replace the economic efforts of citizens but to act for the common prosperity in ways that no individuals or particular groups of citizens could do by themselves — by maintaining procedural stability so that people may plan, and by opening new channels of commercial endeavor, encouraging new enterprises and acting to bring all citizens into the productive life of the nation. Repudiating an atomistic economics of laissez-faire license, he urged the new American Republic to extend "the incitement and patronage of government" to the encouragement of manufacturing, to use the power of the whole — and indeed, "the public purse" — to encourage otherwise unused minds to make their own effective contributions to the common prosperity, "to foster industry and cultivate order and tranquility at home and abroad."[148] Government's economic function is to encourage and abet the diversification of economic decision, so that the richest contribution of each may be made to the general prosperity of all, because an ordered productive prosperity "promote[s] the general welfare, and blessing of liberty" the Constitution was pledged to defend and advance.

Within the free area maintained by the cooperative endeavor of an alert citizenry, citizens are to find their temporal horizons open to their own private decisions. Most citizens choose, by necessity or inclination, to devote the time of their free activity to their own concerns — to earning a livelihood and to enjoying their leisure. Relieved of the necessity of being marshalled by their rulers for dictated activities, or alternatively having to protect their liberty by devoting their time to the minutiae of governmental procedures or worry about general upheavals, they yet retain the obligation to inform themselves about public issues so that they can intelligently exercise their constitutional power of employing their deputies and passing judgment on their performance.

The framers had taken time and freedom seriously; they function together as the community concern and in the lives of the citizenry. This freedom to focus individual attention on concerns for livelihood and the leisure that ensues from it, is one prime freedom the authors of the Constitution sought to protect. It is the prime time-consuming concern of most free citizens. To consideration of its own requirements and opportunities, we should now turn.

Chapter **6**

Livelihood

In the constitution of freedom, the principles that ensure its health need to be translated out of the political realm which explicated them and back into the commercial order which originally suggested and sustains them. For it is here that each citizen spends the days of lived time. The meaning of individual life is found in the ways one is permitted to live one's own time, take up one's past, and carve out one's future. The concrete content of one's freedom is found in the ways one is able to expend one's hours.

Everyday existence is focused on securing a livelihood and the leisure that can be enjoyed because of it. Participation in "the general Welfare" and "the Blessings of Liberty" is manifested in the absence of unwelcome interferences as one is enabled to presume the contexts of community and the freedom to handle the time of both work and leisure.[1] Popular control in the choice of officials, delegated to administer constitutional government, permits popular sanction for government policy without requiring time-consuming participation in governmental activity. Most citizens take the freedom to run one's own life as the freedom to spend one's own time on what one deems to be of most concern. This generally means being able to earn one's livelihood as one sees opportunities to do so and to enjoy personal leisure in accord with one's own predilections — providing one refrains from interfering with the like freedoms of one's neighbors.

The American constitutional system developed a sophisticated lesson in the power of liberty and freedom to control and use political power. This was not to operate in a vacuum. Designed to govern a 'commercial republic', a republic in which the prime time-consuming focus of the citizenry is their business affairs, the same principles used to disperse governmental power were already tacitly employed to control the competitive commercial activity that provides its economic sustenance.

The dispersion of property as well as power in a social system of checks and balances — the mark of a free economy — created the conditions for the rapid appropriation of the new technological revolutions about to emerge, and for the flourishing economy that was to grow by means of it. The political arrangement of the new Republic provided the principles by which the new economic powers were to be harnessed. As elsewhere, "the political was godfather to the economic revolution . . ." that rapidly followed in its wake,[2] even as it seems to have borrowed clues for the control of power from the nature of commercial exchange.

i. A Commercial Economy

America's constitutional system was designed for what already was a 'commercial republic'. In contrast to the widespread poverty which shocked Adams, Franklin, and Jefferson on their European travels, of most citizens it could be said that they 'owned something and few owned too much'.[3] Virtually all American citizens owned some property and used it as a means of livelihood in a free-market economy that was largely agricultural or mercantile in nature.[4] Especially in the northern states that largely forged the new nation, most would have been described as moderate in wealth.[5]

By forming a geographically large union, the citizenry of the several states provided themselves with a national free market for their private enterprise economy. Freely producing and distributing goods, they spent their time in manufacturing, exchanging, and consuming activities that provided the source of personal income, wealth, and whatever leisure could be rescued from the new demands of industrial modes of production.

Today's conventional term for a commercial economy is 'capitalism'. This term is unfortunate, but we appear to be 'stuck' with it. Notably, it was never used by Adam Smith, the Scottish philosopher who is generally regarded as its prime prophet. It was not coined until 1854,[6] and then as a term of opprobrium. In truth, such an ideologically loaded term does not fit into dispassionate discussion of what has proved to be an open-ended, "experimental, often pragmatic, economic approach . . . [which] has often led to policies and practices quite different from" ideological forecast or textbook description.[7]

The word 'capitalism' focuses on only one component of an inherently complex and interrelated system for meeting modern economic needs — a system that brings together, primarily under private auspices, the requisite of adequate capital to fund expensive productive machinery, the raw material and the labor to work it, the management to direct it to chosen productive ends, and the marketing skills to bring its products through complex distributive channels to an adequate number of ultimate consumers who effectively cooperate to sustain it. Inherent in this process are time-investments of educated intelligence in ordering finances, potential market evaluations, product designs, production engineering, distribution arrangements, marketing, salesmanship, evaluation of returns — the time and labor of all concerned in every aspect of this complex of interacting activities.

Capital is but one requisite of this process; labor is another. But entrepreneurial imagination, as well as organization and management skills (not necessarily the same), are initially needed for any enterprise. This complex of abilities is yet subject to technological innovations, consumption requirement changes, and other imponderables — all of which combine to require a continuity of clear-headed evaluations of possibilities and bold, yet prudential, judgmental thrusts into futurity.

No such enterprise has ever functioned in a vacuum, immune from governmental policy, as the 'libertarian' ideal demands. Such a complex of activity depends upon a system of law that enforces contracts, a monetary system permitting the ready exchange of goods and services, and a network of customary procedures and governmental regulations so that each interchange does not require the time to be figured out anew. The most laissez-faire periods in the development of any modern economy have, in addition to presumption of custom, been involved with governmental policies from the outset and necessarily presumed the rest of the economic structure in which it functions. The entire 'infra-structure' already provided and sustained is necessarily presumed in any specific commercial transaction: tariff policies, always controversial, determine the price and, thereby, the availability of raw materials and competing products; monetary policies affect the medium of exchange; legislative acts stipulate procedures and courts enforce trading agreements while protecting the rights of property; and privately sustained institutions — such as banks, markets, and consumer access facilities — are all presupposed in any commercial transaction. Governments subsidized the first railways, and later, highways and airlines in order to promote means of transport, and continue to support agricultural activity. And, always, taxation policies affect the investment of income and the consumption of goods. Early on, universal education at public expense was mandated not only because the extended franchise requires literate citizens, but also because commerce and industry cannot function with illiterate employees.

When stripped of rhetoric and looked at dispassionately, the call, from Adam Smith on, was not to 'eliminate' governmental economic controls but to minimize them, always against a backdrop of governmental policies designed to permit widest possible responsiveness to popular demand consonant with the general good.[8] Even pure market forces, left to themselves, as well as specific governmental policies, favor some and hurt others — and occasionally fall out of balance and need some intrusionary source for correction.

We have seen that the British intrusion into the free market started with reforms designed to protect industrial workers. In America, early contests over tariff policies and debates over silver coinage dominated its early politics; in 1890 the Sherman Anti-Trust Act, designed to maintain the freedom of the market — by mandating the 'checks and balances' of competition and thus foreclosing monopolies of economic power — represented a direct intrusion into the marketplace.[9] Many would justifiably argue that governmental protection of market forces after the Civil War, as the early unions contended, was carried so far that the poor and the weak could barely survive, that the principles of 'social Darwinism' ('let the successful prosper and the others fall by the wayside') prevailed for a time, to the detriment of the society itself.

Following the Great Depression of the 1930s, all industrial economies that continued to be governed by representative governments finally accepted heretofore unacceptable governmental intrusions into the ordering of their economic processes. These pervasive reforms effectively reconstituted the free enterprise system without surrendering the essentials of a free market economy.

These intrusionary reforms have generally been of three distinct kinds. The first reformed the relations between management and labor by placing protections around workers unable to negotiate decent working conditions for themselves — such as wage-and-hour laws, legalization of collective bargaining, and requirements for health and safety standards in places of employment. The second reformed the relations between individuals and the society at large by the progressive introduction of requirements for unemployment insurance, provisions for retirement income by means of social security requirements, and more recently, the notion of a communal responsibility for individual medical and health needs. One rarely noted effect of these two kinds of reform has been to ensure a level of popular consumption power that renders a recurrence of complete economic collapse less likely and minimizes the degree of any disequilibrium that might develop.

The third change — in may ways the most revolutionary, if notably least controversial — has been the growing role of free governments in actively maintaining the conditions of market stability by close supervision of the money supply on the one hand, and, on the other, extensive regulations concerning permissible business practices. Such reforms have served to rescue the market economy from the liberty of virtual anarchy which threatened to reduce society to a virtual Hobbesian 'state of nature'; they have also enabled the market and its society to depend upon a greater stability of procedures and conditions and therefore better utilize its ordered freedom.

For any individual, this economic order is very different from what had originally been dubbed 'capitalism'. Early laissez-faire capitalism — a virtually anarchic market with minimal economic controls — radically differs from the contemporary free enterprise system which prides itself on its socially ordered freedom. Today's commercial activity functions within general rules of governmental and consensual policy, continually subject to, and often welcoming, political intrusion — as, for example, in adjustment of interest rates, international monetary exchange levels, and reciprocal trading agreements with other nations. Current discussions of proposed revisions of anti-trust laws, acceptance of the proper role of governmental sanction for major mergers, rules governing advertising, the introduction of medical products, and regulations of the securities exchange system — all attest to general acceptance of the principle that government, as voicing the general interest, rightfully oversees the economic activities of free citizens. Deviating in fundamental ways from what preceded it, the economic system of this post-Depression era represents such a pervasive reconstitution of early 'capitalism' that it is grossly misleading to continue describing it, as revolutionary ideologues are prone to do, in terms originally used to condemn its initial nineteenth-century English form.

Depending on private initiatives to serve as the economy's directive force, degrees of governmental intrusion into the economy have been accepted as manifesting its rightful role to protect the common good in ways that, after some political as well as economic battles, are now generally deemed helpful to the mutual interest in the general prosperity.[10]

The modern economy emerged from a commercial revolution that developed principles of free markets and private property. These principles were originally developed to loosen up European 'mercantilism', a system whereby centralized governments managed their economies by closely regulating permitted independent enterprises — by setting 'just wages' and prices for labor, rules for guild membership, services, and manufactured commodities.[11] Such policies, justified by the claim that they were undertaken for the sake of the community as a whole, were governed by the conviction that *the amount of wealth was static:* insofar as one's gain was at the expense of another's, it seemed legitimate to set up standards for what was deemed to be an equitable sharing of scarce goods and resources.

The crucial difference of the modern era, one without historic precedent, is that a modern free-enterprise economy works with *the experience of creating new wealth.* Expectation had been that, by removing many controls and leaving individuals free to respond to market forces of supply-and-demand, greatest rewards would accrue to those who do most to expand the wealth of the community.

But, as we have seen, relaxation of governmental controls could never have been complete: not even minimal economic policies of an organized government are without effect; it seems inconceivable to imagine policies of a government that would have no economic effect whatsoever. What actually transpired in the loosening of the late-medieval reins — which we today term the emergence of a free-market economy — is in some ways a democratized development of mercantilism: opening up new benefits to the whole people *because* they are geared to expanding productivity rather than remaining content with redistributing parts of a 'static pie'. The government of even the most loosely organized modern society is generally expected to follow such economic policies as will best contribute to the common prosperity, the common good; the overriding concern of the electorate of a democratic society is that the policies of its governmental administration contribute to its overall economic development and sense of well-being.

Modern economies, as they developed, initially sought to remove most overt governmental interferences inherited from a preindustrial age, while providing a stable monetary system of exchange and, depending upon perceived need, some kind of tariff protection for local industry. With the rise of popular governments, control of the economy was progressively taken under popular, rather than monarchical, control. The modern economy of most industrialized nations represents, then, a democratization of the public interest — with nations such as Britain and the United States in the 1800s effectively opting to minimize, but never completely forsaking, societal controls. The pervasive reforms since the late 1920s provided socially protective procedural rules within which economic activity is to function while leaving that functioning, within those limits, to the free actions of their citizens. Despite all ideological rhetoric, governments of free societies are expected to 'manage' the rules of the economy so as to facilitate economic prosperity.[12]

The truly descriptive divide is not between a completely laissez-faire economy, in which the government does nothing at all, and a fully controlled command economy, in which the government makes all economic decisions: our actual existential choice is between a 'demand' economy, where market forces are left free to operate *within* a wide range of socially responsive governmental regulations that govern its procedures while providing its stabilities; and a 'command' economy where governmental officials pre-empt all decisions and direct every facet of economic activity.

A government that lays out procedures without pre-empting private initiatives is a 'demand' economy which moves on the requirements of its consumer-citizens rather than governmental production quotas. Such a 'demand' economy characterizes all free nations today. The 'demand' is that of the market citizens provide — restricted, ruled, governed, and buoyed up as it may be — and not governmental requirement. But, within those rules and regulations, citizens, individually and in groups, are left free to direct their own economic activities, their own quests for livelihood, and their own enjoyments of its proceeds.

A 'demand' economy is characterized by the looseness of governmental controls, by a sophisticated system of commercial distribution which guides its productive processes, and by its *deliberate dependence* upon the free initiatives of its citizens to fill those distribution channels. It is inherently driven by willingness to purchase, by customers and clients who choose to exchange time-earned purchasing power for specific goods; its successful production and service facilities function, not by acting upon orders of its governors but by responding to a freely perceived capability of meeting the free consumption of its distributed products. Free-market enterprises are geared to the distribution channels their production plants are to feed; they require a comprehensively efficient system for distributing goods to their consuming partners. Industrialization, *per se*, provides the means for 'mass production'. But that 'mass production' depends on a 'mass distribution' system — which is a sign of a free society, because it is based on unenforced options that drive it toward innovation and quality production.[13]

Our contemporary commercial economy, as any other social development, emerged as the response of our predecessors to the problems they faced and the opportunities they saw lying before them. We will find it easier to anticipate our own genuine possibilities if we first glance back to see how and why this achievement came into being.

ii. Roots of Development

It is usual to associate the publication in 1776 of Adam Smith's *The Wealth of Nations*, providing the first systematic rationale of a free-market system, with the rise of capitalism. In fact, "by then the basic western economic institutions were in place, and economic growth was well under way."[14] Smith was not the prophet of a new vision; he was a moral philosopher who provided a rationale for what was already emerging.

What had, indeed, nourished the development of the new economic system for the three hundred years preceding the Industrial Revolution was, first, the emergence of commercial enterprise and, later, an agricultural revolution. The rise of a commercial culture began in the Renaissance when the rise of commercial urban centers with their innovative banking and trading systems broke through the localization of economic activity. Impulsively, it transcended the perceived barriers and initiated the rebirth of culture, the rise of science, and the courageous explorations that opened up a new world to what had been a very parochial vision.

Built on exchange of goods, the new commerce developed the need for a money system to free it from time-consuming barter. Requiring a handy system of computation for quickly reckoning these monetary exchanges, "the Hindu-Arabic numeral system and its methods of computation" quickly displaced use of the cumbersome Roman numerals. By 1478, twenty-eight years after Gutenberg's invention of movable type, commercial need elicited the first textbooks to teach the new arithmetic that we today take for granted. One long-term result of this new method for handling commercial transactions was the unleashing of the rapid advance of mathematics, upon which modern science depends. More immediately important, was the demand by the new counting houses and commercial establishments in Italy for clerks who were able to use the new system of number and computation; to meet this demand for arithmetic competence, enterprising Italian teachers set up new schools. Because these new centers of learning drew students from north of the Alps, they helped to break down a general parochialism and to internationalize European commerce. Leaving the use of Roman numerals to universities and monasteries, these new training facilities "eliminated a monopoly on knowledge and gave great impetus to the rise of a middle class,"[15] which increasingly depended on becoming not only literate but 'numerate'.

Cardinal Cajetan, an antagonist of Luther, had already urged that compensation for work should be shifted from a "just wage" based on one's station in a static order, to "what was appropriate to one's contribution" (shifting with changes in worldly conditions).[16] A new commercially productive order of economic activity was coming into view as horizons broadened. Rather than emerge according to a vision prescribing a new kind of society, the institutions and procedures of the new commercial culture were animated by a novel awareness of the openness of a future newly furnished with novel possibilities. Gradually evolving without any specified ideology, the commercial order evolved out of new contacts with different cultures which increasingly opened new vistas toward an expanding future. Its practitioners were "wholly pragmatic . . . [without any ideological] commitment to any economic principle other than economic effectiveness and survivability."[17]

Stimulated by new horizons, commercial enterprises opened those horizons further and developed independently of the scientific revolution also emerging at the same time. By the time of Galileo, western Europe's economic development had for the first time already by-passed all other cultures. It would be another two hundred years before any direct link "between economic growth and leadership in science" would develop.[18]

What had 'caused' this new and unique historical development was not the 'factory' system of production (which traces its development to the mechanized clock in fourteenth-century Germany). Western Europe had already achieved "economic advances that had even then divided the world into the 'have' and the 'have not' nations."[19] This advance certainly was not due to any western cultural advance and integration: Islam dominated the western world intellectually (e.g. by its retrieval of Aristotle and adoption of the Hindu number system) at least until the expulsion of the Moors from Spain in 1492. And Chinese culture, on virtually all levels, seems to have been generally more advanced and sophisticated than Europe's until the emergence of the modern world in the late middle ages — marked by the Renaissance and Reformations.

One standard answer to the question of 'cause', derived from Weber, is that Calvinist Protestantism precipitated the emergence of early capitalism — by its espoused virtues of frugality, sobriety, industriousness, and a work-ethic; by its individualization of moral conscience and responsibility; and by its sanctification of prosperity and this-worldly labor, together with other middle-class values.

Although it is hardly contestable that Calvinism was a major contributory factor in the development of a commercial culture, it is hardly a full explanation.[20] If Calvinism were 'the cause', early capitalism should have emerged in Switzerland, Holland, Scotland or the Calvinist communities of Hungary. Actually, the commercial revolution built on "a new social contract . . . gradually hammered out" in Holland which developed the idea of contractual rights of private property and the development of "large-scale *markets*."[21] In fullest force, capitalism then developed in England and America — both of which included influential Calvinist elements, that were yet a minority in each — and then in the German states, where Calvinists represented the lesser branch of the Protestant Reformation.

Presumably there was no 'one cause', but a multiplicity of developmental factors conjoining to precipitate this unprecedented revolution in human affairs, with varying factors exercising specific contributory influences at different times. This likelihood is apt to be overlooked because

> the external events of the present are part of a 'realization phase' of a past and closed period, while the incubation of the future has quietly been taking place for many years along different lines and is influenced moreover by the weight and form of our participation in it.[22]

At least three developments, important to this essay's concern, joined together into a unique temporal convergence to precipitate this new upsurge of human activity in western Europe:

First was its unique political pluralism.[23] Feudal Europe was no monolithic entity; it was a collection of separate local duchies and principalities united, prior to the Reformations, only by an acknowledged fealty to a common spiritual throne with which its adherents continually disputed about the rights of temporal domain. As each locality was governed by its absolute prince, no political power could bring them all together. The Protestant Reformations added a plurality of religious loyalties to the multitude of political allegiances. The pervasive pluralism of power provided the foundation for an advance, once some precipitating input stimulated it. One factor, then, was political: it was this set of competing "political forces which made the Industrial Revolution possible"[24] as it brought new wealth to competing centers of political power.

Second, the continuing competition for power and primacy had abetted the emergence of a commercial trading class enriching diverse localities. Buttressed by the new democratization of literacy, ability to handle numbers, and general knowledge opened up by the printing press, merchants encouraged the great explorations and, by virtue of the trading channels they had developed, sought new merchandise to fill these markets. Commercial trading groups stimulated the European reaching-out to, and then taking in, new relations with other countries and cultures. Explorations had been initiated to find trade routes to the Indies because of *consumer demand* for their exotic products. But once Columbus had discovered the new world,

> the [Atlantic] Ocean became the most profitable trade route for European vessels. . . . All of this [was] . . . the masterpiece of the mercantile middle class, the Renaissance's enterprising class of burghers. In 1500, the world was already oriented toward the merchant.

Seeking to expand their commercial operations, this new middle class provided "the motor behind the Great Expeditions," prompted continued explorations, and later settlements of the newly discovered territories. These, in turn, provided their previously unknown products for commercial exchange, for markets, for intensified trade, and commercial expansion.[25]

Third, the agricultural revolution "in the dense network of towns in the Netherlands, first, and then in England," made it possible "for the first time in human history to nourish more people *better* . . . [and] for the first time exempt [them] from the traditional famines." This increase in agricultural production, indeed, engendered a new idea in the history of mankind, the idea of economic growth. "Growth was not caused by the Industrial Revolution. Rather industrialization would never have begun without [the new idea of] economic growth."[26]

This change "from manorial agriculture to an agriculture of individual peasant holdings had materially improved the food supply." A rising population, coupled to a decline in the need for rural labor, fed into the growth of the cities, an outgrowth not of industrialization but of the revolution in agriculture, "a point sadly illustrated in our own times by the analogous struggle of Third World metropolises to cope with a flood of desperate immigrants from the countryside."[27] The new society was the

> grafting [of] an urban world onto a rural world, and this process was well under way before the Industrial Revolution. By the middle of the eighteenth century . . . by most tests Europe had developed, in early mercantile capitalism, a full-blown economic system that had already superceded feudalism.[28]

The new emerging social system was inherently pluralistic. Religious, scientific, political, literary, and economic activities were in different hands — largely autonomous to each other, not only as distinctively different realms, but also as individuals participating within them — and no class so clearly dominated the others as the feudal aristocracy had done. Increasing pluralization of authority was manifested in every segment of society. The change from a feudal to an encompassing commercial culture took up the political divisions of medieval society as its cue; dismantling its cultural integration, it ushered in a pervasively pluralized society, in which different kinds of authority and power were not only dispersed among different social elements but fragmented within them.

By the early nineteenth century the new industrialization produced a radically increasing productivity together with visible concentrations of urban poverty and distress. Previously scattered about the rural landscape, poverty was now centered in the towns where it was dramatically exposed to view. And so it "engendered a new *sensitivity* to the problem of poverty."[29] For the first time, poverty became, not an enduring fact of social reality that was to be accepted in resignation, but a 'problem' to be solved.

Britain's wars abroad but served to augment the misery of her new domestic condition:

If it was political forces which made the Industrial Revolution possible, it was also political mistakes which made it needlessly costly in
human terms. The tragedy is that in the three critical decades in the
middle of the take-off, Britain was not only carrying through a massive investment programme but fighting, and paying for, the costliest
and one of the longest wars in her history [the American War of
Independence followed by the Napoleonic Wars: 1775–1815]; work-
ing-class private consumption was squeezed in consequence.[30]

In due course, as we have seen, liberalism's economic license,
which had developed in full force, was itself to be tamed — by the
'positive freedoms' that thinkers such as T. H. Green advanced as new
'prescriptive rights' entitled to governmental protection in Britain,
and in America by new intrusionary supervision of the market-place.
Such reforms of early capitalism were initiated in each case, against
the 'social Darwinism' of liberalism's received atomistic doctrine, *by
conservative governments.*

The *means for* these reforms had grown at the same time. The
growing autonomy of economic activity brought with it a new autonomy and a new vibrancy to the sciences and the arts, a new increase in
social wealth to sustain them, and a widening generalization of education which is itself a force for further dispersal of authority. As economic activity found greater autonomy from mercantilistic controls,
so it, too, was pluralized among competing firms and conflicting economic interests. Intrinsic to this general development, the modern
representative state had *already* emerged as the product of the
Commercial — not the subsequent, Industrial — Revolution. Coming
to represent "the most efficient and pervasive organization of political
power in history,"[31] it has also been, to the complaints of some, one of
the most restrained. Nurtured by the urban middle class, the growth
of democratic republics established the conditions for autonomous
decision-making that enabled the new free-market economies to
develop and to function within newly broadened procedural restraints.

Democratization — breaking down inherited social barriers,
equalizing opportunities for the citizenry, and extending the popular
voice to the choice of governmental officials — was necessary for the
new economy. As a money-economy, it requires popular support for
procedural stability, continuing protection from arbitrary governmental actions, and the diversification of decision-making power needed in
order to function. As a socially mobile middle class provides its center,
a commercial economy requires governmental protection of the

dynamic of temporal processes and of the freedom to utilize them in accord with individual judgments.

These modern commercial enterprises, and the capital they invest, seriously attend to the meaning of time. They function by investing money, an inherently abstract and intangible token for wealth, for long periods of time. Popular acceptance of the prescriptive rules by which businesses may function, and the stability of the currency which is to be invested in the hope of future returns, are both preconditions for the transformation of accrued wealth into capital.

> To the medieval merchant accustomed to keeping wealth in a form easily buried against the hazards of political extortion, war, revolution, and other forms of banditry, such a tie-up of capital for a period far beyond the range of foresight would have seemed insane. There was simply no way to calculate the future stream of benefits.[32]

That 'time is money' we have all been told. For a modern economy, time is no longer a placid backdrop to a cyclical round of selfsame activity. Time itself comes to be understood as that "through which money might be used." The new "ethos . . . saw in idle money a resource for transforming the future."[33] Present investment looks toward future production that *will then* be consumed, just as present production depends upon past capital investments which emerge from appropriating either earlier sequences of investment-production-consumption as savings for a future increased return, or the deliberate accumulation of debt to be repaid out of projected future returns. A future-oriented temporal perspective, drawing on the result of past endeavors and anticipated future results, is intrinsic to the entire process. Unless "the existence of investment opportunities" provides, in the first place, "the incentive for the accumulation of capital,"[34] we should wonder why capital should be accrued for future investment instead of just being enjoyed.

The temporal sequence, in the mind of the potential investor — whether an individual planning his education, or an entrepreneur, an investment banker, or a government assessing new tax laws to encourage capital formation — is first to envision an as-yet unrealized future possibility for economic benefit, and then to gather together savings and credit capabilities, the capital (as in a modern corporation by accrual of profits, stock and bond issues) in order to pursue and actualize it. The "role of practical intelligence" had been profoundly altered, as it has come to involve itself in the deliberate 'manipulation' of tem-

poral sequences.[35] Any investment on any level depends upon a forward-looking temporal perspective and a present commitment to a
course of future activity.

The temporal perspective of the individual, whether consciously invoked or 'pre-conceptually' activated, is intrinsic to all commercial activity. Individuals spend "on themselves in diverse ways, not
[merely] for the sake of present enjoyments, but for the sake of
future pecuniary and non-pecuniary returns." Such expenditures
may be for education, health, quest for suitable employment, or
gathering the information needed for any of these. From a personal
point of view, this time-expenditure may well "be viewed as investment rather than consumption."[36]

Indeed, the Marxian textbook picture of the frugal 'bourgeois'
accumulation of capital, through individual savings from past income,
hardly accounts for the growth of banking, the *new* notion of credit,
or the great surges of capital that went into the rapid rise of modern
industry. Important as accumulation of profit from the past may be,
modern industry largely rides on what it perceives as *now to be
retrieved from the future*. Major investment was and is continually animated by hope for future dividends and by public and corporate debt.
Just such a public funding of debt — a prime "source of capital for
the great industrial expansion that was just beginning in England"
through the newly established Bank of England — Hamilton had
commended (in his controversial proposal for a national bank) to the
new American Republic as the key to an ordered national development.[37] Hope for dividend return from *future* profit animates investment for the future; and debt financing is a borrowing *from the
presently anticipated future* for present investment activity. Whether
investment be from savings (that are an accumulation from the past in
order to realize a possibility seen as future) or from borrowings (that
will be repaid later), the whole temporal process exemplifies the temporal structure of human decision — operating primarily by means of
bringing visions of possible futures into the constitution of the present activity and selectively using lessons from the past for that purpose (cf. Chapter 2).

It was Leibniz (who initiated the German Enlightenment),
Johnson has argued, who first expressed the ethos of this entire development by suggesting "that the selfish deeds of each combined into
social forms for all." As Johnson notes, Leibniz had seen the universe
guided by "a beneficent providence"; the harmonizer of individual

efforts was seen as "divinity."[38] Johnson's intuition sees further than he
states: for Leibniz not only saw that the actions of each are socially
bound as both a response to, and an influence on, what happens to us
all; he was also one of the first of modern thinkers who recognized
that the ultimate importance of each person lies in the human capacity
to provide a distinct perspective while at the same time reflecting his
own social milieu in distinctive temporal ways. Leibniz thereby provided a metaphysical ground for the emerging theory of a free society:
a conceptual model by which to understand ourselves as distinctive
individuals who are, at the same time, inherently members of a time-
ordered society. Deriding the notion that we are each self-contained
'atoms'(completely independent of all others), he urged that we think
of ourselves as 'monads' (uniquely individual beings) who are, in
essence, *continually* engaged with others — always feeding from and
feeding back into the society to which we belong.[39]

Leibniz' 'monadic' notion of human individuality urges the
democratic thesis that each brings a peculiar gift, as an individual evaluative perspective, to the life of the social whole; as such, each is of
vital importance to the whole insofar as he maintains a unique individuality dependent upon the social whole for its ongoing continuity. Into
this conceptual model of authentic individuality[40] is packed a plea for
the importance of protecting the expression of differing viewpoints, for
social protection of individual creativity, for recognition of the pervasiveness of temporal development on both an individual and a social
level, and for the orderly procedures of republican government.

Significantly, Leibniz was the first philosopher of the modern
epoch to take time seriously. By insisting on the primacy of time in
human experience — all our physical activity is guided by the temporal cast of human thinking which always acts within the framework of
time-bound living, planning, travelling, anticipating, fearing, hoping
— he had come close to describing the temporal form of modern life.[41]

Leibniz had urged the import of looking forward, of anticipation,
in precise social terms: "it is much better to prevent poverty and misery, which is the mother of crimes, than to relieve it after it is born."
Seeking to foreclose "arbitrary power," he argued that the proper form
and "definition of the state . . . [is] what the Latins call *res publica*"; its
function "as democracy, or polity," is to engender agreement on what
constitutes the social good. Just as a republic attracts to its membership
those who seek freedom and individual diversity, it is the one form of
government that deliberately makes "the common good the first object

in [its] social catechism"; therefore, the prime task of a republic's "politics, after virtue, is the maintenance of abundance, so that men will be in a better position to work in common concert."[42]

Early commercial societies enunciated such principles and developed the new mode of republican government while dissolving traditional class lines into a new social mobility that brought those of many backgrounds into the new middle class. The modern democratic republic is as much a middle-class creation as is the private-enterprise market system. The reason seems plain. Both require a wide freedom of evaluation, debate, and preference. Both represent, on different levels, social diversification and social mobility. Both require a greater stability of continuity than any autocratic rule can rightfully promise. Both work on the essential precept 'to make haste slowly': for popular government, by virtue of the number of persons who have to be consulted about any proposed change, as well as the vested interests that many have in opposing specific innovations, is essentially conservative and looks upon radical change with suspicion — it takes the uninterrupted continuity of temporal flow with utmost seriousness. As de Tocqueville noted, "in democratic communities the majority of the people do not clearly see what they have to gain by a revolution, but they continually and in a thousand ways feel that they might lose by one."[43]

In contrast to a command economy, a demand or market economy presupposes the freedom of each, as a socially prescribed right, to depend on his own prudential judgment regarding what products, services, and ideas should be chosen for acceptance, consumption, or production. Individual consumer choices, on any level, are a kind of 'voting' on the perceived array of alternatives:

> The process of the market economy is, so to speak, a 'plebiscite de tous les jours', when every monetary unit spent by the consumer represents a ballot, and where the producers are endeavoring by their advertising to give 'election publicity' to an infinite number of parties (i.e., goods).[44]

The fundamental demand of a market economy is analogous to the fundamental demand of popular government — the ability for each to be guided by individual judgment within the context of the whole. In both cases, each needs 'candidates' to make themselves available and to have their advantages proclaimed and debated, so that by each one's own selection each voices an individual judgment that expresses a 'vote' that is a 'demand'.

The question, of course, arises as to how these diversified voices and demands issue into a harmonious, if dynamic, social order — whether conceived on an economic, political, or intellectual level. Leibniz had, Johnson suggested, seen a "beneficent providence" as the unifying force to guide the diversity of the members into the unity of the whole. It was not long before this was secularized in Adam Smith's famed phrase of 'the invisible hand' — to be accepted, but not to be explained, as the harmonizing force of a political economy. Polanyi suggests, perhaps more perceptively, that this mutual adjustment and congruence of individual wills represents a "spontaneous order" (as distinguished from a 'directive order'); and it depends upon a "self-adjusting order of distribution"[45] to be explained by social processes of general reciprocity and a sharing of self-interest just as the conflict of political wills results in a general consensus.

However the fact — that competition for influence and power results in the cooperation of social harmony — might be explained, "There was never any doubt in the minds of those fighting for the free economy [as for free government] that it would and must be operated in the spirit of Christian justice, as they understood it. It was not an amoral world" that they sought;[46] the quest for social freedom on each level, being concerned to open futural possibilities for human development, was conceived as being preeminently a moral imperative.

iii. The Moral Imperative

Any rational test of an operating social system should be on two coalescing grounds: first, how well its announced goals are met, and second, how those goals are to be evaluated. These are essentially pragmatic and moral tests: how well does the system function to produce what it sets out to do, and, are the goals used as the measure of success themselves approvable? On both counts the commercial economy's industrialization has proved to be a redounding success.

The great promise of commercialization, and the Industrial Revolution it spawned, was progressive elimination of its newly recognized 'problem of poverty'. If poverty may be judged as the most callous of human injustices, the moral imperative clearly calls for whatever system of economic organization, commensurate with its ground of human freedom, allows us to reduce or eliminate it. As industrialization promises new opportunity, the prime moral judgment concerning alternative economic systems, that is, alternative ways of handling a community's economic activity, should be the pragmatic question of efficacy: on the basis of garnered historic experiences and the genuine possibilities still held forth, which appears most likely to progressively eradicate the condition of poverty from any valid description of human existence?

The industrialization that commercialism developed has provided a historically unprecedented opportunity to accomplish this goal. The freedom which brought it into being is not a detriment to, but the necessary condition of, our continuing success in doing so.

This unique historical opportunity, and the moral obligation to undertake it, is without precedent in human history. Poverty had traditionally been presumed to be an integral part of the human condition: that 'the poor we will always have with us' was a standard rubric of all pre-industrial thought. That poverty might be eradicated instead of being shared had traditionally been seen as a commitment to futility; never able to conceive of the new power to create new wealth, pre-industrial thought, facing no alternative but to reconcile itself to its omnipresence, could thus never see its inherent injustice. Accepting poverty as irremediable, our ancestors took the concept of 'distributive justice' as the only moral response to their only economic experience, that of a static economy. *That wealth can be newly created for wider distribution is a new idea with no pre-industrial precedent.* This new vision is revolutionary.[47] No longer confined to finding a formula for a 'fair' distribution of a scarcity we must somehow share, we are finally enabled to look to encompassing all within a prosperous common good — by augmenting the creation of new wealth through the free cooperative endeavor of creative competition for its development and use.

The dream of free men had, indeed, from the beginning, always included the idea, not of the elimination of poverty, but at least its personal conquest. Presiding over the ascendancy of the Athenian democracy, Pericles had said: "We regard wealth as something to be properly used, rather than as something to boast about. As for poverty, no one need be ashamed to admit it: the real shame is in not taking practical measures to escape from it."[48] Initially proposed as the goal for any individual, we are now able to *require it* as a moral mandate for any responsible society.

The real choice, as our historic experience demonstrates, is *not* between freedom and the elimination of poverty — but *their neces-*

sary conjunction against all alternatives: societies organized on the basis of political freedom have already provided the surest, *demonstrated* road to the conquest of poverty. Whenever the popular voice has been enabled to direct the general policies of government, the priority, as could have been anticipated, has been to demand what is requisite to raise the level of the common prosperity. It is no historic accident that the most prosperous peoples in the world today are the free peoples.[49] And whatever else may still motivate depressed peoples, the goal to which they all seem to aspire is the free prosperity of the industrialized democracies.

In the face of history, it is unnerving that this still has to be argued out. If the function of an economic order is to produce the greatest prosperity possible, then the pragmatic test of efficacy should take priority. Rather than doze in ideological slumbers, one should abjure abstract conceptual formulas and accept from actual human experience those economic procedures that have worked most efficaciously to this promised end.

At the end of the twentieth century we have seen at least three comparative 'experiments' in socio-economic development unroll on the world scene. Each forcefully speaks to the lesson at hand. If we are to take the history of time seriously, we need to attend to these three comparative historical lessons:

First, the one whose duration parallels the 'rise of the west', is that of the New World — the contrast between the 'English' and 'Iberian' Americas. "These two Americas, North and South, equally colonies and equally underdeveloped, were founded upon two radically different *ideas* of political economy."[50] Despite the earlier settlement of Iberian America, dating back to the 1500s, the Rio Grande has continually been the boundary between prosperity and poverty. Even as some of the nations to its south, buoyed by petroleum-based or other economic advances, have started to join into the modern economic world, their own slowly emerging middle classes have started to demand the substance, and not merely the form, of republican government. But the Rio Grande, still marks the divide between countries founded in the heritage of feudal agriculture and those founded as commercial polities, still marks a sharp divide not only of the stability of freedom and representative government but also its concomitant of economic achievement.

The *second* is a comparison of Russia and Japan. In 1868, in St. Petersburg, Nicholas II ascended to the throne of "all the Russias;" in that same year, in Japan's Kyoto, the Meiji Emperor resolved to displace the Tokugawa Shogunate, which had effectively ruled for almost 300 years, and restore imperial rule — with a commitment to take Japan into the modern commercial world. Both were backward peasant countries, virtually embalmed in medieval feudalism. Russia, despite some cultural affinities with the West, maintained its 'autocracy'; Japan, despite being, to the West, an 'alien' culture, embarked on a bold program of westernizing its political and economic institutions.[51]

Both were 'allies' during the First World War. Both were subsequently subjected to dictatorship — the first, in the name of Marx, by a *coup d'etat* against the Provisional Russian Republic of 1917;[52] the second, under the Tojo dictatorship, prosecuted the war first against China and then the United States. Both were allied with Germany's National Socialist regime — Russia until its alliance was betrayed; Japan to the end. Both were literally devastated in the Second World War. Despite Russia's initial defeats, it emerged victorious with control over a new empire of conquered if restive lands in eastern Europe; Japan, after a bold conquering sweep across much of East Asia, was forced to retreat into its initial island-nation status.

In the ensuing forty-odd years, the two have forsaken any similarity. Japan, functioning since the end of the War with a private-enterprise economy under the parliamentary constitution MacArthur imposed, has emerged as one of the world's leading free industrial nations. Russia's Soviet Union only now appears to be discovering utilitarian virtues of 'open-ness' and degrees of 'democratization' (in which it had always boasted it surpassed 'the West'), even as its leadership calls for the radical 'restructuring' of its faltering economy.[53] Japan has functioned as a freely open society; while Russia's Soviet Union has functioned with a network of slave-labor camps and ruthless repression of all dissent. Japan developed its own rich culture as it assimilated foreign 'influences'; while a rigidly closed Russian society only reluctantly admitted, even from its own past, what can pass the rigors of (even newly relaxed) state censorship. Japan, an island nation scarcely able to produce its own foodstuffs, manages to feed its people well; while the Russians, once providing the 'bread basket' of Europe, can barely feed its own population even with imports. Japan, without natural resources of its own, has yet enabled its citizens to enjoy one of the world's highest standards of living; while Russia's Soviet state has hardly brought its immense natural resources into use and still struggles to provide its people with minimal modern comforts.

The *third*, and perhaps most important, of these historic experiments is seen in the record of the free industrialized western nations. Emerging from a fragmented political structure and a poverty-stricken economy in the late Middle Ages, they succeeded, despite intermittent and often consuming wars among themselves, in developing the principles and standards to which other peoples aspire. What have they done, and how have they done this?

It is essential to appreciate just what the industrialized democracies have accomplished in scarcely two hundred years — because those of us who are the beneficiaries tend to take the accomplishment for granted. By every tangible standard — of health, housing, and education, infant mortality and life-expectancy — "every single country of Europe and North American was a 'Third World' country two hundred years ago, and several were very poor indeed much more recently."[54] Their stories are the stories of most of our ancestors; they were "by modern standards . . . a story of almost unrelieved wretchedness. The typical human society has given only a small number of people a humane existence, while the great majority have lived in abysmal squalor."[55]

Emerging from this common condition, free countries moved to some form of popular control in the form of republican (often parliamentary monarchical) governments, accompanied by political, commercial, cultural, and religious freedoms. They have enjoyed growing literacy, educational, and health standards together with a level of general consumption and economic well-being rooted in a free existence undreamed of in the past.

This is no staid accomplishment, on the laurels of which we can now rest. "Rather, it is not only continuing but is continuing at an accelerated pace, and at least to date there is no indication that the acceleration is diminishing."[56] Relieved of the continuing struggle against poverty, most free citizens can turn their attention to other concerns; they prize their private lives which earlier housing conditions would have rendered beyond reasonable hope, while transforming the cultural activities of a select aristocracy into a 'mass-market' dependent on monetary and temporal expenditures which their grandparents could not have imagined. Against all previous history, free societies have transformed poverty into a minority-condition, regarded as a prime, but progressively soluble domestic problem. The economic gap in the world today is between the "wealth and the poverty from which [free industrialized economies] have escaped" and the condition in which "most of the world's people still live."[57]

Outperforming every alternative economic ordering of human affairs, modern capitalism has advanced "the material welfare of human beings, as measured by the means available to the great majority of individuals to choose and shape the quality of the lives they lead."[58] This massive freeing of personal time for individual self-control is no mean accomplishment.

Indeed, this economic system, uniquely, has regarded time itself, whether it be social or individual, as an inherently scarce resource to be prudentially 'spent'. Part of the cost of every engagement is its "transaction costs," the time that needs be expended to secure the "information, and resources" any particular exchange requires. "The price of time," is "a key concept in understanding how modern value systems and production systems have come into being";[59] it is crucial in the conduct of any free society in which each individual must be free to decide just how to invest, apportion, and use individual time.

Seeking to keep open options for the future, free nations have utilized this time-structured economic order to radically diminish the degrees of poverty in their populations, while finding themselves capable of effecting the most widespread welfare systems of 'cushions' or 'safety nets' ever known. Not only have they been able to afford to do so; their democratic polities *demand* that they use newly developed wealth to do so.

No self-styled socialist regime in the world has been able to come close.[60] It is indisputable that the politically free capitalist countries have gone furthest in minimizing poverty and ameliorating its humanely subversive effects — while, indeed, raising the level below which poverty is defined.

The thrust of a free-enterprise system, encouraged by free nations, is to continually expand mass-markets. The function of a mass market, by definition, is to meet the needs of the many. It is to these that modern industrial productivity is largely geared. "The largest and most successful industries are those which aim to supply everybody, in every family."[61] The great innovations of mass production go, not to meet the needs of the wealthy, but of the population as a whole. The activity of free-enterprise economies has been directed to raising and meeting consumption expectations on the part of the great mass of citizens — not the luxurious needs of a few wealthy patrons who, even without technological advances, could have had their needs met by a continuation of individual handicrafts.[62]

It is, therefore, somewhat ironic to find that some middle-class beneficiaries of this economic largesse bemoan the rise of 'consumerism'. After all, it was against the perceived failure of a generalized 'consumerism' that the early criticisms of capitalism had arisen. Whether the enjoyment of consumer products has gone 'too far' is an open question (and one of moral judgment upon the 'proper' uses of an individual's lived time) — but it is one that can only be raised for debate in 'capitalist' countries. For those who bemoan the condition of the 'lower classes' to complain about the common person's desire (to consume what modern industries are able to produce while receiving wages that increasingly enable them to do so), expresses heights of intellectual 'bad faith'. It is equally ironic for such critics to proclaim their antagonism to the social benefit of the advertising campaigns, directly or indirectly, supplying their livelihoods: for which they work and whose entreaties they honor while enjoying the latest espoused products. Meanwhile the self-styled 'socialist' economies they often seem to prefer, are newly discovering, against the weight of Marxian emphasis on 'the means of production', the economic importance of encouraging growing distribution and consumption networks and are adopting the product-promotion agency of advertising in order to do so.

Some critics claim that these indisputable results come from 'exploitation'. This criticism arises from the thesis that the full value of any product is that of the labor that went into creating it, the 'labor theory of value'[63]: the capital that animates the advance of industry comes from 'capitalists' securing for their own use part of the product of their workers' labors. Conceivably, this could explain that part of capital coming from profit — although it would seem that some credit is due to the organizational talent of those able to provide raw materials and machines and bring them and labor together with marketing skills, enabling the products to reach customers. But this explanation alone cannot account for the radical rise in workers' wages and the continually higher consumption levels they are thus able to enjoy.[64]

Such criticisms, as already indicated, do not only overlook the import of non-labor factors in modern production. They also ignore the complete dependence of sustained production on a marketing and distribution network to effectively direct its output — crucially lacking in socialist countries in accord with the Marxian focus on 'control of the means of production' as the answer to all social problems. And they cannot explain why capitalism's evolution from labor-intensive industries to the capital-intensive industries (which progressively reduce the contribution of employed labor to the emergent product) has served to raise general living standards. This evolutionary transition, rather than confirming 'levelling' fears, has created new industries, consequent new employments, and a vastly improved quality of life.[65]

Some argue that the rising standards of living in free countries depend upon 'colonialism' — the exploitation by the industrialized nations (including their working classes) of the backward countries of the world. This thesis, ironically, emerged in the mid-nineteenth century as the *original* colonial empires were dismantled; the last of them, that of Portugal, the poorest of all western European countries and the least entitled to be called 'capitalist', lasted for another hundred years (while the *new* British and French empires collapsed after World War II). It cannot explain the dramatic rise of either post-war Japan or the newly independent states of East Asia; neither can it explain the continuing dependence of socialist countries upon importation of western technological innovations and manufacturing expertise. Underdeveloped countries are, in most ways, of less economic importance to developed countries than are other developed countries.[66]

Some argue that capitalism can only prosper because of the 'alleged dependence of advanced countries upon those that are less advanced' (the 'dependency theory'). To this, Berger points out that "the development of the capitalist societies of East Asia is the most important falsification of dependency theory."[67]

On any theory of neo-colonial dependency, conquered-Japan (as conquered-Germany) should have been rendered into a dependency of the United States. But Japan has risen in forty-odd years to challenge American industrial supremacy and is now investing into segments of American industry, increasingly dependent for their futures upon decisions made in Tokyo. Need one add the stories of Korea, Taiwan, Singapore?[68] Japan's democratization was imposed upon it by military force.[69] In both Korea and Taiwan, the emergence of a commercial middle class — which an industrial economy eventually produces, if it does not already have one, because it requires the services of commercial development and marketing arrangements to distribute its products — has engendered strong pushes to democratic rule.

The development of these countries — along with India, left by the withdrawal of British imperial interests with a nascent middle class and a democratic form of government — "disconfirms the widely accepted notion that democracy [even "in a non-western culture"] cannot be imposed by force of arms."[70]

The significance of the Asian experience of democratizing capitalism has a broader significance:

[it] is bad news for Marxists. . . . [it] is also not very comforting to ideologists of capitalism who still adhere to some laissez-faire notions to the effect that state intervention is bad for economic development. All of these societies are characterized by massive state interventions in economic life. They are heavily *dirigiste*, and have been so from the beginnings of their respective modernization processes.[71]

Industrialized capitalism can, and has, developed under governmental direction — certainly in the Far East. One could argue that this was, even in sublimated form, also true in the West.[72]

Whether seen as the product of commercialism or as a 'democratized mercantilism', contemporary capitalism depends upon governmental policies, which, in the name of the common good, identify popular liberties and freedoms with general prosperity and entrepreneurial opportunity. Encouraging industrialization and commercial enterprise without directly engaging in those enterprises, it limits itself to setting procedural rules encouraging their enhancement by tax policies and market incentives.

Whatever particular criticisms this kind of system, or any particular aberrations of it, merit, specific reforms should be limited to being corrective. Intelligent reform that is morally responsible to all those lives that benefit from this unique historic development should not seek to subvert it because *some* have been 'washed onto the shore'; rather than divert the entire stream, responsible reform confines itself to channeling the flow and bringing those 'wafted aside' back into its progression.

The prime function of an economic order is to supply material needs; effectiveness in doing so is a first criterion for rationally evaluating alternative systems. Before one renounces a free enterprise economy, one should be able to demonstrate how any proposed replacement could meet its manifest record of accomplishment. Without equivocation, it can be asserted that no system for providing for the material needs of a people has been more successful than that of commercial capitalism. This is no accident — precisely because it is geared to a market system of distribution, it is immediately in touch with popular needs as they are generally perceived; the continuity of its institutions is justified by their effectiveness in meeting them.

iv. Ownership

However a free economic system may be described, it places a premium on private property ownership and translates the social value of things and of time into the medium of monetary exchange. The livelihood of its citizens, left to their own choosing rather than government directive, depends upon the utilization of private property for the public benefit.

The 'right' to property has been seen, from the outset, to be crucial to any notion of individual rights and public liberty. Locke succinctly explicated this by consolidating the rights to 'life, liberty, and estate' in the right of 'property'. Its general dispersal through the citizenry is the surest guarantee that the delegated power of government is exercised for the freedom of the citizens. As Rousseau explained:

> It is certain that the right of property-ownership is the most sacred of all the rights of citizens, and more important in certain respects than liberty itself; either because it lies closer to the conservation of life, ... or because ownership is the true foundation of civil society and the guarantee of the commitments of the citizens . . .[73]

Built on the idea that the public advantage lies in the productive use of private property, a modern commercial economy is an industrialized economy geared to the driving force of economic growth. This idea, which came out of the agricultural revolution, was itself made possible by the "definition and development of *property rights*." This idea of private property called forth a system of law to govern the enforcement of contracts and exchanges together with the whole range of regulations that govern social as well as commercial relationships. The use of private property to augment one's own holdings has resulted in the economic growth, the benefits of which our prosperity enables us to enjoy. This economic growth is itself "inseparable from capitalism and from modern 'propertarian' society,"[74] and depends upon the protection of private property.

Ownership and control of property is a source not only of growth but also of power, as it provides a source of employment, consumption, and influence. As a vested interest distinct from that of governing authority, it provides a source of independence from the concerns and, above all, from the authority of others. As Röpke points out,

> whenever the lamp of freedom, of the enquiring mind and of humanity has illuminated the darkness, it was when a sufficient number of

people had a modicum of private prosperity and were therefore in a position to shake off their economic dependence on the state or the feudal lord.[75]

Society's recognition of individual property pluralizes loyalties within the common concern and thus becomes a bastion against the arbitrary actions of government officials. By investing the rights to property with the legal safeguards and protections of the organized community, a community has effectively disbursed sources of power; it thereby affords itself the protection of these disparate sources of power against its own officialdom, as well as other power centers it encompasses. The right to acquire and use property thus becomes an important safeguard of individual independence against excessive governmental intrusion, as well as against usurpation or tyranny.

Private property is not only a community safeguard against political encroachment and a means for personal enjoyment. Its prime economic value is its utilization for creating new wealth. This economic utilization, in addition to its immediate political import, provides its ultimate social value. For it is primarily as a center for the production of wealth, along with the vested interest in its protection, that private property becomes a bastion for liberty.

An economy, built on freedom to initiate and pursue new economic activities, brings the principles of political freedom into the marketplace that governs a free economy. Dispersing the economic power to inaugurate new initiatives in production and distribution of goods and services to its citizens, the contest of economic competition is essential to economic freedom. As the safeguard of political freedom is ensured by a constitutional system of political power checks and balances, so a free economic system fragments economic power; by maintaining the structure of competitive markets, by encouraging individuals and groups to enter the competitive contest for economic return, it brings the principle of checks and balances into the economic life of free citizens.

Monopoly by economic oligarchs is as offensive to public freedom as is any monopoly of political authority. As in the political realm, the principle of a commercial economy is competition for public favor. In this sense, the American 'Sherman Anti-Trust Act' of 1890 was centrally important: one function of a responsible free government is to police the marketplace so that no one power may dominate it. Economic power, as political power, is to be fragmented and dispersed while contests for influence are to be ordered. In defending the principle of a competitive economy, the political lesson had been learned well.

Any monopoly of power is to be feared: power is to be fragmented if it is to remain free. In economic terms, as in political terms, this mandates maintaining a structural balance between contending forces while protecting each to voice its own concerns. For the sake of the common good, the first principle of a 'commercial republic' is that economic power, as any power, is to be dissolved into a contest of competition. As Röpke noted,

> it is the indispensable function of competition within the market economy to adjust opposing interests by insisting on equal value of service and counter-service and by forcing the producers to pursue their own advantage only by way of furthering the interests of the community.[76]

The prime economic function of a free government is not to provide directives for economic activities which it leaves to the initiatives of private individuals; it is to sustain them with a stable currency which permits them to plan ahead and stable laws prescribing acceptable procedures which it is to police, thus ensuring that commercial activities are honestly conducted without foreclosing new innovations.

A free commercial economy is a money economy, and the value of money, as the medium of all exchanges of goods and services, becomes central to its functioning. Translating rights to tangible property, and control of time into monetary terms provides a fortuitously impersonal evaluation of community service, wealth and its exchange. A uniform monetary standard of economic value translates any claim of economic value into an economic abstraction. Advantageous because it facilitates handling contracts — for any kind of exchange of property, time, or services — it also lowers the "transaction cost" of any exchange by minimizing the time required to arrange it.[77] By translating commercial exchanges into the dispassionate language of money while maintaining the stability of exchange values upon which commercial interaction is based, each citizen is permitted to face the future with the confidence needed to plan ahead. Money not only permits an orderly exchange of goods to take place; it also provides a stable order in which investment may prudentially be made into a yet-open future.

A monetary economy *dis*engages any evaluation of moral worth from economic contribution. A wage system is *not* an evaluation of the individual person; rather it is, within even a controlled market, only an evaluation of a person's socially recognized, specific contribution to the economy itself. Were wages not variable, so that they can induce voluntary filling of both distasteful tasks and acceptance of special responsibilities, compulsory labor (as in the late Middle Ages and in totalitarian nations today), would conceivably be needed.

The impersonal nature of monetary evaluation minimizes the priority of family status or other inherited right, and thus opens up an arena of social mobility in which no one is necessarily bound to the occupation of the parent — historically the first liberty of an emerging modern society. Freed from inherited rank and status, each individual, by engaging in economically productive activities, enters into a monetary world in which all contributions are translated into the abstract standard of monetary worth. Access of all activity to a monetary measure thus enhances the social fluidity and democratic classlessness of modern society. This use of money as a universal medium of exchange is, *fortunately*, "cold, impersonal, insensitive to station, class, creed, race, or person. . . . its use opens the political economy to men of every class, race, and creed."[78] As a democratizing medium, it recognizes no inherited class but takes each individual into the economic society as it gauges the import of proffered instrumentality to the particular project. A money economy thus enables each to "transcend his own biographical starting point," and thus "frees the individual from the bondage of [inherited] concrete social allegiances."[79]

Gross as some of its manifestations may be (especially when viewed in contrast to the formalized courtesies of an entrenched nobility), a money economy generally subverts any rigid class structure built out of inherited wealth or power. Insofar as each person acquires monetary wealth in accord with a standardized market value, each is free to find his own place in the dynamic order of the society. Free societies are essentially fluid in their class structures and social mobility has become a generally applauded norm.[80] The status of each is relatively consonant with the social evaluation of what he has done, however the operating norm for this evaluation may be judged. Before one protests this, one should consider the sole feasible alternatives — not an aristocracy of talent, but an oligarchy of either inheritance or entrenched directive political power. The general democratizing tendency of modern free-enterprise economies lets each stand on his own — with what he has done with what has been given to him, in terms of wealth, education, or status. The result is a fluidly mobile social structure in which social stratifications are continually dynamic.

One might well denigrate this as placing undue emphasis on wealth, but wealth ideally indicates the socially perceived economic import of how one expends personal time by employment in a socially useful enterprise, and thus, in contributing to the general economic good. To the extent that this rewards system is misappropriated, it calls for reform of the particular rewards system itself, not of the principle that economic status should be dependent upon contribution. However the rewards system of any society may be skewed at any particular time, this kind of compensatory system ensures that the society as a whole does not harden into rigidly separate social classes: children are not condemned to share the status of their parents — whether they sink or rise depends on how they appropriate the opportunities opened to them. However unfairly this may seem to work out at any particular point, it does insure a fluid social order, the avoidance of permanent stratification, and a continually open invitation to members of each generation to do better for their society, and thereby for themselves.

Differentiation of monetary rewards capitalizes on the virtues of some degrees of inequality, while it hedges in the economic system with political and cultural controls.[81] It has — a few contemporary moral philosophers to the contrary — *not* equated the value of the person with personal income; rather it squarely insists that personal income is but a reflection of the negotiated social judgment of economic contribution, not of personal worth.[82]

A free enterprise system is not merely concerned to open economic channels of productivity to the free initiative of citizens so that their livelihoods may be adequately supported. It is also concerned to open up areas in which their leisure time may be freely spent. By encouraging free initiatives in the provision of alternate ways for the expenditure of leisure time, areas of professional employment not directly related to the production of material wealth are created. As such, these enable citizens to become 'audiences' for performances — athletic competitions, dramatic and musical presentations, and television shows which require 'mass' consumption in order to occur. They also enable individuals to individuate their leisure by how they choose to spend their free time: private reading and participation in freely chosen associations — union and professional associations, religious and charitable organizations, hobby groups, public interest societies, and varied political clubs. Each of these freely competes with all others for the personal time of their 'clients' — knowing that no individual can accept all their invitations because inherent temporality compels choice among them. These different ways of spending leisure time usually involve divergent kinds of social involvements and, by leaving each free to construct one's own, educates a citizenry in ways importantly discrete from the structured time frame of most direct economic involvements.

These, and especially the less institutionalized leisure-time activities, provide a very different time frame from those generally associated with economic employment. For most individuals, the difference between work and leisure is most radically marked by a dramatic change of temporal pace — for some, an escape from the closely knit metrical time schedules of factories and offices; for others, a refreshing change that enervates the return to the economic arena.

To the extent that a society permits a wide range of intellectual freedom by removing itself from ideological censorship of those activities carrying ideational content, it pluralizes the intellectual life of the citizenry by opening their horizons to a free exchange of ideas and perspectives. This opening quickly feeds back into the society itself by bringing new ideas and imaginative projects to bear in a richer mix of personal activities.

These different leisure-time activities, encouraged in a free society, set up a complex system of alternative and often conflicting loyalties. An individual, in addition to participation in the economic unit which engages employment and loyalties of economic interest, generally belongs to several voluntary groupings. Some of these are in accord with, and some are opposed to, specific proposed or current governmental or other social policies. Whatever else the pluralization of groups within a society does, it multiplies loyalties — and leaves it to each individual member to resolve the conceivable conflicts between them. In a society whose government ultimately depends on a popular consensus, this dynamic — the confluence and conflicts of diverse inner loyalties — pluralizes the subordinate loyalties and thereby variegates the sources of political power.

On both the level of economic livelihood and of leisure time activity, a modern free-enterprise or capitalist economy sets up a multitude of power centers, in the very nature of its enterprise. It opens the door to free leisure-time activities, often with a direct bearing on contested social policies Its organization of its economic life, perhaps more centrally, sets up a diversity of economic power centers. Effectively 'delegating' basic economic decisions — concerning separate initiatives in manufacturing, distribution, and services — to individuals prepared to undertake them, a free society refrains from directive control of its economy by maximizing the authority of its members to exercise those social decisional responsibilities.

The political function of public, private, political, economic, and social centers of popular loyalties — the multitude of voluntary leisure-time associations and the number of public corporations and private entrepreneurial companies — is that together they serve as alternative centers of popular power. Its historic source, as Polanyi noted, was the new concept of individual contract that enables each to control his own time:

> The first step toward liberation is the fixing of feudal dues by custom, law or written copy. And finally, by the commutation of these dues in terms of money, the copyholder [of a free contract] becomes a tenant, entitled to dispose freely OF HIS OWN TIME and person, and to select according to his own judgment what is most congenial and profitable for him to do.[83]

A free society thus enunciates a principle rarely voiced — *one prime property right is the right to one's own time.*

Property is power, as both Locke and Rousseau understood. Private property, as the power of private allegiances to a multitude of voluntary organizations, provides diverse centers of opposition to governmental encroachment. This complex of centers of interest and allegiance comprise a vast plurality of ways in which citizens come to meet and work with each other and assess the varied institutions of their polis. The maintenance of liberty and freedom depends upon this social cooperation in maintaining an arena in which these fragmented centers may engage in a continuing struggle for influence, and a fluidity of class structure so that each person may yet envision being, in some regard, in another social position. To distribute the power of a society among a plurality of power centers, while yet retaining to the voice of the whole the ability to check any aggrandizement of subordinate powers, is to preserve the stability of freedom while yet allowing freedom to function.

When governmental officials are given complete control of the economic order through nationalization of industry, as well as the political influence that, as government spokesmen,they already possess, it is difficult to see how their concentrated power could be contained. For all accesses to control are then in one set of hands and no power center in the social order can possess the strength to oppose and constrain them.

The nineteenth-century intellectual dream of a socialist society was conceived as a protest against the human misery brought to light and exploited by the anarchic license once permitted in the newly freed economic sphere.[84] Seeking to reserve the productive power of property to political direction was but a dream of unverifiable human beneficence, to be directed by a beneficent government solely concerned to allot to each a share in its vision of their good. Its advocates never considered that a directive bureaucracy quickly develops a life of its own, that it is a 'new class' whose class interests can be expected to take understandable priority before its appointed social mission; being unchecked by countervailing power, it remains free to incorporate all power to itself. Insofar as socialism's advocates could spell out no institutional restraints on the bureaucrats called upon to manage this social beneficence, their thinking effectively ignored any serious attention to the nature of power. They were never to think through, in the light of their vision, the problem of balancing economic and political powers. The socialist experiments of the twentieth century amply document the inherent danger.

If 'all power corrupts', then adding all economic to political power can only lead to the most absolute corruption of power — something to be avoided for the sake of freedom at almost all costs. In contrast, the tradition of free republicanism has insisted that the only way to control power is by its institutional pluralization — checking each center of power with countervailing force: the more concentrated political power becomes, the more important is it to augment economic powers *outside* it.

Conceived in some of the most humanely beneficent idealism of which man is capable, the socialist dream was thus conceptually flawed and misconceived at the outset: it never reckoned with either the dynamics of power or the virtue of creating social inducements or creative incentives to engage private advantage to the service of the public good. And because it would have concentrated all power within the hands of a somehow chosen few to provide beneficent guidance for the rest, it is, despite protestations to the contrary, essentially anti-democratic in the fullest sense of the term. Flagrantly, it denied *the property right*, not only of tangible assets, but *of lived time itself.* Conceptually it chose *not* to leave 'the people' free to work out by their individual endeavors their own visions of their own goods — but to entrust a benevolent elite to direct them in the 'proper way'. Taking into account the lessons of the dynamic of power, that elite, as any bureaucratic group, should be expected to rapidly develop its own self-interest by perpetuating its own mission in a new tyranny. Yet this is the inherent message of those who today invite us to a 'rationally planned' society.

The livelihoods of members of a free citizenry necessarily presume the social and economic health of the entire community, because all citizens must function together within its compass. As they do so, citizens are pledging themselves to maintain their freedom to act freely. As an employee of a corporate enterprise, of a private entrepreneur, public-interest organization, or governmental agency, as an entrepreneur or an organizational officer, each is a participant in the economic order. In principle, each citizen is left free to be an individual entrepreneur with a socially recognized right to his own time — which may be expended by utilizing personal capabilities to maximize personal advantage, directing one's own investment of time and money, and subjecting oneself to an evaluative faith in the forces of the ordered market — which are, when all is said done, the combined consumer demands of the society's members, as the society comprehensively perceives them. "The necessities of the entrepreneur become the rights of the individual, and vice versa."[85] Each one, as one's own entrepreneur, handles a personal economic condition as seems fitting — by accepting available employment or a dole, by starting a business or seeking to enhance one. Each has a vested interest in seeing one's own time and money-investment prosper — and a vested interest in the societal organization that sustains it.

Whether in terms of voluntary leisure-time organizations, or in terms of economic centers of gainful employment, each center of citizen activity becomes, by virtue of those involved in and with it, a center of political power. These are intermediary institutions which stand between local individual citizens and their centralized government.[86] They provide alternative centers of loyalty, divergent focuses of interest, and thereby, centers of popular power against the encroachment of political and bureaucratic authority. They provide a central defense of freedom — just insofar as they stand ready to withstand encroachments on their own time, tangible property, and ability to function. They provide a continuing demonstration of the need a free society has to encourage, within its midst, the growth of a plurality of viewpoints with organizational strength. It is finally this pluralization of centers of power that prevents any one of them from overwhelming the rest.

The price of freedom is the continuity of contest. That this continuity ensues in a social harmony requires a procedure by which each such contest may be resolved. It is the interest of the unity of the society that the possibility of divergence by each member, within the bonds of the general social agreement, be preserved and extended by the power of the entire community.[87]

Augmenting constitutional promises, the distribution of property ownership helps to ensure that those promises will be kept, by providing each citizen with a vested interest in seeing that they are.[88] To use Polanyi's term, a 'polycentric' system of power — ensured by widespread private property that can not only be enjoyed but can also used to create new sources of economic development — multiplies centers of power and influence while providing a system of checks and balances to bring them into harmony. This diffusion of economic, together with political, power has engendered and sustained ordered freedom; oriented to what yet may be, it brings social diversity into the play of a free social order.

v. Developing a Middle Class

However 'capitalism' may be understood, its advocacy is usually attacked as inherently 'conservative', if not inherently 'reactionary' and 'inhumane'. In actual fact, however, capitalism has proven to be the most radically revolutionary and humanely beneficent of all historical movements. Echoing the call by Walter and Russell Davenport, in the 1940s, for recognition of the 'continuing revolution' in human affairs which the American experience proclaims, Berger argues:

> . . . from its inception capitalism has been a force of cataclysmic transformation in one country after another. Capitalism has radically changed every material, social, political and cultural facet of the societies it has touched, and it continues to do so.[89]

In point of fact, no one has provided a more effusive endorsement of capitalist enterprise than did Marx and Engels. Writing during its infancy in the revolutionary year of 1848, and using their favored pejorative term of 'bourgeoisie' for what we would today refer to as 'the upper middle class' (that produced the entrepreneurs who came to be called 'capitalists'), they said:

Our epoch [is] the epoch of the bourgeoisie . . .

Modern industry has established the world market, for which the discovery of America paved the way. This market has given an immense development to commerce, to navigation, to communication by land. This development has . . . pushed into the background every class handed down from the Middle Ages. . . .

The bourgeoisie . . . *has been the first to show what man's activity can bring about*. It has accomplished wonders far surpassing Egyptian pyramids, Roman aqueducts, and Gothic cathedrals; it has conducted expeditions that put to shame all former Exoduses of nations and crusades.

The bourgeoisie has through its exploitation of the world market given *a cosmopolitan character* to production and consumption in every country. To the great chagrin of reactionaries, it has drawn from under the feet of industry the national ground on which it stood. . . .

The bourgeoisie, by the rapid improvement of all instruments of production, by the immensely facilitated means of communication, *draws all*, even the most backward, *nations into civilization*. . . .

The bourgeoisie, during its rule of scarcely one hundred years, has *created more massive and more colossal productive forces than have all preceding generations* together. Subjection of Nature's forces to man, machinery, application of chemistry to industry and agriculture, steam-navigation, railways, electric telegraphs, clearing of whole continents for cultivation, canalization of rivers, whole populations conjured out of the ground — what earlier century had even a presentiment that such productive forces slumbered in the lap of social labor?[90]

If 'bourgeois' capitalism in its first hundred years, had indeed "created more massive and more colossal productive forces than have all preceding generations together," one might then expect it to have been seen as the liberator of mankind — which, in fact, it proved itself to be, rather than its enemy. Whatever criticisms of capitalism's conquests may be valid, one should not, in the words of the familiar aphorism, 'throw out the baby with the bath water'. A new creative force had been unleashed. It should be harnessed, as in fact its recent history has demonstrated it has been, not repudiated as Marx demanded. Indeed, during its second hundred years, it accelerated its advance while harnessing itself by the reforms which the democratic capitalist countries all continued to make since the Great Depression of 1929. It has curbed the power of concentrated wealth by setting out stringent rules for the conduct of its commerce while providing its workers an increasingly vested interest in its growing prosperity.

The Marxian expectations generating the reasons for absconding from approbation of early 'bourgeois' capitalism have proved to be false. Capitalism did *not* divide society into a hopeless divide of rich and poor; that is the state of affairs it inherited. Rather, by the entrepreneurial efforts intrinsic to its functioning, it has progressively raised the level of the poor by raising real wages and allocating to labor an increasingly larger share of income and influence. Particularly as it has begun to pass into a post-industrial age in which wealth is produced less by labor and more by sophisticated machines, labor's ability to 'exploit capital' — in the reformed free economic order — has progressively brought labor into an expanding property-owning middle class.

Because a capitalist, or free-enterprise, economy places a premium on entrepreneurial effort, because it has learned to control monopolistic tendencies and to police the market to enforce competitive practices, it has served as the most innovative system of economic order the world has known. It has exhibited the ability to relieve human society from dependence upon accident, and from merely fortuitous convergences of progressive factors, by opening channels for new advances; it has, indeed, developed into an engine of progress that, in its technological advances, is providing increasingly imaginative ways in which to relieve the drudgery and tedium of routinized labor.[91] Because its technological advances require increasingly larger numbers of sophisticated employees, it is also providing a demand that responsible educators should welcome — pervasively raised educational levels of the citizenry.

This continual pull to rising educational standards feeds one of its most significant results — the increasing tendency of 'bourgeois capitalism' to bring increasing numbers of its citizens into 'bourgeois' ranks by transforming its society into a pervasively middle-class social order — one in which, increasingly, every citizen 'has enough but not too much', one in which the levels of poverty are being raised while the upper level of middle-class status enters into a higher level whose ability to fund new investment is crucial to the social health. Raising educational standards raises the livelihood level of its citizens and improves their spiritual as well as their material quality of life. As members of an expanding middle class, individuals find increasing interest and opportunity to engage in cultural, religious, and political affairs. Such noneconomic leisure-time pursuits are made possible by the increasing allotment of free personal time which a forward-looking industrialized commercial society produces. These technological advances and the consequent freeing of leisure time join to provide each citizen with new opportunities to use his own time with increasing latitude of decision.[92]

As this developing economy has become increasingly more sophisticated in its functioning procedures, it may have indeed begun to master ways to even out the extreme cycles of 'boom and bust' that marked its first hundred-odd years. By bringing 'floors' under minimum income to provide a creative 'input' into the ebbs and flows of the market, and ceilings on excessive investment activity by controlling the cost of money, it is developing techniques to tame the demand-and-supply vicissitudes of a free-market system by general policy increasingly aimed at an augmented prosperity for all.[93]

This accomplishment has been largely attained by continued expansion of mass-market strategies. A mass market depends upon expanded purchasing power — and the more successful industry is one that can envision more societal members as potential clients. In place of an oligarchical order in which the artisan would sell a few products, as de Tocqueville pointed out, "at a high price to the few," a mass market encouraged the innovation of mass-production because it invites the innovative practice of "conceiv[ing] that the more expeditious way of getting rich is to sell them at a low price to all."[94] Free-market economies aim at producing products, not for those who could have afforded them in any event, but for the greatest possible number. The "largest financial rewards [have gone] to innovators who improved the life-style not of the wealthy, but of the less-wealthy many."[95] By developing this practice of merchandising to the many, a free-market economy transforms an increasing proportion of its society into the middle-class status of those increasingly engaged, as producers, merchants, or consumers, in market activity.

Essential to capitalist economies has been its focus on market development and distribution of products. In contrast to the Marxian focus on productive forces, it is the market-oriented economies that have evoked the mass-productivity which enables capitalist economies to prosper. By expanding markets for particular consumer goods, industries expand their own productivity — and thereby the number of those employed in the manufacture and distribution of their products — thus generating another round of rising living-standards. In a very succinct way, by logic of the process, the general prosperity of the community as a whole redounds to the prosperity of its members.

By a generalized pattern of income distribution across wider spectrums of the population, generally raising living-standards for all, a high degree of social mobility, and increasing attention to those who feel themselves not 'counted-in', countries justifiably characterizable by Novak's term of 'democratic capitalism' are increasingly becoming pervasively middle-class societies. This is the kind of society that, through history, has demanded democratization — and which proponents of freedom have consistently insisted provides the only social base that can sustain a society devoted to the liberties and freedoms of its citizens.

These societies are built, not on a moral assessment of each citizen, but on the presumption that such an assessment is not within proper social purview — which is to be restricted to maintaining a proper material modicum for free humane living. The purpose of social organization, as Green (echoing Kant) insisted time and again, is not to instill morality, but to create the general political and material conditions that encourage individual morality to assert itself. Morality depends, not on social enforcement of strict codes, but on enabling individuals to freely direct their own lives within the context of social harmony. This limitation of social judgment of the moral status of others has indeed led to a society that is freer, with increasing free time for all, more generally prosperous, and more open to diverse considerations of moral perspectives on particular practices than any we have known. By radically reducing poverty, it has, against all utopian protests, indeed removed the greatest detriment to individual morality. By progressively affording its citizens the opportunity to rise out of poverty and forge their own futures with a sense of human dignity as responsible human beings, it has shown its own 'good faith'.

Ironically, as 'capitalist' economies found themselves increasingly able to properly feed, educate, and house their citizens, their critics employ an increasingly moralistic voice. Rather than face specific present problems by acknowledging the new possibilities which this development opens for the future, they romanticize the pre-industrial past — a human condition, in which most people's waking time was wholly preoccupied by 'grubbing' for food or sparse shelter — a condition of many 'third world' countries today.[96]

Nothing is really new in the thesis that generally responsible living requires material sustenance: Aristotle had already explained that 'virtuous activity' "needs external goods . . . for it is impossible, or not easy, to do noble acts without the power of equipment. . . . happiness [then] seems to need this sort of prosperity" (1099b). A free economic order has, indeed, increasingly provided the material basis for moral or virtuous behavior and for a social commitment to individual happiness consonant with responsible social life.

The economic lives of our ancestors were nothing that we, who know something better, would want to envy. Romanticization of the life of the past does not face either the new possibilities of the present or the living conditions of the past; rather, it appeals to a literature concerned to depict those who were fortunate enough not to be part of the large sustaining and illiterate mass of their societies, and who were thereby able to provide us with their vision of something better — while it frequently glorifies revolutionary protests against those conditions rather than focusing on the progressive accretion of changing conditions requisite to a better social order. The 'knights of the round table' were illiterate and, as the later patrons of the arts, they lived on the drudgery of serfdom labor; the craftsmen, whom many Marxians glorify as having been able to take pride in the products of their labor, worked, only after undergoing the virtually slavish status of apprenticeship, under conditions today's workers would never rightfully dream of accepting.

It is ironic that in the very period when Leninist governments are seeking 'to restructure' the meager fruits of socialist economies,[97] and democratic-socialists entrusted with power in the Western democracies opt for programs of 'privatization', that the call for the socialist ideal should be still heard. Wherever it has been tried, 'socialism' has *failed to work*, while, yet in its name it is being implicitly repudiated by its faithful adherents who seek to augment their failed experiments by adapting the methods of capitalist achievement.

This is 'the' pragmatic judgment. The varied economic 'experiments' of concurrently divergent development, which constitute a good part of the twentieth century,[98] have established standards of workability that can be marked against each other. Different explanations may be offered, but by the test of general quality of life of the citizenry, the first test for which the critics of an emergent capitalism called, no rational assessment of historic fact can question the fruitfulness of temporally open-ended free economies in securing a high level of human livelihood. When we add to this the expansion of intellectual and cultural freedom and the freedom of leisure, intrinsic to its development, we must justifiably demand the reasons for any judgment other than approbation on moral grounds.

History is, itself, not experienced as a predetermined unrolling of a gigantic screen on which all that will ever appear to the human observer has already been somehow recorded. History appears to us as a continuing opening into the future, which ever reveals the unexpected. But it also shows that procedures that have been tried — those trials which have succeeded and those which have failed — tend to replicate. By any pragmatic test in which the general welfare of the average person is taken as the test-case, no historic evidence suggests that any alternative economic-political arrangement can honestly promise more.

'Democratic capitalism' has sustained general prosperity by insisting on general liberty and freedom — by transposing the political principles of diversifying power, harmonized by a system of checks and balances, into an ordered system of competitive commerce in a free polity. Maximizing individual control over individual time, it thereby invites the more creative among us to develop further innovations that may benefit us all.

Whatever deficiencies may be acknowledged, however far we may yet be from a fully equitable social order, remediation is to be found within these parameters that two or more centuries of social experience have opened to us. Modern free commercial societies, are, by any equitable count, the most fruitful that mankind has so far, in some five thousand years of recorded history, East or West, yet achieved. This historic accomplishment has been epitomized in building a middle-class society in which disparities of wealth are minimized in their import for the future and are less divisive than in any antecedent mode of organization, while the diffusion of wealth is being maximized so that an increasingly large proportion of the population becomes property owners who thereby participate in the generalized prosperity of a free citizenry.

A growing middle class represents the diffusion of the power of property among a citizenry whose members increasingly claim a vested interest in their society and the freedoms it entails. As the power of property is generalized, a society of property-owning citizens develops, and the power of freedom that nurtures it is increasingly secured.

vi. Building Free Societies

All countries with a free, or republican, government have worked with a market, or demand, economy. Developed in the 'West', it marks those countries of the 'East' whose living standards soon rapidly exceeded those of their neighbors. These Asian countries, in accord with the requirements of a free industrialized society that depends upon commerce for its functioning, have developed increasingly important middle classes; in due course, the middle-class push for democratic liberties should have been anticipated.[99]

Two questions, at least, still appear open. The first is why what we call 'capitalism' has functioned so well with, and even enhanced, the republican kind of government which nurtured it. The second question is whether this relation has been an accident of history or something more. In fact, to answer either question is to answer the other.

A free-market, or capitalist, economy has proved to be the most efficient way yet devised to enhance the kind of productivity that sustains a growing standard and quality of living for its people, the richest the world has ever known. Breaking old class barriers, it inaugurated a degree of social mobility inconceivable three hundred years ago; it has built the most 'classless' — the most open and lest stratified — society history has known, with minimal social barriers changing in each succeeding generation. It has been able to afford to treat its poor generously while opening the doors for advancement for all (if not for them so much, then at least for their children). Indeed, it has served what some churchmen today term the "option for the poor"[100] more effectively than any historically viable alternative, however stridently advanced.

What Montesquieu designated as the prospect of a "commercial republic" has come to pass. It has succeeded in building a notion of private life in whole areas of activity, deliberately sequestered from governmental, and even public, intrusion. It has thus, while creating some of the most powerful governments in the history of mankind, nevertheless succeeded in *using them* for commonly agreed upon purposes while limiting the scope of their functioning and their pertinence.

Effecting the highest living standard ever known, it has generalized sources of livelihood and universalized access to education while promoting standards of leisure never known before. It has built upon, and in turn nurtured by its own modes of operation, the freedom upon which it depends. It has been uniquely innovative and, as historic experience now stands, alone holds open the road to progress, not only in the technologies it has developed out of its educative opening, but also in the promises it offers for a quality of human living that is culturally enriched because it increasingly needs stringent standards of education for its citizens.

This innovative effect has come about, in some part, by ceasing to regard this market system as a self-contained autonomous entity properly removed from the popular controls supplied by the political order. Markets operate *within* a society and often need to be restrained so that they do not operate against it. Important as free markets are for the prosperous life of the society, the power of market freedom, like any other power within an interrelated society, needs to be restrained by a disciplined concern for the good of the whole.

One reason for this success of a system based on unchanelling diverse sources of social power — while simultaneously defining their functional freedoms by constraining them within the boundaries of the common good — lies in the open recognition of the nature of power itself. All social arrangements are arrangements for the allocation of power within the community, and any allocation of power must be limited for the sake of the community's own good.

Two radically different rationalist perspectives still beset us. One demanded that all powers be left free to function without the constraint of concern for the common good; it led to an anarchy which demanded pervasive reforms of the system of freedom so that freedom might yet prosper. The other proposed a *deducible* system of centralized planning to avoid the pitfalls of economic anarchy; it led to some of the most pervasive tyrannies the modern world has known. The moderate alternative to both principles is not conceptually 'neat'; it honors Montesquieu's call to moderate and compromise any rationalist vision. The governing principle of free societies knows that concentrating power in a few hands is intrinsically pernicious; the effective means for developing the common good is to generate a procedure for dispersing power in an orderly way through the community, while retaining to the community's own governmental organization the authority to supervise the free exercises of those powers so that they may function together for the freedom, the common good, of the whole.

The political system of checks and balances — the sharing of power by diverse agencies while yet focusing responsibility in discernible areas — directs this politico-economic system of socially encouraged, competitive forces. This is no accident. The lessons learned about the controlled utilization of power have come to us out of political experience and have been generalized. Every corporate board room and union meeting hall, as every parish, congregation, fraternal lodge, and political club, is, while divided on some matters, a center of citizen loyalty and thereby a countervailing power to the potential power of the state *and* of other social groupings. By deliberating, encouraging, or permitting a multitude of intermediate and, often, contesting organizations among the populace, as in their government, the reach of any particular center of political or economic power has been limited, even while each has been endowed with the power that the society judges needed in order to carry out the public purpose.

Free governments have continually functioned together with the capitalist economies they generate because they both utilize the same principle for the control of power. A free commercial economy under republican government incorporates into its economic structures an analogous division of economic power. Their coalescence provides a reciprocal strengthening of the processes and procedures of freedom. The pluralization of power, with each group seeking to augment its own, results in that crucial struggle for power that is requisite for the maintenance of political freedom. This continuing struggle for economic power and political influence is necessarily open-ended to the future — in terms of long-term investment of capital, time, expertise, labor and, above all, of faith in what the prescriptive specification of procedures for developing a free future can accomplish. The way to the expansive freedom of free societies is clearly marked.

All countries in the world today that are called 'democratic republics' (whether in presidential or monarchical form) have free-market economies. Yet some countries that have authoritarian governments, under growing pressure for liberation by their emerging middle classes, maintain growing capitalist economies. If recent history has been any guide to what we may reasonably expect, such societies will eventually develop duly representative institutions — so the West's historic procedure shall be reversed and economic freedom will engender political freedom.[101] The logic of the case is to anticipate their eventually doing so — and especially in Asian societies where a generalized Confucian tradition of consensual participation is coupled with a respect for legitimate authority (which is being increasingly popularized) — because the economic (and often the religious) lives of their citizens are being increasingly lived in a commercial culture in which choices, negotiated consensus, and the exercise of judgmental freedom are increasingly manifested as constituent to a progressively pervasive, free 'way of life'.

To maintain a society in which the diversity of freedom, openness to temporal futurity, and the appropriation of previously unforeseen possibilities, together with even a reluctant encouragement of difference within a unifying harmony — all conjoining to advance the common good — requires a social dedication to a high degree of cooperative activity. The *social cooperation* of a free political structure, as of a free-enterprise economy, is a cooperation of competition, of mutual striving, in which all cannot win the final awards but all share in the rewards of the contest.

This is what has been termed 'democratized mercantilism', 'bourgeois', 'reformed', or 'democratic capitalism' — a free commercial economy that developed an industrialization and learned how to take it in hand. This kind of open economy is inherently and essentially animated by the same generalized spirit of temporal openness to the future, cooperation of competitiveness, and freedom that makes popular government possible. It takes lessons from its past, as it seeks new horizons from its vision of the future, while making the best out of the living present. It ties temporal perspectives together for the benefit of the socially grounded freedom it utilizes and enjoys. In its exercise, individual citizens find their freedom as socially constituted temporal beings. Structuring by its sense of community its republican system of government, which it has developed and upon which its future depends, it remains open to such peaceful reformation as its constituents may freely deem desirable.

Part III

The Discipline of Freedom

Our freedom is socially framed within the living present. But the present is no static autonomous 'now'; the present is the 'meeting-ground' of the possibilities of the future as they are taken up into the forward-thrusting heritage from the past. The living present we each share with our contemporaries presents itself in the nexus of decisions we are continually called upon to make. Rooted as we are in the heritage we take with us, this continual call for new decisions is the voice of futurity pressing in upon us.

We face the options of the future with hope or foreboding, but we know we cannot avoid the decisions demanded. Continually in mid-passage between what has-been and what may-be, we are always helping to create what is not-yet. To this continuing decisional nexus that comprises our dynamic present, we bring and redirect the whole course of historic development of thought and deed which has wrought the present day as we plan ahead.

Our time opens onto an array of specific alternatives before us. Our freedom to decide is no haphazard license, but the opportunity for a self-imposed discipline so that we may become our own masters, creators on a scale that may be great or small of what yet shall be. We exercise this opportunity by time-committed projects that engage our lived time — joining to shape the future we will share. If we are to do this, as intelligent beings who are able to decide, to plan and do, we need to discipline the continuity of our judgments, decisions, and commitments. Within the framework of a coherent vision, we develop

227

the discipline required for the fruitful exercise of a socially bound, time-ordered freedom.

The preceding pages have sought to develop the framework within which we are called to make specific judgments — for ourselves and for others — as we face our concrete situations. Our ability to make judgments is made possible by the social ground of a free society. If we are to maintain our ability to continue to make the decisions that mold our lives, our first loyalty must then be to securing the temporally structured social freedom that enables us to do so.

As freely disciplined beings who seek to make the most of the opportunities that present themselves to us, we face the necessity of self-discipline on at least three levels. Each of the three principles which have been developed, entwined as it is with the others, suggests a normative outcome.

First, as essentially social beings who continually depend upon the social contexts in which we function, we need to recognize in our specific decisions that we are always acting *together within* history. Intelligence demands that we maintain continuity with our past by taking its lessons into our decisions which are concerned to forge the future. Our responsible decisions, as history-making beings, takes up a responsibility for the future of freedom.

Second, as temporal beings who continually evaluate prescriptions for the social policies which will occupy our ongoing time as citizens and as private individuals, we are repeatedly called upon to offer or pass judgment on proposals for social policy. These specify courses of activity to which our ongoing social temporality is to be committed, delineate the areas in which our further free decisions will be situated. These decisions will focus on perceived ills to be corrected and those possibilities of the presently looming future deemed most pressing. As we address these problems and concerns, in our advocacies and dissents, we effectively formulate the agenda of prime concerns which free citizens commend to their society so that their freedom may continue to flourish.

Third, as citizens with a responsibility for our enabling freedom, we need to ensure that our judgments concerning proposed social policies be coherent and responsible; to do so, we need a method of rational evaluation — one that recognizes the social nature of all decisions and the temporal commitment of all social prescriptions, one that enables us, in the light of our prime loyalty to the furtherance of freedom, to differentiate those programs which 'succeed' from those which 'fail', those which correct perceived problems from those which but compound them.

In the preceding discussions, the pragmatic method has been repeatedly, if only implicitly, invoked. Because of the careless ways in which this term is frequently used this needs to be explicated. For responsible attention to the problems of a free people requires fidelity to a continuing pragmatic evaluation of the proposals and programs it considers for carrying on its own historical development.

Chapter 7

History

∿⟡⟐⟡∿

Our essential sociality, expressed in temporal terms, urges that we take history seriously. Each of us represents a developing biography within a historically developing, political society. Each of us comes out of a common past that is presumed in every aspect of the particular person who voices an experience as 'mine', as the experience upon which every 'I' draws. Each of us brings ways of looking at the surrounding world, of evaluating the import and desirability of what is perceived, of determining where to go from here. We define the dynamic of each present situation by the variety of possibilities that can be integrated into the evolving outlook we each bring along.

As we acknowledge the heritage of the past and the lessons it bears, we are increasingly enabled to evaluate the offerings of futurity. The continuing task of our freedom is to reconcile them. Our future cannot be created *de novo*. It can only be built out of the genuine possibilities which the historically rooted present presents as viable options. And the past can neither be discarded nor taken whole. Each of us is continually deciding which strands out of the past are to be carried forward and which are either to be rerouted into the fabric of the future or aborted along the way.

As free citizens who are charged with building the future, we bring out of past development the education and evaluative norms we use in our judgments, the potentialities and talents already developed which enable us to go on. We are heirs of untold generations and remain in their debt for everything we find ourselves to be. Their experiences, when creatively used, guide our own. Those who do not acknowledge what the past has provided are not only poverty-stricken but historically irresponsible: having deprived themselves of the ability to lean back on

the social time that has bred them and imbued them with some historical foresight, they can only look dimly ahead. Continually distilling the
lessons of our heritage to build what will mold the heritage of future
generations is one task of responsible freedom.

As social beings, as citizens of historically developed cultures, we
are each *in* history from the outset. As free citizens, we live in a contractual society that is itself an ongoing process. Our 'contract' is not
merely with our contemporaries; as Burke urged, this living social
contract is a "partnership not only between those who are living but
between those who are dead, and those who are yet to be born."[1] By
acknowledging the present to be an ongoing process, we retrieve the
lessons of the past and build them into our responsibility for what yet
can-be. Immersed in the present, we are in the midst of the process
that is our history. Simultaneously, we are both heirs and creators.

History is not something 'over and done with'. History is the living present. We are not external observers watching its development.
We are part and parcel of it — and are charged to continually make it,
by everything we say, think, and do. Our historical being *is* the process
of evaluating what has been given to us, selecting from it the lessons
we find applicable, imaginatively projecting it forward, and, as thus
continually refined, carrying it on.

Our history is structured by those possibilities we deem as fated
and those we envision as yet open-ended. We can ascertain the factual
details of what has been while we continually reevaluate their significance. But the construction of the future, our historical task, proceeds
into the unknown: how our efforts will turn out we have no way of
knowing. Our only choice is to abide by principles of decision which
we can justify, and hope for the best — always cautioned by that wisdom which realizes that, because of a multitude of unknown factors
feeding into the present, nothing ever works out quite as expected.

To acknowledge that we are *in* history does not mean that we
should join a cult that venerates it. That we face real decisions into the
unknown, that we bring a variety of alternatives into the present, that
we do not know just how even conscientiously conceived courses of
action will work out, that we find large events often turning on small
decisions — all point to the open-endedness of our historical development. "History," Aron noted, "is the tragedy of a humanity that creates its own history but does not know what history it is creating."[2]

To some among us, this is eminently unsatisfactory. They insist
on *knowing* just what the endpoint is, just where lies the promised land.

This is really secularized mysticism. And it is a dangerous delusion because it seeks to evade the essential finitude of human understanding. Those intoxicated by their own vision of some utopian ideal too often compromise their absolute devotion by seeking to secure it by a relativism of means: If the envisioned end be such a perfect state that it will have eliminated all human tribulations, then *any* means might seem justifiable. When utopia is seen as waiting at the end of the road, it is easy to regard anyone who defies instruction as to the proper conduct of the journey as inherently betraying genuine beneficence; such an 'obstructionist' is then deemed as justifiably dispensable: "The sublime end excuses the revolting means. . . . The revolutionary myth bridges the gap between moral intransigence and terrorism."[3] It is no accident that the mass imprisonments and mass murders of our time transpired under regimes that, abjuring both the finitude of human perception and faith in what freedom can accomplish, instead have claimed a trans-historical insight into 'the goal' of history — thereby endowing themselves with rightful absolute power as the faithful guardians of the 'only' road to it. The more secure in its vision the party seizing political power seems to be, the more ready it is to dispense with those it deems morally blind to its own privileged vision.

Some claimants to such dogmatic certainty use it to provide themselves with a psychological benefit while holding themselves aloof from 'the fray': as 'true believers' who place themselves on the sidelines as 'god-lettes' who watch the unrolling of the historical scroll, the gospel of a clairvoyant grasp of the whole of all history frees them from all responsibility. The more grandiose the explanation, the more inexorable its developmental laws — whether economic, racial, national, or cultural — the more relieved they are of attempting partial solutions to the concrete problems of the here-and-now. Calling for total or final solutions, they abjure partial ameliorations of justifiable grievances. And if they themselves do not seek power to effect particular changes, they afford themselves the intellectually moral luxury of condemning what is distasteful in the present situation and excoriating those who try to manage it, while they grandly and irresponsibly sit back to watch the inevitable slowly unfold.

The first lesson of historical experience is that we have access to no final solutions. Every action, no matter how carefully prepared or intelligently planned out, can be expected to produce consequences unintended, side effects unforeseen, responses that could not have been anticipated. We are always faced with a finite number of possibilities whose farthest repercussions can only be guessed at. We are always *in* complex situations opening up courses of development that reach beyond our possible vision.

If God be God, then God may know what yet can be. But no one of us is external to a particular historical human situation; we are each part and parcel of one. Any human view is from *within* the particular perspective of its situation. We can only weigh alternatives of which we are aware. We can only compare seemingly similar antecedents to see how they worked out. Within the finitude of the human situation, we can have no encompassing insight into the 'whole of history', into any all-encompassing 'final end' or absolute 'first' or 'final cause', of how or why what is transpires the way it does.

The discipline of freedom is the discipline of beings who are inherently fallible. It is "the *discipline of the finite* which human genius submits to when it grapples with the harsh reality."[4] One is well-disciplined when one recognizes the finitude of the scope of human vision — and acts on principle in loyalty to prime values, rather than on expectation of idealized outcome. As Robert Burns nicely described our existential condition:

> The best laid schemes o' mice and men
> Gang aft a-gley;
> An' lea'e us nought but grief and pain,
> For promis'd joy.[5]

The discipline of freedom faces our being *in* history with humility. It seeks no final outcome — only the best one that appears available. It seeks no monopoly of decision — conscious of its own inherent limitations, it seeks to augment them by calling into play the perspectives of others. Its concrete commitments may, on occasion, need to be daring but they must be prudent — as it wisely recognizes that its ventures into the future are ventures into the unknown. It, therefore, seeks to keep the future open for corrective action — by not over-extending its decisive commitments — so as to permit alternative routes of escape from presently unforeseen miscalculations that may only show up later.

The pragmatic value of enriching our judgment by employing a multiplicity of perspectives mandates that responsibility be pluralistic. Most specific social quandries can be ameliorated in a variety of ways. What is important is not some one particular solution to a current problem but one that resolves it by maintaining the freedom that permits further correction. Many different ways present themselves for restructuring a particular problematic situation. It is not the particular mode of rectification, but the principles of decision and the anticipations they justly project that are crucial. We say that we look to a more democratic society — there are diverse ways in which this can be achieved. We say we believe in a republican form of government — but no two republican constitutions are identical. No particular solution to a given problem is sacrosanct; what is always crucial is that the accepted solution represents a prudent yet courageous fidelity to freedom and its open future.

Our commitments are made in the form of temporally exclusive decisions — to pursue one course we exclude all that might ensue from other alternatives. But if selective commitment and decision are meaningful, they involve "options among alternative courses of action [and] some attention has to be given to the criteria for such options."[6]

The criteria for such decisions, the preceding essay has urged, must be not a precise blueprint of a future state of affairs, but a set of guiding principles or evaluative norms of a socially temporalized freedom, which we seek in each historically concrete context to endow with embodiment. By avoiding, as Kant urged, "premature measures" which arise out of demands by "despotic moralists [who] . . . act contrary to political prudence,"[7] we do not invite the disruption of social upheaval. By demanding moderation of judgment, we persistently seek to keep the future open to perspectival changes, reassessments and readjustments, as unknown contingencies feed into the future options progressively coming into view. The flexibility of a moderate course, which always distinguishes what 'can be' from what is ultimately desired, signifies the prudence of finite beings whose convictions of certitude may prove to be mistaken, whose judgments along the way may prove erroneous. Commitment to the principle of freedom is a commitment to a steady course toward its enhancement, even though particular directions may alter — as a sailboat may tack first this way and then that against a changing wind, in order to reach its port.

Each immediate decision along the way can be expected to yield new problems together with unimagined constraints and possibilities. Each proximate goal, in turn, becomes but a new point of departure. Particular means and particular ends form a continuum, as Dewey often observed — a continuum of the reality of the temporal. Our present already began in the past, and what we now do carries over into what will actually ensue.[8] If our animating principle is to maximize

freedom — to emancipate the temporal tomorrow for new assessments and decisions — constant acknowledgement of the force of
temporal continuity should guide our evaluations of particular alternative solutions that we must face along the way.

This one commitment to the openness of freedom is a commitment to what makes our evaluations and value choices possible. For
freedom, as such, is not one value among others; it is that which
makes evaluative activity possible. As such, loyalty to freedom over-
shadows all conflicting priorities — precisely because it permits them
to be sorted out and selectively adopted. Whatever specifics we may
seek — health, wealth, peace, equality, happiness — are sought
because they are deemed requisite to being free to become and be
ourselves. As members of a social order, as citizens of a republic, as
private persons who seek an adequate livelihood and an enjoyment of
leisure, we seek to maximize the freedom to control our own time.

We identify our freedom with our own being. We judge the
social order by the extent to which our social freedoms enable us to
use our time to be ourselves, to function as autonomous beings. For
freedom to be mutual, it must be ordered. An ordered freedom, in
which particular values and aspirations may be sought, is the
enabling condition for their possibility. In seeking specific reforms,
the enhancement of free existence is the only rationally acceptable,
motivating reason for the subsidiary values on which we usually
focus attention.

An old adage says that one of the most short-sighted of all self-
defeating actions is to eat the hand from which one is fed. If the exercise of freedom enables us to be the rational, moral beings we believe
we are, if freedom is the key to making ourselves what we seek to be,
then it is a matter of self-loyalty, in the fullest sense of the word, to
hold a loyalty to freedom, as the essential potentiality of man, to be the
highest loyalty — against all competing claims — to which we are
called. The continuity of temporality, joined to recognition of our own
fallibility of judgment, suggests the corollary: the ensuing obligation, in
the midst of decision, to opt for keeping the future as open as possible
so that misfires can be corrected before they become disasters.

Freedom, we must recognize, is not a *mere* 'property' with which
we can readily dispense. It is no accidental accretion that can be discarded like an old handkerchief which can be replaced. Freedom is the
enabling condition for us to be what we are, what allows us to become
what we yet can be.

The discipline of freedom recognizes that, as social beings, we are already involved in history. We inherit it, learn from it, evaluate it, and build it — while using its lessons as we strive ahead. The first responsibility of the self is to the possibilities of the self which are grounded in the possibilities of the society to which it belongs. The first responsibility, the first loyalty, which makes other loyalties possible, is the freedom to be free: to develop ourselves and our society, to enhance the meaning of the individual lives it brings forth, nourishes, and sets upon their own free ways.

The discipline of freedom thus mandates an ethic of stewardship, a taking concernful care of the freedom we share together. This means a commitment to look out for freedom when it is endangered, even by persons of good will; and, perhaps above all, to guard the autonomy of others, as intrinsically as important to us as our own.[9]

In the midst of history we are building history, on levels often seemingly trivial and sometimes profound. However unknown our futures may be, free citizens of a free society can only effectively build them together in a spirit of mutual responsibility for a freedom that is necessarily shared. Free citizens face their present, animated by possibilities yet to be selected and realized, as offering once again the opportunity to weld the future together as the history of people who are free.

Freedom is responsibility. As we build our futures, we are building the heritage we will be passing on. Our actions today set out parameters for the generations yet to come. A fidelity to freedom, a stewardship over freedom, is then a responsibility to hand that freedom on, to keep the future open for free decisions by those who come later. Being in history, building history, our social responsibility is to bequeath a future that will become a past that free beings can proudly inherit.

As citizens of a free republic we build this mutual historical development together. As citizens, we are called upon to endorse policies, support programs, debate issues, resolve debates in elections — all concerned with specifying our future course. Our common social history is centered on that agenda of specific social policies and priorities which we enact into the rules governing our future course.

Chapter *8*

Agenda

Social temporality is incarnated in the citizens of a free republic. Their time is delineated by the specific agenda of prime problems and aspirations they decide to address. This social agenda sets policies to be pursued, which lay out the temporal horizon in which the society sees itself functioning. By prohibiting certain kinds of activities, mandating a few, and encouraging others — a society sets out the temporal parameters within which individuals can live their time, form their own temporal horizons, and find their freedoms.

No agenda, accordant as it may be with common concerns and ensuing policy decisions, is value-free. Any agenda presupposes criteria for evaluating alternatives and making hosts of either/or decisions. These decisions, as the problems from which they arise, are grounded in the commonly perceived contemporary situation.

We live today in a world our grandparents would barely recognize. The glories of the ages that produced ours, as we have seen, only encompassed small elites served by an anonymous population that labored without hope. Out of this limited accomplishment, modernization's pride is that it brings societal members forth as individuals.[1] One prime test of a society is to be the kinds of individuals it produces, the free lives they are able to lead; this is a distinctly modern notion.

Nothing in life is cost-free. Commercial civilization developed in three historically quick stages — preparation by commercial and subsequent agricultural innovation, industrialization, and the contemporary technological revolution. This development has extended the normal life-span while creating an unprecedented prosperity that sustains limited work-weeks, vacations for all, a spread of educational time that can last into one's thirties, and sustain a retirement that begins in one's sixties. By restricting the time of gainful employment to some thirty-odd years of life, it has ushered us into an age of generalized free leisure unprecedented in human history. (What previous generations could have taken for granted a work-life of limited vacation-bound, five-day weeks consuming less than half of one's expanded normal life-span?)

This expansion of individual freedom, the opening of individual determination of how to spend one's time, no longer restricted to eking out a livelihood, is increasingly concerned with how to spend the time that one's livelihood enables each to call one's own. This new freedom, once reserved to a small elite, is rapidly becoming the general condition of all free people.

That our educational institutions have sorely failed to prepare most of us for this new freedom augments the general indictment of their performance. They have failed to bring most of us into the conceptual framework of an increasingly cosmopolitan world in which unprecedented leisure and consequent opportunity for cultural development more and more becomes a norm for human activity. What was once the vaunted freedom of the few thousand free citizens in ancient Athens is progressively becoming the legacy of free citizens in a world with increasingly wide geographic, as well as historical and cultural, horizons.

Paradoxically, the same technological advance that sustains an unprecedented advance of human freedom has also called into being new bureaucracies enabled to control every aspect of human life — epitomized in the historically unprecedented totalitarian state.

> One of the most fundamental traits of modernization is a vast movement from fate to choice in human affairs. . . . The paradox here is that modern technology also supplies the means by which powerful institutions can control the lives of individuals. Thus the totalitarian state is made possible by modern technology. The great drama of modernity is this dynamic tension between liberation and re-enslavement.[2]

This great drama is being played out all around us. While increasing the free power of free citizens, it has fostered an interdependence among nations that draws us all more closely together by transforming previously autonomous areas into neighborhoods.

This development forces us to bring the principles that have been developed to bear as we look out in two divergent directions:

First, with regard to our relations with other peoples, and second, to our domestic concerns. Let us face each in turn:

1. We find ourselves today in a newly framed world. Writing at the end of the Second World War, Jaspers noted, "Today, for the first time, there is a real unity of mankind which consists in the fact that nothing essential can happen anywhere that does not concern all."[3] The old Stoic vision, the 'explosion of the framework of the polis' to include all of mankind,[4] has finally become acknowledged fact.

The growing interdependence between nations has ended the days of absolute national sovereignties. Almost imperceptibly, a new attitude has developed regarding the independence of nations, an attitude rarely voiced in any general terms. Little is any longer said about the propriety of 'not interfering in the domestic affairs of others'. Without explicit discussion or debate, the call for what some call 'human rights', others the demand for 'democratization' or 'liberation' — what I have termed the 'freedom to be free' — has come to transcend national boundaries. The fate of each of us is finally coming to be acknowledged as the fate of all. To respect another people is no longer tantamount to respecting whatever repressive government they may have had thrust upon them; those who protest this new cosmopolitan concern are usually the oppressors. Loyalty to the idea of freedom is to insist that others, too, have a rightful claim, morally equal to one's own, to be free citizens of a free republic. Loyalty to the idea of freedom has unwittingly come to be accepted as an obligation of a free people to defend the possibility for freedom for those who are not yet free. Whatever the prudential wisdom of any specific call for intervention, by economic or diplomatic pressure or military means, it has come to be generally presumed that a free people has not just a right, but a moral obligation, to intrude into the internal affairs of other countries (at least when it is requested or its tyranny offends the freedom of others) in order to ensure *their* own freedom.

However we may judge the prudential wisdom of any specific call for intrusion into the internal affairs of other nations — the Helsinki Accords, bringing pressure to bear for free emigration from enslaved lands, foreign support for Poland's Solidarity movement, the demand for sanctions against South Africa, United States' support for the popular uprising against dictatorship in the Philippines, the 1987 Guatemala City accord for peace in Central America as well as the American Government's criticisms of it — they reflect one principle: the freedom of each is the responsibility of all. Rarely, if ever before, have such gross 'interferences' in the 'internal affairs' of other nations in the name of a political principle been generally countenanced as legitimate, much less as duly proper or morally obligatory.[5] Yet a precedent was set by the Western allies' determination to forcefully 'impose' free representative governments on Austria, Germany, Italy, and Japan at the end of the Second World War.

The principle seems to be clear. Freedom *is* responsibility, accountability for what one chooses and decides. No one has a right *not* to be free — because to abscond from freedom is to refuse responsibilities to others. In an increasingly close-knit world, the irresponsibility of not-being-free is a luxury which free nations, for their own sakes, can no longer accord to others. Erich Fromm's famed statement that there can be 'no escape from freedom' means that no one can be free from the responsibility of participating in a free government. Whatever else may have contributed to the devastation of the Second World War, the destruction of Germany's Weimar Republic was a crucial contributing factor, as was military dictatorship in Japan. Free nations have an obligation to be concerned about the state of freedom, and thereby of civic responsibility, in other countries — because the freedom of others impinges on their own. Beyond all other moral concerns, such an interest is, at least, one of prudential self-protection.

This consideration raises the overriding question of the realistic prospects for world peace. At the beginning of the modern age, a few prophetic thinkers saw that the security of freedom and of peace are mutually dependent. Because free governments require security against aggression, they will seek peace between them so that they may devote themselves to their prime concern: maintaining the general peaceful commerce of their citizens, who must disrupt their lives to engage in foreign wars. Peace thwarts the militarism that breeds authoritarianism, and freedom only prospers with peaceful exchanges.

Rousseau, insisting that the only form of "legitimate Government is republican," rejected peace projects, such as those of the Abbe de St. Pierre, because they depended on agreements between monarchical states with dynastic ambitions rather than between democratic republics.[6] Kant quickly developed this theme in setting out principles seen as providing the necessary condition for the attainment of world peace:

> *The Civil Constitution of every state shall be Republican.* . . . [For it] is the only constitution which can be derived from the idea of an original contract, upon which all rightful legislation of a people must be founded. Thus as far as right is concerned, republicanism

is in itself the original basis of every kind of civil constitution . . . [and] it also offers a prospect of attaining the desired result, i.e., a perpetual peace. . . . *The Right of Nations shall be based on a Federation of Free States.* . . . Each nation, *for the sake of its own security,* can and ought to demand of the others that they should enter along with it into a constitution, similar to the civil one, *within which the rights of each could be secured.*[7]

Only free states, he argued, are unlikely to war with each other, because their citizens are concerned with peaceful commerce rather than the expenditures requisite for military adventures, and their governments are beholden to their citizenry, as their citizenry acknowledges a general responsibility for what their governments do.[8] With some two hundred years of historic experience to guide us, we now know that free peoples are likely to develop a prosperity which, only with the greatest reluctance, do they endanger by war with each other. Peace between free peoples can be expected as their natural condition. Kant's cosmopolitan republicanism was conceived not only as the projection of the principle of free government but also as the security for free societies to develop, each in its own way, and thereby as the necessary concomitant of peace among nations.

But the conditions that make freedom possible must be well-anchored. The modern tragedy is that as undeveloped peoples have joined the growing world order and yearned for lives of free citizens, the push has been for their rapid industrialization with the expectation that they would quickly come to enjoy the prosperity and freedoms of free societies. What was forgotten by their rulers, as well as by industrialized nations in their aid programs — which are, again, a sign of a sense of responsibility for the development of others — is that free societies developed out of commercial middle-class societies which only subsequently underwent that industrialization which depends upon responsible distribution channels for real increases in productivity. To export factories to a backward people may not necessarily be the greatest of blessings; indeed, doing so can short-circuit a historical course of development. To export factories to a historically laggard people ignores the lessons of time and history: without a commercially based middle class to sustain and develop their distributive outlets, factories produce frustrated hopes, false promises, and oppressive governmental power. An industrialized system, if it is to be successful, needs to be grafted onto the historically developing society into which it is introduced, and requires a developing distributive system ('infrastructure') able to bring its benefits to its populace. Before the seeds of this mediating commercial structure are in place, introducing industrialized production into a society not already equipped to handle it is disruptive of the social fabric. The conditions for an advance must be emerging before the advance itself can be expected to have the hoped-for beneficent effects.

Free industrialized countries depend upon a fragmentation of their economic interests and employ only a small proportion of their workers in manufacturing; their work force is largely employed in mining, agriculture, transportation, communications, private and governmental services, the professions, and in the commercial trades concerned to promote consumer interest in proffered products and their distribution. Attainment of such a historically developed, variegated economy may be expedited, but it is questionable whether its development can be short-circuited.

If the industrialization of 'backward' countries is to enable them to emerge as new free nations, the requisite modes of thinking need to be developed. The 'psychology' of commerce and of industry are not the same. Industrialization depends upon a factory system which is, in each instance, even when organized into worker-teams, a small command society which sets out goals, and assigns work to meet them. It is little wonder that hierarchical governments, be they military or bureaucratic in nature, have demanded immediate industrialization; i.e., factories organized on hierarchical principles. And it may be small wonder that in so many cases — such as Kennedy's vaunted "Alliance for Progress" — these industrialization programs, which depend on this type of organization, fell so far short of anticipated success.

A commercial society, because it is *not* a command society, depends for its economic engagements upon individual commitment, initiative, negotiation, evaluation. Commercial activity breeds the activities of individuated judgment intrinsic to a free society. Industrialization, as an adjunct to a commercial society, serves its purposes and reinforces the freedoms it requires as the condition for its proper functioning. But unless grounded in a middle-class commercial society, industrialization alone cannot produce the kind of individualized thinking a free society requires. Without a commercial culture to sustain it, industrialization only too readily serves an authoritarian or totalitarian state.

The emerging industrial economies of East Asia all come out of cultures deeply imbued by a Confucian tradition which, whenever its people were free to do so, promptly developed a commercial culture.[10]

Without the freedoms and the commercial base that serves free countries, they have nevertheless successfully industrialized and raised their living standards. This industrial development has elicited, as in the communist states, new middle classes now calling for 'democratization'. One crucial difference is that, in contrast to communist Russia and China, the free economies of East Asian countries have developed not bureaucratic but commercial middle classes, and it is on their success in effecting international lines of distribution that their industrialization success has depended. In an inverse way, Korea, Singapore, and Taiwan[11] have replicated the Western experience: rather than first developing a commercial middle class that demands the political freedoms that find expression in a free-enterprise economy, they have by governmental policy directed the development of free-enterprise economies which, with industrialization, developed the commercial classes — needed to organize their production and distribute their products — that now demand democratization.

As commercial interchange loosens political structures it is no surprise that these middle classes are now demanding political freedoms and a consequent voice in the affairs of state. If this inverse development proves anything beyond the capacity of industrialized capitalism to raise living standards, it shows that a free-enterprise economy requires — and produces where it is lacking — that kind of fluid class structure which is the social grounding of democratic freedoms.

If the concern to universalize freedom is to meet with success, it should focus on generalizing its enabling conditions. To do so would be to take these lessons of time and history seriously. Without a commercial middle class, historic experience suggests no prospect of institutionalized freedom. Our efforts toward freedom in developing nations need to be directed toward building a commercial infrastructure and its concomitant, a strong commercial class, as a counter to omnipotent government that can use new industrial power as a means of suppression instead of liberation. If emerging free nations choose to encourage industrialization first, that industry needs to be founded on a complex of individual initiatives, not governmental procurements, so that it may foster an emerging commercial class to organize its production and the distribution of its products — and thus provide a vested interest in the development of a free society.

If a free people may justify their own freedom, they have an obligation to the cause of freedom wherever it may appear. How this obligation may be pursued is to be guided by justifiable principles of prudence; the moral obligation to do so whenever the possibility arises would seem to be beyond reasonable question.[12] Their justification in the freedom they prize is rooted in the need of free nations to sustain,rather than threaten, the prospect of a peaceful world by helping to bring forth its conditions. Their obligation to protect the exercise of freedom transcends any notion of a selfish cocoon by manifesting a loyalty to the idea of mankind.

And they may be sustained in this responsibility because they find themselves, as the end of the twentieth century approaches, without any viable ideological contest. Even those leading nations which had proclaimed alternative courses for human development seem to be folding their tents away; their public avowal is that they are now attempting to accommodate what the exercise of freedom has actually wrought. As one prime principle of a free people is to be vigilant for the stability of freedom, the task is to encourage this accommodation with the hope of eventually welcoming them into a community of free nations.

2. When we turn attention homeward we must always acknowledge that what is done at home has international import. America is no longer a continental island whose domestic policies do not affect others. Continuing to serve as a beacon to beleaguered individuals around the world, its policies have a direct impact on, as they are increasingly impacted upon by, the policies of other nations.

The ways we address our domestic problems yield resolutions in terms of policy proposals rejected or accepted. None of these policy decisions can be value-neutral. Evaluative judgments not only mean favoring one policy alternative over another; evaluative judgments are already involved in discernment of the problem the proposed policy is supposed to resolve. "No prognosis," as Jaspers pointed out, "is harmless."[13] Any policy recommendation implicitly brings evaluative priorities into play and seeks to redirect development in their light.

> The theorist who claims to know what uses his insights should be put to arrogates to himself the rights of others . . . to live their lives in accordance with their own values. Such arrogance is not morally neutral. . . . the idea that theoretical insights provide a warrant for moral judgments and practical guidance is intrinsically antagonistic to democracy. It is an idea that implies an intellectual and moral elite, which has the right to rule because of its superior theoretical insights.[14]

Rather than allocate basic policy decisions to experts, a free society cannot afford not to open crucial alternative courses to public debate and subject them to the sanction of public opinion. Uneducated as public opinion often is, a free society endangers itself when its officials arrogate to themselves the right to decide what is 'best for others' and deny the citizenry the responsibility for decision. The defense of alternate policy proposals should be examined in the light of their impact on the freedom of the community as a whole and the temporal horizon within which its citizens function. That defense, which must be constant, is subverted when the freedom that government is designed to protect forecloses the impact of public opinion on the policies it sets out to pursue. Once these basic directions are set, it is then, and only then, that the modes of administration are to be left to those charged to conduct the public's business.

Freedom needs a strong, if restrained, popular government that always places the good of the whole ahead of any of its particular components. The principle of the fragmentation of power requires that, whenever possible, social initiatives be left to local agencies, private individuals, and groups. But the corollary is that responsive government, while acknowledging its obligation not to do what others can do as well, steps into those situations which can only be handled by the collective strength of the whole. We thus need, Lepage urged, to reject the "Manichean view . . . that denounces the 'vicious' state and extols the 'virtuous' market." Responsible free government intervenes when "it is evident (if not conclusively proven) that the market solution *really* is more costly to society than public intervention."[15]

Whatever else a national government be restrained from doing, a prime obligation is to police the marketplace itself, to maintain honest and fair competitive practices, and to forestall tendencies for control of corporate power to centralize. Valued as market solutions should be because they encourage the free initiatives of individuals, markets, too, are imperfect instruments that occasionally become skewed. Although modern economic needs require strength in industry as in government, these, too, need to be moderated; for concentrations of corporate as of governmental power offend the principle that freedom is only maintained by the continuity of contest.

Checks and balances need to be maintained in economic as in political life. The principle of counter-vailing power entails the principle of counter-vailing responsibility. To throw all burdens onto either the private side or that of governmental intrusion into the free market is to destroy the balance necessary to that continuing contest requisite for the continuity of freedom. What seems to be evolving is a mutuality of cooperation, rather than head-on conflict — between public and private sectors, between management and labor, between local and national government — to meet problems which, in many cases, have arisen for lack of mutual foresight. The government of a free people will utilize the contributions of all segments to the health of the whole.

One prime principle of republican government is that the good of each member is to be realized in the good of the society itself. Subsidiary maxims for discerning and addressing particular contemporary concerns emerge from the preceding discussion. In each case the problematic situation should be pragmatically addressed — always using as a chief criterion that of ensuring the general freedom and its horizon of open temporality. The first responsibility for freedom is to maintain the conditions which make it possible, the operational context within which it is to be secured. To this end, let me suggest a summary agenda of six domestic concerns which the principles that have been developed seem to suggest.

a. Any outlook that insists on the import of context must be concerned for the environment. Its impact is on everyone — including those who direct 'polluting' facilities. As industrialization has progressed, the environment has suffered; no one seriously questions that. Yet society as a whole has benefited from the progress of industry, and no particular segment should be punitively handled — in what would effectively be ex post facto legislation for what was socially accepted behavior at the time of its performance. The usual way in which a public responsibility for a private correction is handled is by tax relief and market incentives. Disputes about responsibility, especially as they come to questions of payment for past errors, may be expected. But to the extent that public policy did not foresee environmental problems, public policy shares the responsibility.[16]

b. The concern of all of us must be the human lives that are fractured by increasing technological advances. Any 'levelling' movement — 'destroy the machines'! — in the long run hurts us all. Our prime operative principle must be not 'to level down' but 'to raise up': the central concern of a free society is that all citizens are brought to accessing the common good; continuing technological development redounds to the general benefit of all. To the extent that any citizens personally suffer from these advances, their fates rightfully become a common concern. Increasing technology, by its very nature, discomforts those dependent upon replaced modes of operation. As some citizens lose employment because of increasing technology, the social responsibility ensues to make sure that they do not bear the full brunt of its cost. Ameliorating the conditions of their transitions to new modes of employment, including retraining for required new skills and techniques, is a responsibility to be shared between those private sectors that immediately benefit from the new technology and the society that, in the long run, reaps its rewards.

c. An especially insidious threat to the domestic social health is the presence of an underclass. Aside from a moral concern for these individual citizens themselves, the presence of any sizeable group that sees itself excluded from participation in the common good is a threat to the health of the common good itself; attendance to its presence is an act of prudential self-protection. Some degrees of individual alienations may, indeed, be healthy for progressive development, but pervasive alienation from participation in the common good,when left unaddressed, threatens to subvert the general health of the society itself. To the extent that such an underclass is racially homogeneous, this becomes a special danger; for society's own benefit, they must be provided special inducements, education, and training that encourage them to seek their places as *individual* citizens in the society at large.

This kind of attention needs to be tempered by a refusal to reduce any individual citizen to treatment as merely a group member. Fidelity to the principles of a free society requires adherence to Emerson's plea that freedom requires individuation: encouraging individuals to emerge as such forestalls the suicidal fragmentation of the social whole into a multiplicity of warring group interests.[17] A free society is committed to regard its members as individual citizens and welcome them as such into the common endeavor. To open opportunity to some individuals by discriminating against others violates every principle of a free society and precludes a common dedication to remedying past injustices. A society of free citizens engaged in expanding its productivity has no need to punish the innocent to bring those deprived into the fullness of citizenship. Rather than seek to appease one group at the expense of another, a free society insists on calling each forth to stand as an individual citizen within the complex of the whole. The richer a society becomes, the more need it has to enlist all in its common endeavor. And, in the long run, a free commercial society can least of all afford the luxury of harboring paupers who have not been enabled to pay their own way to enjoy the common prosperity.

d. The echelons of higher education, to an extent without historic precedent, have been opened to all, while denigrating the quality of education for those who, for a variety of ascribed reasons, are counting themselves out. Economic incentives, because they are often primary motivating factors, could be brought to bear. Vocational education was seen as one way to do this by opening opportunity for specialized employment to those without skills or more than minimal schooling. To the extent that our schools may have trained people for old skills that were being outmoded while they were being taught, the lack of temporal foresight regarding oncoming employment opportunities provides one serious instance of the import of a future-oriented, temporal outlook.

Whether unemployability, welfare abuse, and criminal behavior can be traced to misguided governmental social policies, inadequate schooling, or a combination of these and other contributory factors, is not immediately clear. Whatever the contributory factors may be, the danger to the health of the society — already recorded in crime and drug-use rates — is threatening. The minimal function that legitimates government, Hobbes, Locke, and Rousseau joined in urging, is to provide security of person and property. When a government declines to handle this elemental problem, one is tempted to question its legitimacy!

One contributory problem may have been the general tendency, strongly encouraged over the last few decades, of looking to the national government as an omnipotent agent capable of curing all social ills while not familiarizing citizens with its cost.[18] The function of limited government is to do only what individuals cannot do for themselves. One function of a national government is to set out specific goals designed to integrate any underclass into the society itself while providing encouragement to local governments and private groups to contribute to this effort. In doing so, the basic goal of such integration is not to create new wards of the state but to encourage self-control and self-reliance on the part of those being raised up to full citizenship. One way to do this might be to follow the precedent of the education-enhancement laws for veterans, by 'vouchering' each and enabling each to patronize the particular agencies which appear most suitable to meeting his or her individual developmental needs.

e. We face the danger of growing social bureaucratization. "Bureaucracy," as Jaspers noted, "is a means. But it tends to make itself its own end." It is, he explained, "sovereignty based on regulations and orders issued by officials of the civil service. It functions like a machine, but the implementation of these regulations is determined by the nature and outlook of the officials."[19]

Bureaucratization of government is not only to be found in its administrative bureaucracy. It is also to be found in a body of representatives that has transformed itself from a representative body into a more or less permanent legislative bureaucracy. That incumbency of office should entail presumed continuance in office, is an offense to the Constitution that grants it its authority. Important as the maxim of seniority may be to the effectiveness of a legislative body, it would be well if popular resentment rose up to foreclose the incumbent advantages for electoral office and that the people's representatives should be limited to a limited duration of service.[20]

Bureaucratization of managerial personnel is not only true of government — where it provides a fourth 'check and balance' to the traditional three — but of industry and commerce as well. A mature capitalism, as frequently noted, pushes "forward a managerial type of individual quite different from the free entrepreneur."[21] Bureaucracy encourages the managerial mind that does not create but wishes to routinize; inherently suspicious of innovation, it seeks to administer 'without waves'.

Entrepreneurship, the courage of imaginative creativity, produces 'waves' as it invents new products, envisions new sources of prosperity, and thereby alters the dynamic economic balances of power. On this innovative creativity, the future of freedom depends. It brings to the common good a mentality that seeks new modes of meeting current problems, develops new modes of productivity, and initiates the kind of progress from which all benefit and on which the hopefulness of a better future state of affairs depends. As it sets new outlooks into place it is replaced by managerial minds to administer what has been already accomplished. Good managers are necessary, but they rarely produce new advances.

A society whose freedom encourages the continuity of innovation on which it feeds, thus, needs to guard itself against managerial masters. Whether in government or in business, they become a new and privileged class increasingly dependent upon "administrative rather than market methods of resource allocation."[22] They may be a small group of the population but, sharing a common interest that is more often better versed in the intricacies of policy questions, they are often able to move as a united party against an often inchoate body of public opinion. The larger they grow, the more important a segment of the voting population they become. Seeking to attach themselves to each new emergent interest, the general tenor of their increasing power is to attach themselves to a mutuality of protection which generally comes to locating centers of decision in a governmental authority that works with bureaucratic counterparts in private organizations. "Time," de Tocqueville warned, is "on its side; every incident befriends it; the passions of individuals unconsciously promote it." Thus, "the older a democratic community is, the more centralized" will its centers of power tend to become.[23] A bureaucratic officialdom, in business or government, is expected to work as it is intended to work — but it also invariably works for its own self-interest, as should have been anticipated, against the narrow confines for which its labor was originally employed. It does not produce anything beyond efficient management of such innovation as has been handed to its care. Its function, as it sees itself, is to distribute among its charges the benefits of what it has been assigned to administer, which is always conceived to include itself.[24] Necessary to any enterprise, private or public, is an administrative directorate that must be continuously curtailed as it proceeds. For the managerial mind-set is ultimately bureaucratic: concerned to administer what we already have, it generally protests any innovation that would break current patterns. Yet it is on innovative creativity that we ultimately depend, a mentality that seeks new productivity and initiates the kinds of progress from which we all benefit and on which our futures depend.

The irony is that, though reluctant to accept change, bureaucracy on a governmental level only too often fosters it in the name of liberalism's elitism which, always in the name of egalitarian pronouncements, looks for specially qualified persons to manage that equality and seduces society's new intellectuals into the prospective managerial class by assuring them a directive role in managing the development of the egalitarian ideal.[25] One sign of this mind-set is eager acceptance of the idea of a 'zero-sum' society — we have achieved all that we can and should proceed to let a set of officials manage what we already have. Its root and result is a focus on redistribution of the current 'pie' rather developing a larger one. Management of what is already accomplished is a bureaucratic specialty which usually takes offense only at disrupting innovation.

American society at its best, has lived on the encouragement of innovation. Hamilton's vision, at the initiation of this Republic, was that of governmental fiscal initiatives to encourage it. Indeed, he had urged that "the incitement and patronage of government" ought to be given, not only to the encouragement of manufacturing, but that "the public purse" be used to invite the imaginative contributions of each to the common good of all by encouraging otherwise "unused minds to make their own effective contribution to the common prosperity."[26] Government was not to pre-empt responsibility for commerce and industry; rather its function was to provide an economic stability for commerce and industry while setting out national goals and providing such inducements (in the form, for example of tariff, tax, and monetary policies) as might be fruitful for the continued private economic development of the nation as a whole. One central function of the government of a free society is to serve as its chief coordinating facility: its leadership function is to lead, assist, and encourage citizens, individually and in voluntary combinations with each other, to undertake such actions as are deemed contributory to the general welfare, the common good.

f. We need to face, with utmost seriousness, the deterioration of the quality of education. As already suggested, a free society's first responsibility is the education of its citizenry — to recognize its course of development and adhere to its principles while becoming useful citizens who engage in the freedom which is its common good. Many current commonplaces could be cited about the sad state of what American educational practice produces. Recent best-selling books have bemoaned its current state. Too often, our students know no history and think the world began with their parents — if that long ago. They know little of the intellectual heritage that binds them together into a common vision of what is being accomplished, of where they come from, and of the values and commitments that brought them here. And they are shamefully ignorant of even their geographic, much less their historic and cultural, situation. All this could be repeated and adumbrated. Even dismissing much hyperbole, most of this is true. Without a keen sense of heritage, and the lessons to be learned form it, how can any generation be equipped to face its future, to bear the responsibilities of the freedom they are taught to cherish?

But why? One answer might be that we have been too consumed by utilitarian demands for immediate means and ends. "Utilitarian theory restricting itself to the means-ends relationship, says nothing about the relations of ends to one another, nothing at least about ultimate ends.[27] In accepting a means-end dichotomy we tend to focus on the 'means' and forget the 'ends' for which they were originally justified. Our educational institutions have seen themselves as vocational institutes: consumed to equip their students for an immediate end of useful employment, they have largely neglected the life-ends that make lives worth living. Our educational institutions, teaching techniques, have ignored the cultural ethos which gives them meaning; focused on techniques, they have ignored the broader questions of what techniques are for.[28] The virtue and meaning of education — originally an invitation to general participation in a rich culture, which modernity has progressively been able to open to all — has been cheapened as a kind of vocational training, on a low- or high level as the case may be. Reducing the horizon of its vision, it has been self-defeating.[29] While opening education to a clientele wider than ever before invited to enter into its institutions, American educational institutions have generally failed to meet even these immediate vocational objectives on many levels while neglecting to open the grander vision of a culturally developed citizenry. This 'accomplishment', effectively depriving their student-clients of the education owed to them, has failed the responsibility entrusted by a democratic society to open the common cultural heritage to all; its effective accomplishment bespeaks betrayal of the trust and responsibility it had eagerly accepted.

Life, as Paul Schilpp once admonished, is to be concerned "not with making a living but living a life." It is this which much of contemporary education has grossly neglected — and at great price: it has thereby foreclosed parameters of possible experience which should be opened to each as each is able to take them in. Each individual's educational experience should open up a perceptive appreciation of the culture being voiced while making possible a broader look within wider horizons; it should enable each new citizen to be cognizant of the immense debt, as Royce pointed out, now owed to the entirety of one's historic culture, which has enabled each to be what each now finds himself to be, and of the possibilities to which he still looks forward. This debt is not merely to the history of scientific development, only too often presented as accomplished fact rather than as history in process — but as an ensuing responsibility to the possibilities of the future. Our heralded technological advances are still historically conditioned on the religious and moral, the political and economic, as well as the literary and humanistic, strains of our historically still developing culture, and the future they still offer as well.[30]

The proponents of free government always recognized that free citizens can only remain free insofar as they maintain their cooperatively competitive institutions of freedom and respond to their calls as persons dedicated to standards of virtue and to transcendent demands for moral fidelity. To disparage these, as many contemporary heirs of liberalism have done, is to cut the root from under the tree of liberty which rests on grounds upon which our faith in freedom is justified. Without a deep religious faith in the import of freedom, one may wonder whether the faith in freedom, central to any free people, can long survive.[31]

Democratization has always asked for a universalization of education — with the consequent generalization of intellectual authority. But its full promise has been seriously compromised by its too frequent reduction to something defended as 'vocational instruction'. Above all, our schools need be seen as a truly socially responsible means of developing a cultured citizenry. To restore a focus on a catholicity of serious content is to honor the democratizing function that public education serves. In contrast to a specifically vocationally oriented education which tends to freeze social stratification, a generalized cultural education enhances the vocational possibilities and consequent social mobility of all in a dynamic social environment.

The first requisite of a democratizing education is to insist that the discipline of the student, rather than the satisfaction of an amusement-patron, be the foremost virtue to be exhibited by its charges: It thus endows them with a renewed sense of responsibility for carrying themselves forward as free citizens disciplined to create a free future still unwrought and unknown.

A society increasingly dependent on sophisticated opportunities for enhancing its livelihood and opening up widespread leisure requires citizens whose shared cultural roots are fully opened to them so that they may more fully utilize the common heritage as they face their social callings and their private lives. Seriously attending to this task represents a two-fold obligation that is really one. As a matter of social self-protection, a comprehensive polity, alert to the need to guard tis own future, should make sure that its citizens are equipped to undertake and creatively develop the occupations and civic responsibilities of decision that will have to be filled. As a responsible polity concerned about the lives of its members, it acknowledges a prime responsibility to educate each of its citizens to the fullest lives of which they are individually capable. The educative task of a free society should be, as de Tocqueville had urged, to "try a little more to make great men;" by placing "less value on the work and more on the workman," its educational system should be geared to developing "an energetic people . . . out of a community" so that the free polity will not be burdened by "pusillanimous and enfeebled citizens."[32] The vibrancy of an educated citizenry can only redound in increasing their society's level of life.

The experience of 'living a life' should be itself richly rewarding — but it depends on the resources provided to it. Such experience requires a sense of responsibility by each recipient to utilize his enabling sources to create his own bequeathment to what will come after. Opening this sense of history-making responsibility is the due of every citizen of a free democratizing republic.

It may, perhaps, be a fantastic hope. But it is not something to be reserved for a new elite class of the children of the prosperous in 'the best universities'. For the sake of the polity itself, it is the due of all members of a free and deliberately open society that they be equipped to accept its invitation into the fullness of its citizenship. An open society invites every citizen into its future and has the obligation to provide, and the right to expect, that its educational institutions enable each, to the fullest extent of ability, to participate in its outcome. Only so can each citizen joyfully join into its equality *in* freedom, and recognize himself as a free citizen who finds individual meaning and the meaning of individual life in the open temporality which is the inheritance his society is responsible to equip each to enjoy.

To approach questions of policy is to examine the ways in which public agencies, by the programs and directives they propound, frame the temporality of the citizenry. To seek to emancipate this temporality for all without imposing more than minimal requirements on each, is to exercise a maximum responsibility by the whole for the freedom of each. By equipping, and thereby inviting, each to forge an individual contribution to the activity of the whole while finding sustenance in doing so, we open the doors to a socially mobile society, the most classless free society we can realistically envision. Such a society shares an equality of freedom to be enjoyed, developed, and attained without any specific form of that enjoyment being imposed on any. It offers its citizens a vested interest in its future as it encourages its citizens to be responsible in their freedom, to take their freedom and the temporal opportunities it offers with utmost seriousness as a public trust.

Chapter **9**

Pragmatics

Fidelity to our freedom requires that we think our problems through in a methodically responsible way. The preceding discussions have implicitly employed the method of pragmatic evaluation: self-consciously loyal to the principle of being open to the future, while acknowledging the contextually limited nature of concrete freedom, it orients itself to what ensues from a fidelity to its evaluative principle. Crucial to the explication of social policy, it insists that the real meaning of any proposal is what actually transpires when it is put into practice. However we may judge the generalization of the pragmatic method for theoretical concerns, it is crucial for any responsible thinking about social policies — just because they always encumber our responsibilities for others.

If our freedom to think through the problems of our times is to be responsible and fruitful, we need to seek, out of concrete situations, the truly attainable future possibilities which are presently available. Disciplined and practically oriented thinking recognizes that it is conducted in community with others which it will affect; it looks to temporally open situations it seeks to resolve, and is loyal to the freedom for the future which enables it to function. Directing itself to specific attainments in redirecting the onward flow of history's development, responsible thinking *continually* tests itself by the way things 'work out' as it translates thought into practice, always remembering that what one does invariably affects others. Responsible to take care to avoid seductive abstractions and ideological formulas, it tests itself by carefully observing what transpires when it brings itself into employment in concrete situations. Holding itself true to its enabling principle of freedom for the future, it acknowledges responsibility for its operational relevance to the present actualities and futural possibilities with

255

which it finds itself able to deal. As Kant, for example, urged, we need to continually exercise our "reason which is *pragmatically capable* of applying the idea of right according to this principle [of freedom which] constantly increases with the continuous progress of culture."[1]

To commend this kind of sober thinking regarding social issues is to commend the pragmatic method, often identified as the American creed, which Charles Peirce propounded. When we regard the concepts in our proposals as prescriptions for acting, it provides the principle for disciplined, free, creative thinking by deliberately focusing on the specific practical problems to be 'henceforth' resolved. As such a method for responsible thinking, he offered this as 'the pragmatic maxim':

> Consider what effects that might conceivably have practical bearing you conceive the object of your conception to have. Then your conception of those effects is the WHOLE of your conception of the object.[2]

The *practical* meaning of a proposal is not its logical consistency, its internal coherence, or its emotive attraction — but what actually happens when it is put into practice. This means, *not* the goal that it seeks to attain, but *all* that ensues from its implementation — all that is entailed in the process of bringing about its actualization — including the side-effects of the efforts to do so and the impact of other events simultaneously going on upon the entire process. A true attention to results requires us to take the continuity of temporal development seriously, be open to unknown contingencies, and remain aware that any particular process we instigate is but part of a dynamic context in which other developmental influences will bring themselves to bear.

Can the 'pragmatic maxim', in any ultimate way, stand alone? Can it properly be used for 'grander' questions of speculative concern. I am inclined to join many thinkers who would say "no" to both questions. But, that is not the point here. Taken on its own *as a mode of social practice*, as a guiding rule for practical reason, the 'pragmatic maxim' commends no specific doctrine; it *does presume* the reality of the temporally structured experience of freedom which permits it to function. It is a method by which to reason in a responsible fashion concerning the practical decisions we must continually make. Too often, we are asked to consider proposals that seem 'fine on paper' but which, when put into practice, produce effects that can only repeat old disasters or invent new ones. To the extent that the concepts which guide a proposal yield unsatisfactory results, such concepts, and such proposal is faulty and to be distrusted. When dealing with political and social programs and proposals, it would be salutary if the 'pragmatic maxim' were taken as binding.

Journalistic use of the term 'pragmatism' too often identifies it with unprincipled opportunism, on the one hand, or the utilitarian subordination of 'means' to 'ends' on the other. It is neither.

To the charge of 'opportunism', the reply is that without guiding principles, no rational means of evaluating success or failure are available. Unless one has criteria by which to evaluate the outcome of an attempted program or a process of endeavor, one cannot rationally pronounce it as a 'success' or a 'failure'. One needs a clear idea of judgmental criteria before a rational judgment can be made of whether or not the attempt 'works'. Taken as a principle of action, the pragmatic maxim is geared to evaluating any attempted program or solution in terms of what it actually brings about, the state of affairs its actually produces; it is a maxim to take our social decisions seriously, as freely made decisions that are truly building the future.

This means that the stages of a process are not to be regarded as merely useful 'means' to an independent 'end'. Doing so yields a temporally false dichotomy of 'means' and 'ends' — and misleading queries such as the endless debate over whether 'the end justifies the means' — as though 'means' and 'ends' are not always integrally tied together into the continuity of a temporally orchestrated process of achievement. The choice of 'means' is not separate from what is to be effectively achieved; rather 'what-is-done' constitute the steps in *producing* what will actually result.

The usual spatial analogy of 'a road' to be travelled is misleading. A responsible proposal does not postulate an endpoint to which we seek to travel and, *separately*, then ask the question 'which route do we take to get there?'. A serious proposal is a program of *temporal continuity* to be envisaged, *not as a journey* but as a temporally structured *production*. A better analogy is the medical one: the responsible reformer, like the conscientious doctor, first elicits a 'history' and only then 'prescribes' a 'procedure' to cure a present problem; in following it through, he considers, and watches over, all the likely reactions and responses along the way — and is quick to change if unwanted side-effects ensue.

Pragmatism is neither opportunism nor utilitarianism. It admonishes us to conform to the temporal reality of the given historically developed situation. It presumes that time is, not a series of points on a man-made graph whose segments can be separately evaluated, but the real continuity of events without any breaks between them. The methods we use to achieve an end *feed into* and become part of what we eventually achieve. Pragmatic judgments realistically anticipate the possible outcomes of present expediencies and are continually responsive to stages along the way.[3]

Freedom to think is the enabling condition of thinking; it is socially bound and temporally structured. When true to itself it does not abscond responsibility for thinking through the temporal dimensions of the practical problems which practical thinking about human problems always faces. At least three strictures should guide any serious proposal for responsible public policy:[4]

First: We always start within an actual situation which has arisen out of a historic development and carries propulsive strands of the past along as it looks to the possibilities for future development. No proposal arises in temporally isolated autonomous situations. Any situation is socially bound and is itself within a historically developing context. Rare is the proposal that is so radically innovative that it is without historical precedent. Responsible reforms carefully consider how similar proposals have worked under comparable conditions and also acknowledge other aspects of the actual developing situation in which they are to be incorporated. Any change will not only affect other aspects of the historically developing society but will, in turn, be affected by what is transpiring in its environs.

The first pragmatic test, then, for any specific social proposal is to consider its conceivable effects upon the constituents and genuine possibilities presented in the actual present, in the light of historically similar efforts, and to consider its potential interaction with other ongoing social developments.

Second: Any proposal calls not only for a specific outcome but, integrally with it, a procedure to attain it. In contrast to all utilitarian doctrine, pragmatism refuses to divide 'means' and 'ends'. In a real sense, the question 'do the means justify the ends?' is a fallacious question, for the two are never distinct. In a temporal continuum, the procedures by which we seek to attain a goal become part of what we may eventually attain. The goal, is not an isolated situation at the end of an imagined 'road'; what will result will be the *product* of its own temporal development and will incorporate whatever has been fed into it.

The second pragmatic test is twofold: to examine the procedures requisite for ameliorating the present problematic situation *and* the concrete embodiments they may be expected to produce. Rather than 'adjusting means to ends', one ought to ask about the complete process of change being advocated: Are the specific procedures truly productive of the contextually encumbered solution that is sought? Are any of these procedures likely to lead astray, produce unwanted by-products or have side effects on other aspects of the social whole? Any proposal for change, when seriously considered, is a prescription for a history-writing process that commends a specific continuity of incremental development. And, to avoid the perils of utopian gambits, it must examine just what the institutional nature of any proposed outcome can be together with the human costs that may be necessary to produce it. No one of us is likely to attain an immortal state of perfect health: the 'medicine' along the way, prescribed to improve a patient's present state, can yet be expected to produce side-effects, even while effecting the 'cure' of the present illness together with the ensuing problems that the 'cure' itself will then pose. The 'cure' and the resultant state represent, not a journey distinct from its endpoint, but the development of a continuum of a productive procedure.

Third: Human judgment is fallible and deals with possibilities, not certainties. The ability to foresee all the ensuing details of any action is intensely finite. Any decision to accept the proposed reform, to enact it, is an act of freedom. Like any act of freedom, it is an act of faith in the possibility of change, a commitment into a future which is unknown and inherently unknowable beyond the realm of 'educated opinion' — which has often been wrong. Just as a constitution necessarily incorporates an amendment procedure so that it can itself be changed, so any responsibly free commitment holds open the possibility of disengagement, of altering course or aborting the project with minimal damage, should the decisional judgment begin to produce unanticipated side effects while in process. Just as a good doctor readily alters the prescribed medication if it is producing unwanted reactions, so the responsible social reformer designs the temporal procedure of his proposal so that its efficaciousness can be *continually* tested, and if need be, radically altered along the way.

The third pragmatic test for any proposal demands an 'escape' procedure so as not to condemn its survivors to mere retrospective judgment. Although all commitments are temporally irreversible, they are generally alterable in midcourse. The integrity of the freedom upon which decisions always depend is to maintain the maximum degree of temporal openness along the way. The continuity of freedom depends upon the continuity of evaluative reasoning, the continuing confession of fallibility, thereby a built-in openness to moderate course, and the determination to change course, if necessary, while still in 'midstream'.

These three pragmatic tests join together to demand that we recognize that social reform is always social experimentation and that social experimentation involves living human beings. What we do affects others, just as what others do affects us. Just because we do not live alone but live in an organized society with others who share our time and our freedom, we are deeply interdependent even while developing our own individual lives. Loyalty to our own moral judgments, evaluations, and commitments needs to be deliberately pragmatic, because what we do continually alters the freedom and time not only of ourselves but also of those with whom we live.

The pragmatic method of social reasoning looks to the *tangible* results of social policies. It seeks to permit us to control our future by disciplining the ways in which we go about creating that future. It recognizes the limits of our perspectives, our need to function within them and within the social contexts which always define where we are and what we can truly do. It accepts the continuity of the need to decide while keeping an eye open to vicissitudes of 'chance' (or unknown contingencies) always entering into our anticipated continuities.

Kant, commonly regarded as one of the most rigorous of thinkers, identified the "pragmatic" with the "prudential," as he called us back to the ethical wisdom "of the ancients (Aristotle)" by urging that the morally responsible way to bring principles into practice is to practice judgemental moderation.[5] To moderate our moral certainties is a moral virtue to be practiced especially when our actions impose our views on others — as all of our social prescriptions do. The social responsibility of the individual citizen is to insist on moderation in social practice: to moderate expectations and moderate commitments to achieve them. Moderation of social policy is itself a moral virtue, because it is cautious about binding the time and freedom of others to any one person's individual convictions, commitments, and evaluative judgments.

The threefold (really tri-une), pragmatic test is a way of exercising prudence in our social advocacies by binding ourselves to a discipline of responsible moderation. Prudentiality is itself a socially necessary moral responsibility we have an obligation to demand — because it is a way of exercising a watchful stewardship over the future of freedom by seeking always to keep the future open to each for free development.

The discipline of freedom, in social practice, exercises prudentiality of advocacy as a social imperative; it is suspicious of any proposal which forsakes a premium of self-corrective moderation in action by opting for extremes; and it calls for dependence upon consensus rather than majority dictate — just because taking the views of all into account tends to moderate any dogmatic dictum and binds each to the good we are joined to share. Prudential judgment is pragmatic because it continually acknowledges that its proposals are to be tested by what they produce; it freely assumes a responsibility not to intrude on the freedoms of others beyond what the social health manifestly requires; it exhibits concern for a responsible structure of the temporal continuum of social processes, a recognition that temporality is ingredient to any serious development; and, it is loyal to the freedom that makes it possible by recognizing its essential finitude and thereby moderating its commitments so that errors and mistrials can be caught before they become disasters.

As free responsible citizens, we are, in a real sense, involved with others and necessarily responsible for each other. That responsibility cannot pre-empt the free autonomy of others in the name of a higher or privileged insight. As we respect each other we should be concerned to maintain that framework of our being-together which enables each to pursue personal dreams and aspirations as free and thereby responsible citizens.

This communality of the temporality of freedom is the common good we seek to advance as the condition in which we all may prosper. Our care for each other is manifested by maintaining a custodial stewardship over the freedom we share so that, separately and together, we can avail ourselves of the openness toward the future in which it is to be exercised, so that we may each be free for the opportunity to make our time our own. The temporality of freedom is that openness to the future which enables each of us, as a socially bound individual, to maximize the specific, historically presented opportunities of the freedom to be free.

Notes

Introduction

1. Röpke, p. 21.

2. Kant, "Perpetual Peace," in (ed.) H. Reiss, p. 117; (italics mine).

3. Ricoeur, *Political and Social Essays*, p. 268.

4. The distinction, between 'republican' as primarily referring to a mode of government and 'democratic' to the nature of the social body, is used through this book. It is de Tocqueville's; for comments on it, see Aron, p. 165.

5. "[Athenians say that they] are not slaves of any master, that they perform their civic duties out of love for their *polis*, without needing to be coerced, and not under the goads and whips of savage laws or taskmasters (as in Sparta or Persia)." Berlin, p. xl.

6. Friedrich, p. 28.

7. Dallmayr, *Polis and Praxis*, pp. 8–9.

8. Cf. Rousseau: "But beyond the public person, we have to consider the private persons who compose it . . . [and] distinguish . . . between the duties which [Citizens] have to fulfill as subjects and the natural right which they ought to enjoy in their quality as men." *Social Contract*, par. 80, p. 28.

9. *N.B.*, Stated in somewhat technical terms, this is to approach the social problematic in a generally phenomenological way: rather than focus on the 'empirical' objects of experience, to start from the 'experiential', the ways in which those empirical objects are actually experienced: instead of looking to some ideal ordering of society, to ways of individual participation in society; instead of expounding the time of history, to seek insight into the temporality of the individual's historical outlook; instead of enunciating abstract 'rights' and 'liberties' a

263

society should proclaim, explicating the concrete freedoms the citizen may indeed experience by effectively belonging to it.

10.   "[Government's legislative power] not only commands the purse, but prescribes the rules by which the duties and rights of every citizen are to be Regulated." Hamilton in *The Federalist*, # 78, p. 523. *N.B.*, If time-produced income, time-consuming duties, and time-optional rights are governed by the polis, the governmental system determines how a citizen's time may be structured and expended; the structure of 'temporality' in the 'dynamic of free polity' then depends upon a mode of governance that harmonizes the freedoms and powers of the community and those of its individual citizens.

N.B. The original spellings and capitalizations as rendered in this edition have been retained in all citations. Citations henceforth are merely to author, article number, and page(s).

Chapter 1. *Membership*

1.   The philosophic response was soon developed on various levels by Leibniz, Rousseau, and Kant: one can only think as an 'I' because of the 'we' to which the 'I' belongs.

2.   See, for example, Part III of Descartes' *Discourse on Method*, where he suggested a 'tentative' or 'pre-scientific' ethic, clearly recognizing that, however far into individualized thinking he might proceed, he still was bound to function as a member of his own society.

3.   Divided, for example, as John Rawls and Robert Nozick may be in their contemporary ideological loyalties and programmatic proposals, their common adherence to the basic presuppositions of an atomistic liberalism, and the nominalism on which it rests, belittles the controversies between them and also highlights the normative ambiguity of their premises. Without thinking out the nature of social existence, they have each pursued a 'logic' of social relations without any foundation in the nature of those supposedly engaged in those relations.

4.   Locke, *Second Treatise*, par. 87; cf. pars. 123, 124, 138.

5.   See Machiavelli, *Discourses*, III.i., p. 297.

6.   See Mosca, pp. 358–59: "It was in ancient Greece that, for the first time, only that people was regarded as politically free which was subject to laws that the majority of its citizens had approved, and to magistrates to whom the majority itself had delegated fixed powers for fixed periods. It was in Greece that, for the first time, authority was transmitted not from above downward . . . but from below upward, from those over whom authority was exercised to those who were to exercise it."

7.   Although, in a neglected and seemingly undeveloped passage, Aristotle identified the experience of the self with the experience of time: "It is inconceivable that a person should, while perceiving himself or aught else in a continuous time, be at any instant unaware of his own existence . . ." (448a).

8. Cf., Rousseau, *Social Contract*, pars. 55–57, pp. 18–19.

9. See Bergson, p. 157: "Man is a being who lives in society. . . . By language community of action is made possible."

10. Only in 1781 did the Habsburg Empire, which comprised much of central and eastern Europe, begin to proclaim, under Joseph II, religious toleration throughout its realm; See Tapie, pp. 218ff.

11. See McDonald, pp. 42–43.

12. For example, religious prohibitions on medical practices deemed necessary for community health, social teachings found to be politically subversive, or animal sacrifices that offend its sensibilities.

13. That man is always a being-in-the-world most dramatically comes into modern thought from Heidegger's sustained attack on philosophic remnants of our Cartesian heritage. More forcefully than anyone else, he brought to the attention of the philosophic community the import of the fact that we are always in-a-world constituted by relationships with other people and with things. *But* he never really seems to have noticed that this general enveloping context is itself always within the complex of civic, economic and other layerings of a politically organized society.

14. Royce, who presided over Harvard philosophy in its prime, regarded himself as a 'pragmatic idealist'. Often passed over as some peculiar kind of 'American Hegelian', his fundamental development of pragmatism, like that of Peirce, clearly built out of Kantian grounds; he not only anticipated crucial aspects of Heidegger's existential phenomenology, but in important respects which show in what follows, saw beyond them. For some explication of this, see my paper, "Royce's Pragmatic Idealism and Existential Phenomenology," pp. 143–64. Cf. Marcel & Apel.

15. Royce, *Studies of Good and Evil*, p. 94.

16. Royce, *The World and the Individual*, II, p. 260.

17. Royce, *The World and the Individual*, II, p. 170; (italics mine).

18. Royce, *The World and the Individual*, II, p. 168, 166; (Royce's italics).

19. See Royce, *The World and the Individual*, II, p. 177.

20. Royce, *The World and the Individual*, II, p. 188 (italics mine); cf. Heidegger, *Being and Time*, pp. 78ff.

21. *N.B.* This term is Edmund Burke's; it is developed in Chapter 4.

22. *N.B.* This distinction is crucial: as I am using these terms, 'reaction' is an automatic action *caused* by an *external* stimulus — as in a 'knee-jerk' reaction; a 'response' is to be explained, not by means of the external environment, but by the individual's own judgmental evaluation of it. It depends upon *Spinoza's classic definition of 'freedom', which is presumed henceforth:*

> That thing is called free [i.e., 'responsive'], which exists solely by the necessity of its own nature, and of which the action is determined by itself alone. On the other hand, that thing is necessary, or rather con-

strained [i.e., 'reactive'], which is determined by something external to itself to a fixed and definite method of existence or action.

Def. VII, Part I, of Spinoza, *The Ethics*, p. 46.

23.   Sullivan, p. 39.

24.   Schutz, p. 54; cf. p. 52.

25.   Cf. Röpke, p. 5: ". . . society, its many components and manifestations notwithstanding, always forms a whole in which everything is integrated and interdependent."

Chapter 2. *Temporality*

1.   See, e.g., Rosenberg & Birdzell, p. 58.

2.   See, e.g., Gurvitch, esp. pp. xxii–xxv.

3.   For a detailed presentation of this fascinating story, see Landes, esp. pp. 67–69. *N.B.* See Landes, pp. 77–8: "Medieval man . . . was innumerate as well as illiterate. How much reckoning could he do in a world that knew no uniformity of measurement? . . . Even the learned were not accustomed to using numbers. The calculations of the calendar, for example — a crucial aspect of liturgical discipline — was confined to specialist computists."

4.   See, Decartes, "Meditations," III, I, p. 168; & "Arguments Demonstrating the Existence of God (Addendum to Reply to Objection II)," Axiom II, II, p. 56; and "Reply to Objections, V,"II, p. 219, sec. 4.

5.   See, e.g., Locke, *Essay Concerning the Human Understanding*, Bk. II, 1. "Idea of Duration and Its Simple Modes."

6.   See, my *The Human Experience of Time*, [hereafter *HET*], pp. 103, 105–09, 134–42.

7.   See, *HET*, pp. 109–21, 143–52.

8.   Kant, *Critique of Pure Reason*, A278=B334, p. 287.

9.   One could, indeed, develop the relationship between their views of time and of society beyond the purview of this essay: Locke's 'atomicity' of separate ideas in consciousness is consonant with the atomism of his social theory; the emphasis by both Leibniz and Kant on the primacy of time as a continuity of process, within which *we* 'mark off' 'moments', correlates with their views of society as grounding the individualities appearing within it.

10.   See, *HET*, pp. 167–74, 218–38.

11.   See Schutz, p. 35: "the life of the human mind [is] *in time*, that is to say, in the *'durée'* ['duration'], to use a Bergsonian term."

12.   Röpke, p. 62.

13.   *N.B.* James and Bergson had a mutually acknowledged influence on each

other and on both Whitehead and Husserl. Peirce had set out pragmatism's focus on 'futurity'; Royce and Dewey developed this futural focus in a number of ways. The most incisive examination of the pervasive structure of human temporality was provided by Heidegger and it is primarily on his analysis that mine depends; one might also consult Jaspers or Merleau-Ponty for a developed restatement in psychological terms.

14. Try this in a different language, which uses more than one syllable for the word 'now', as in the French 'maintenant', or "à présent'; or in the Spanish 'ahora'.

15. Cf. Griffin: he suggests that human habits may indeed represent an economy of thought, the lack of need to rethink each problematic situation as it occurs.

16. Schutz, p. 33.

17. Jaspers, p. 152.

18. Jaspers, p. 152.

19. Jaspers, p. 141.

20. Jaspers, p. 152.

21. Kant, *Anthropology*, p. 59.

22. Jaspers, p. 141.

23. See Fraser, p. 362.

24. See Gadamer, p. 279: "Human civilisation differs essentially from nature in that it is not simply a place in which capacities and powers work themselves out, but man becomes what he is through what he does and how he behaves, i.e., he behaves in a certain way because of what he has become."

25. See Gadamer, pp. 107ff.

26. Heisenberg, p. vii.

27. Peirce, p. 284.

28. Ricoeur, *Political and Social Essays*, p. 268.

29. The word 'value' has become controversial in some contemporary, especially phenomenological, circles for reasons that are not always clear — although one is led to believe that the objection is to attributing an 'ontological' status to 'values', i.e., to regarding them as somehow 'things'. No such intention is here suggested. The reader who shares suspicion of this term should substitute something like 'actional norms' or 'justifiable motives' without making an issue of an essentially technical distinction. For, however termed, it would seem clear that without some kind of evaluational guiding norms it is impossible to make any rational assessment of alternative possibilities or even alternate ends.

30. Cf. Gadamer, pp. 279, 287: "A person must himself know and decide and cannot let anything take this responsibility from him. . . . [Prudence is not] mere consideration of expediency that ought to serve the attainment of moral ends, but the consideration of the means is itself a moral consideration and makes specific the moral rightness of the dominant end.". Cf. Chapter 9.

31.   Royce, *Problem of Christianity*, II, p. 37.

32.   Royce, *Problem of Christianity*, II, p. 64.

33.   See, e.g., Fraser, p. 362.

34.   See Whitehead, pp. 72-73: "What is immediate for sense-awareness is a duration. . . . [which] has within itself a past and a future. . . . What we perceive as present is the vivid fringe of memory tinged with anticipation. . . . The past and the future meet and mingle in the ill-defined present."

35.   Schutz, p. 52.

Chapter 3. *Freedom*

1.   Kant, e.g., argued that freedom is so fundamental to human experience that it defies definition: "Freedom of will cannot be defined, however, as the capacity to choose to act. . . . For freedom (as it first becomes known to us through the moral law) is known only as a negative property . . . of not being constrained to action by any [sensory] determining grounds. . . . yet [man's] freedom as an intelligible being can never enable us to comprehend a supersensible object [of our thinking] (as is free will)." *The Metaphysical Elements of Justice*, pp. 27–28. Cf. his similar view about the undefinability of time, in "An Inquiry into the Distinctness of the Principles of Natural Theology and Morals."

2.   Jaspers, pp. 152–53.

3.   McDonald, p. 10.

4.   Arendt, p. 145. *N.B.* Exploration of the metaphysics of freedom is not my purpose here. It is neither the function of this discussion to resolve what is often known as 'the free-will controversy' nor to develop the implications of the experience of freedom for an ultimate speculative understanding of 'nature' or 'reality'. Though these metaphysical dimensions cannot be explored here, they must be touched on in passing; a fuller discussion is therefore reserved for another essay.

5.   Jaspers, p. 153. *N.B.* It has often been noted that when Chinese students began to attend European and American universities in the early 1800s, they encountered the ideas associated with that of freedom for the first time; on returning home, they found that because their own language was devoid of a vocabulary for expressing such concepts, they had to create new terms when they tried to translate writers such as Locke, Montesquieu, and Rousseau.

6.   Pericles, p. 149-150..

7.   Johnson, p. 13; he continues: "There were a very large number of Greek words for slave, and servile status, and infinite gradations of servitude." (The cultural import of a concept is often exhibited by delineations of vocabulary: some African tribes have more words for 'cow', and Eskimos for the color 'white', than we can imagine.)

8.   See, Montesquieu, X, 3, [7] - [9], p. 192 & XV, 2 [2], p. 259.

9.   Indeed, the Greeks and the Romans also took as self-evident the ready availability of conquered populations for compulsory labor in a society dominated by the static economy of a pre-technological age without any market need for advance beyond it. See Johnson, p. 15.

10.   See Montesquieu, XV, 1 [1], 2, [2], [4], pp. 258–60. See Rousseau, *Social Contract*, esp. pars. 20-33, pp. 8–12. That Rousseau universalized Aristotle's delineations of free citizens to include all society members seems clear; in doing this Ricoeur's observation seems very much to the point: "Rousseau, at bottom, is Aristotle . . . in voluntarist language. . . ." *History and Truth*, p. 253. In sharp contrast to the condemnation of slavery by Montesquieu and Rousseau, cf. Locke's, albeit reluctant, justification of slavery in *Second Treatise*, e.g., pars. 23, 178, 189.

11.   *N.B.* Christianity is an individuating religion. It is also, as Johnson has noted, "a time religion." Christianity "owes this historical perspective to its Judaic origin, but early Christianity heightened the sense of the millennium and the idea of an approaching apocalypse in which all books would be balanced and an account rendered. St. Augustine provided a firm historical structure for past, present and future, and his notions became part of the basic repertoire of western thinking. Hence the morality of Latin Christianity is obsessed by chronological factors, and dominated by the sense of urgency, the thought that time is 'precious'." Johnson, p. 32.

12.   II. Cor. 3. 17, Gal. 5.13 & I. Pet. 16. Translations taken from the Revised Standard Version of *The New Testament*.

13.   Arendt, p. 146.

14.   Quoted, in Arciniegas, pp. 117–18. *N.B.* This observation underlines a generally overlooked fact of modern history — the degree of intellectual freedom that generally obtained, even under absolutist governments, before the birth of twentieth-century totalitarianism. Cf. Polanyi, p. 96.

15.   Quoted, Arciniegas, p. 246 (italics mine).

16.   Arciniegas, p. 3.

17.   Arciniegas, pp. 120–21, 130.

18.   Jaspers, p. 160.

19.   Cf. Kant, *Perpetual Peace*, in (ed.) Reiss, pp. 99ff. Cf. Rousseau, *Social Contract*, par. 104, p. 35 & *A Project of Perpetual Peace*; also pp. 240-41 below.

20.   *If* determinism were true, we would still have to explain the pervasive *appearance* of freedom. Even if volitional freedom is an illusion, its experience *is our experiential reality* — our reality with which we must work no matter how it is explained. For *even if* determinism is true, we must continue to live *as if* we are free. The author of a determinist position, *on his own premises*, is not sharing with us a freely thought-out conviction but is merely acting out a predetermined role. Any why should we be asked to heed his arguments? On the determinist premises, whether we accept or reject the argument, we ourselves do no more than play out a role — as a record which only plays what is already prerecorded.

21.   Ricoeur, *Political and Social Essays*, p. 270.

22.   Cf. Polanyi, p. 30: Determinist doctrines, he saw as inherently subversive of a free society, by expressing at least one of three views: "Any [determinist] representation of man . . . if consistently upheld, [i] would destroy the constitutive beliefs of a free society, . . . [ii] denies the very existence of the moral sphere for the sake of which the free society is constituted, or . . .[iii] discredits as mere secondary rationalization the purposes which a free society regards as its mainsprings. . ."

23.   Leibniz, "New System of Nature," in (ed.) Wiener, p. 116 (italics mine).

24.   See Decartes, *Meditations*, IV.

25.   Indeed, one could add, morality presumes to be a certain kind of knowledge; as Gadamer suggested (pp. 287–88): it is "really a knowledge of a special kind. It embraces in a curious way both means and ends and hence differs from technical knowledge. That is why it is pointless to distinguish here between knowledge and experience, . . . [for] *moral knowledge* must be a kind of experience, and in fact we shall see that this is perhaps *the fundamental form of experience. . . .*" (italics mine).

26.   This is essentially what Heidegger meant by 'transcendence', the ability to transcend the limits of the immediate present and bring that reaching-out-into-the-future into constituting the meaning seen in the present situation. Cf. *Vom Wesen des Grundes*, p. 44.

27.   Aron, p. 369.

28.   Dallmayr, "Introduction," Theunissen, p. x.

29.   Aron, p. 122.

30.   See Polanyi, pp. 3–90, for an exceptionally lucid explanation of why sustained scientific work requires a high degree of social protection for intellectual freedom and access to information.

31.   These two words derive from two different originary cultural traditions which have merged into the Western outlook — 'liberty' from the Latin languages and 'freedom' from the German. This indicates that in addition to the derivation from classical sources, there was an infusion of the Germanic idea of freedom which abhorred the idea of slavery. Cf. Johnson, p. 29: ". . . the 'barbarians' themselves regarded Roman society as inferior because . . . it was, manifestly to them, less free. . . . slavery was a very marginal feature of German society. It was in fact an importation, since it was found in developed form only in the most advanced political and social areas, that is those nearest to Rome. . . . [W]hereas in the Roman world the infection of slavery had gradually poisoned the whole body, in the Germanic world the reverse process took place: the dynamic element of freedom gradually cleansed the rest. . . . Within a hundred years, slavery had virtually ceased to exist north of the Alps." Johnson goes on to argue that the resurgence of the West, in contrast to Byzantium and Islam, developed because of this abhorrence of slavery. Indeed, the demise of classical civilization, Green argued,

was due to slavery. See Green, "Liberal Legislation," pp. 371-72.

32. Berlin, p. 127.

33. Berlin, p. 163; cf. pp. xliii–xliv.

34. Locke, *Second Treatise*, Par. 6.

35. Mill, "On Liberty," pp. 72–73 (italics mine).

36. Berlin, p. 139.

37. Green, "Liberal Legislation," pp. 370–71.

38. Ricoeur, *Political and Social Essays*, p. 31.

39. Schutz, p. 33.

40. Ricoeur, *Political and Social Essays*, p. 36.

41. Cf. Dallmayr, *Politics and Praxis*, (quoting Heidegger), p. 114.

42. *N.B.* The concept of 'positive freedom', as any concept that is not moderated in practice, is open to self-destructive abuse: just as the excess of 'negative liberty' tends to invite its society into anarchy, the invitation of 'positive freedom' is to an undue paternalism, a danger to be faced.

43. Some current American examples would be: of the first, rights to choose one's own spouse, job, recreations, or bank; of the second, the newly discovered 'right to privacy' on the one hand, and on the other, the role of the judiciary in much of the civil-rights movement of the 1960s; an example of the third would be the legislative universalization of new educational opportunities for veterans of the Second World War.

44. One of the most pervasive, but not always organized as such, is the linguistic community, which transcends national boundaries — those who share a language normally prefer to carry on their affairs and interests within it — for it betokens a common grammar and vocabulary and minimizes any need to 'translate' what one wants to say into someone else's idiom. Even among those who share a language, many 'subcommunities' emerge around special ways of looking at aspects of the world and spending time dealing with them. Each develops its own 'culture', its own jargon reflecting the unifying outlook and common concern. The physicist speaks a language that, even in English, no layman can penetrate; likewise, the sociologist, art critic, and — alas, too often — the philosopher.

45. *N.B.* The American Union notably found it possible to preserve this constitutional fidelity by conducting a presidential election, in which its President, its Commander in Chief, was openly opposed in a contested election, even while embroiled in civil war.

46. A separate study would be needed to show how, even in attenuated form, societies that are not free still, in some crucial ways, incorporate theese three principles of organized society.

47. See Polanyi, p. 158: "A free society is characterized by the range of public liberties through which individualism performs a social function, and not by the scope of socially ineffective personal liberties."

Chapter 4. *Citizenship*

1.   de Tocqueville, II, p. 95.

2.   Polanyi, p. 34, 36.

3.   de Tocqueville, II, p. 334; cf., p. 282,n.

4.   Aron, p. 352.

5.   For some historically instructive examples of this, see Johnson, pp. 1–51 & 56ff.

6.   One facet of communist societies, ostensibly dedicated to equality, which immediately offends most Western visitors is its open flaunting of its own class privileges; e.g., restricting patronage of, what in the Chinese Peoples Republic are called 'friendship' stores, stores with quality merchandise, to its own directive elite, its 'party cadres', as well as foreigners with hard currency.

7.   See Polanyi, p. 115.

8.   Polanyi proposes a complex but intriguing argument that *because of the nature of time*, it cannot work; see Polanyi, pp. 111ff: "the central planning of production . . . is strictly impossible; the reason being that the number of relations requiring adjustment per unit of time for the functioning of an economic system of n productive units is n–times greater than can be adjusted by subordinating the units to a central authority."

9.   See Polanyi, p. 126, citing Trotsky's 1931 publication, *Soviet Economy in Danger.*

10.   Röpke, p. 162.

11.   See Chapter 6, esp. pp. 199-201.

12.   E.g., consider how recent American welfare policies served to disintegrate the family system among many poor families — the tragic impact on children of single-parent families and their society will ride into generations yet unborn.

13.   de Tocqueville, II, p. 305n.

14.   de Tocqueville, II, p. 314.

15.   de Tocqueville, II, p. 96.

16.   de Tocqueville, II, p. 138.

17.   de Tocqueville, II, p. 329.

18.   de Tocqueville, II, p. 105.

19.   *N.B.* This inequality of rewards follows a long tradition going back to Aristotle's distinction of 'distributive' and 'rectificatory' justice: "awards should be 'according to merit'; for all men agree that what is just in distribution must be according to merit in some sense, though they do not all specify the same sort of merit. . . . For the justice which distributes common possessions is always in accordance with the kind of proportion mentioned above (for in the case also in which the distribution is made from the common funds of a partnership it will be

according to the same ratio which the funds put into the business by the partners bear to one another)." 1131a&b. *N.B.* Also: The goal of the science of government is the establishment and maintenance of a system of justice, i.e. "the common interest" (1282b/12).

20. Mosca, p. 254.

21. Rousseau, *Social Contract*, par. 136 & n. 13, p. 48; cf. par. 40, p. 14; par. 63, p. 21; & *Political Economy*, par. 42, p. 164; par. 58, p. 172; par. 73, pp. 179–80; par. 76, p. 181; par. 77, p. 182. *N.B.* If citizens generally consider themselves as essentially menbers of a common moderate class, then even the wealthier will think in middle-class terms of a work-ethic and the social responsibility of wealth, as Montesquieu and de Tocqueville noted; and, in the American case at least, even the wealthy have felt obliged to work in the economy and devote excess wealth to the common good by developing private beneficences and philanthropies as nowhere else, e.g. the Carnegie Libraries, the various benevolence funds and foundations.

22. Rousseau, *Social Contract*, par. 65, n. 6, pp. 21–2.

23. Isn't this, in fact, the reason why most Latin American countries have been so frustrated in realizing their republican aspirations?

24. I am reminded of a former student, who worked for a United Nations agency concerned with child welfare in underdeveloped countries. She told me, quoting her supervisor, that "those individual initiatives" sponsored by American organizations for "adopting" individual children, paying for support services, and encouraging correspondence to provide personal ties between them, "individuated" their recipients, and "thus interfered" with the plan of the appointed administrator to "keep them all the same for their own good," and also "to ease administering the total benefit."

25. Aron, p. 211.

26. de Tocqueville, II, p. 322.

27. Locke, *Second Treatise*, Par. 123.

28. Locke, *Second Treatise*, Par. 57.

29. Locke, *Second Treatise*, Par. 99.

30. Locke, *Second Treatise*, Pars. 149–54.

31. See, Locke, *Second Treatise*, Par. 190; (italics mine). *N.B.* Into the 1920s, the notion of a 'police state' was not our contemporary term for totalitarian dictatorship; it referred to the minimal liberalist state conceived as "the night-watchman who is concerned only with the personal security of the citizens," *and thus ideally restricted to policing the protection of life and property.* Cf., e.g., Mussolini's "The Doctrine of Fascism" in Oakeshott, p. 176.

32. Mill, "On Liberty", p. 65.

33. Mill, "On Liberty," pp. 72–3; (italics mine).

34. This doctrine of 'social-atomism' is, of course, the social application of that metaphysical doctrine, central to the British philosophic tradition, that the father of American pragmatism, Charles Peirce, repeatedly condemned as 'nominalism'.

35. Perhaps one of the best indications of Mill's unsuccessful attempt to look beyond the strictures of the utilitarian atomism he had inherited is to be seen in his essays entitled "Bentham" and "Coleridge;" his admiration for the insights of the latter, who helped bring German Philosophic Idealism to England, confute his respect for the former, who founded the Utilitarian 'school', and but adumbrate the conceptual confusion in which he found himself hopelessly encased.

36. Mill, "On Liberty," p. 68.

37. See Mill, "Representative Government", VII. *N.B.* The current tendency of his American heirs to promote a Congressional supremacy over Presidential leadership exhibits the historic liberalist bias for parliamentary rather than tripartite government, and the management of parliamentary (legislative) government to be by a ruling majority made up of 'interest' coalitions. Cf. Chapter 5, esp. pp. 162-66 below.

38. Cf. Madison, #10, pp. 56ff. *N.B.* In practice, this system of 'proportional representation' fractures society into groupings; its pragmatic import is that it enabled Hitler to destroy German's Weimar Republic in 1933 while it simultaneously deprived the French Third Republic of any governmental continuity. Its resurrection in contemporary Italy occasions the same disarray of frequent parliamentary crises during which the continuity of policy is left, not to elected officials, but to a governing bureaucracy. Its effective translation into contemporary American debate is the liberalist call for a politics of special-interest coalitions, and the contemporary liberalist tendency to see individuals merely as standing for the groups to which they are ascribed — as in representing 'minorities' in proportioning the members of a school class or employee body.

39. Bentham, *Works*, X, p. 142; note (on the same page) Bentham's acknowledgement of Lockean inspiration:: "O Locke! first master of intellectual truth."

N.B. Although Mill clearly did not want this outcome, there is no logical reason why this utilitarian principle could not be used to justify the enslavement or oppression of the numerically lesser elements of the society.

40. Packe, p. 490.

41. Mill, "Utilitarianism," pp. 9–10; (italics mine).

42. If each citizen has an equal right to have his supposedly irreducible liberties secured, and if this claim is paired with a utilitarian 'greatest-happiness' principle, then the consequent is the expectation of equal right to whatever is desired, without any criterion by which to adjudicate conflicting claims beyond the politics of majority-formation and the placing of a selected elite into directional control.

43. See, McDonald, pp.66. *N.B.* It is, therefore, strange that some fifty years after its first re-publication, we find a retrospective reconstruction of American intellectual life as a continuity of Lockean thinking — despite the Constitution's repudiation of his doctrine of 'parliamentary supremacy', its subsitution of tri-partite government and judicial review (see pp. 151, 157, 160-6), and the prominent roles of thinkers like Emerson and Thoreau, Peirce, Royce and Dewey, who had no philosophic ties to him, in shaping the general direction of American thought.

44.   Cf. McDonald, pp. ix–x, where it is suggested that this new influence came, directly or indirectly either from Jean Jacques Burlamaqui, a Swiss writer, or from Aristotle.

45.   Originally initiated by the manufacture of the thirteenth-century German invention of the mechanical clock, the factory system was already manufacturing textiles in agricultural areas of central Europe in the 1700s.

46.   *N.B.* Burke (who could not have foreseen the nineteenth-century industrial crisis), in contrast to Mill who worked for the East India Company, set an anti-imperialist tone for the tradition deriving from his work — having favored the American cause and having opposed British policy in both India and Ireland as well. He is perhaps best known for his condemnation of the Jacobinism into which the French Revolution degenerated.

47.   Although Locke had named them as "life, liberty and property," he never recognized their conceivable conflict with each other or with the public good; having subjected them to unlimited majoritarian interpretation, he never explained by what guidelines any of them is to be specified: e.g., would he have disapproved of requiring military service in time of war — which potentially entails depriving any citizen-soldier of his 'right' to 'life' and 'liberty' for the sake of the common good of national defense?

48.   Green, "Popular Philosophy in its Relation to Life," *Works*, pp. 116–17.

49.   Burke, in (ed.) Stanlis, p. 330; (italics mine).

50.   But consider: "[Burke's] attack on Rousseau was not a theoretical considera-tion but was expressly confined to the use of Rousseau's theories by the French revolutionaries." Mansfield, p. 692.

51.   Sabine, p. 595.

52.   See Kant, *The Metaphysical Elements of Justice*, p. 13 & pp. 27ff.

53.   Insofar as the "chief end" of government, according to Locke's *Second Treatise* "is the preservation of property" (par. 86), government may legitimately "have no other *end or measure* . . . but to preserve the members of that society in their lives, liberties, and possessions" (par. 171); cf. pars. 127, 222.

54.   Green, *Lectures*, sec. 18, p. 345. *N.B.* A cursory review of the chapter titles in this work clearly shows its design to be a reformulation and development of Rousseauean themes.

55.   Green, *Lectures*, sec. 151, pp. 461–62.

56.   Sabine, p. 433.

57.   Rousseau, *Social Contract* par. 55, p. 18.

58.   Green, *Lectures*, sec. 18, pp. 345–46; (italics mine).

59.   Harold Laski said that this work directed at least fifty years of British social reform: see his *The Decline of Liberalism*, p. 12.

60.   Green, "Liberal Legislation," p. 370. Cf., for a contrasting view, Herbert Spencer, *The Man versus the State*, (Boston: The Beacon Press, 1950), p. 19.

61.   Green, "Liberal Legislation," pp. 370–71; (italics mine).

62.   Green, "Liberal Legislation," p. 372; (italics mine).

63.   And in central Europe, the Habsburg monarchy, under Count Taafle's direction against "the German liberals," simultaneously sought to ameliorate the devastation of unmitigated laissez-faire. See Crankshaw, pp. 272–73.

64.   Textbooks too often describe Green as the first of the British 'Hegelians'. To what extent his metaphysics is consonant with Hegel's, I leave to others to judge. His political writings, however, do *not* draw on Hegel's system; the themes of the *Lectures* are clearly drawn from Rousseau as buttressed by themes from Kant's moral and political writings; his corpus includes essays on Kant, but none that I can find on Hegel or Hegelianism; and his essay, "On the Different Senses of 'Freedom'," provides an incisive attack on Hegel's concept of freedom; see *Works*, II, pp. 312–15.

N.B. He provided a basic theoretical justification for his reconstruction of 'rights' or 'positive freedoms' as 'prescriptive' by an invocation of the tradition of 'natural law' that combines Burke's reaching back to Roman Law as the source of 'prescription' (see Mansfield, pp. 702–03) with Kant's notion of 'regulative ideas' that are not descriptively true or false, but nevertheless pragmatically necessary for coherent thinking.

65.   One prominent example being the American Sherman Anti-Trust Act of 1890, designed to maintain competitive practices in the marketplace, even against its participants.

66.   See Montesquieu, II, 2 [6], p. 108.

67.   Green, "Liberal Legislation," p. 374.

68.   Montesquieu, XI, 6 [68], p. 213.

69.   Plato, *Crito*, p. 50, (italics mine).

70.   Rousseau, *Political Economy*, pars. 37ff., pp. 161ff. *N.B.* The argument concerning compulsory education equally applies to the current concern to control the use of drugs.

71.   "Key Sections from Vatican Document on Liberation Theology," p. 14.

Chapter 5. *Governance*

1.   Cf. Hamilton, #6, pp. 52ff., & Madison #10, pp. 62–64; see, Montesquieu, IX, 1, [3], p. 183.

2.   Cf. Montesquieu, V, 6, [3] & [4], pp. 137-38.

3.   Rousseau, following Montesquieu, was to term this inclusive consensus "the general will," a term which Alexander Hamilton also used as meaning "the deliberate sense of the community." Those political scientists who are concerned to quantify every social phenomenon do not seem to understand that this does not

always mean taking a poll, which too often but reflects a momentary passion; but most successful politicians understand the limits of such a governing consensus and, especially when unprincipled, somehow know how to bend to what they somehow discern as the thrust of generalized opinion. See Montesquieu, XI, 6 [16], p. 203; Hamilton, #32, p. 200; *N.B.* For a brilliant study tracing this political notion of 'the general will' back to medieval theology, see Riley, *The General Will Before Rousseau: The Transformation of the Divine into the Civic.*

4.   *N.B.* At the depth of the post-1929 depression, which some of our students regard as 'ancient' history, Roosevelt could still speak of *only* one third of the nation being "ill-housed, ill-clothed, and ill-fed." It is important for us to accept the fact that by the standards of all pre-industrial economies, that measure of economic failure would have proclaimed a welcome success.

5.   Needless to add, perhaps, except that it is so rarely noted, the 'right to resign' without penalty is still denied to a majority of the world's population as we approach the end of this twentieth century. *N.B.* Before one hastily equates this essential requirement with all 'social contract' theories, it should be remembered that this agreement is *not* an agreement to form a society as by Hobbes and Locke, but is intrinsic to a societal principle of governance; (and, indeed, Locke seriously compromised this principle, cf. *Second Treatise*, par. 191). Rather, this societal covenant is to be understood as the continuing confirmation of agreement to its decisional procedures that the society imposes as its condition for accepting any adult member into it.

6.   It is ironic that so many, from Aristotle to Locke and Jefferson, generally looked to a free agricultural population as the requisite foundation for a healthy free society; whereas as a matter of historic fact, the impetus to democratization has almost invariably come from commercial urban centers.

7.   Lerner, "Introduction," Machiavelli, p. xxxi.

8.   Machiavelli, I, ii, p. 115.

9.   Machiavelli, I, iv, p. 119.

10.   Machiavelli, I, viii, p. 264.

11.   Machiavelli, II, ii, p. 287.

12.   Machiavelli, I, lv, p. 255.

13.   Machiavelli, I, lviii, p. 263.

14.   Machiavelli, II, ii, p. 282.

15.   Machiavelli, I, xviii, p. 170.

16.   Machiavelli, III, ix, p. 442.

17.   Machiavelli, I, xi, p. 146; cf. I, xvii & III, i.

18.   Machiavelli, I, xviii, p. 168.

19.   Machiavelli, I, lviii, p. 265; cf. Madison, #10, p. 60f.

20.   Röpke, p. 96, n. 2.

21.   Machiavelli, I, xxxii, p. 197.

22.   Machiavelli, I, iii, p. 117.

23.   Orr, p. 189.

24.   See Machiavelli, I, xxxix, p. 216.

25.   Orr, pp. 190–91.

26.   Orr, p. 192.

27.   See Machiavelli, I, ii, p. 111. *N.B.* Cf. the comment by de Tocqueville, II, p. 253: "The same state of society that constantly prompts desires, restrains these desires within necessary limits; it gives men more liberty of changing and less interst in change."

28.   Röpke, p. 26, n. 1.

29.   Machiavelli, I, xxxix, p. 216.

30.   In purely political terms, albeit in rudimentary and nontheoretical terms, he anticipated by some four hundred years one central lesson of the phenomenological analysis of human temporality: one is guided by present vision of possibilities which are anticipated by foresight or creation and subsequently evaluated in terms of feasibility by deliberate invocation of germane aspects of past experience. Cf. citation from Kant on p. 36.

31.   One could argue that the general proposition advanced some years ago, that "what is good for General Motors is good for America," helped to lead to the near-collapse of the American auto industry, together with all the ensuing repercussions for American society as well as the ensuing problems of the Corporation itself — by identifying a particular good as the good of all instead of insisting that the good of the community must be identified before the good of any of its component parts.

32.   Mosca brilliantly encapsulated this as the essence of a free society in his principle of 'juridical defense': whereby the power of the community through its government is exercised against the power of the community and its government to suppress the liberties it pledges to protect for each citizen. Cf. Mosca, entries under "Juridical defense" in Index, p. 504.

33.   The young Montesquieu, Rousseau's senior by some twenty years and often invoked by him, was a French jurist, during the early years of Louis XV's reign, who resigned his post for reasons of health and spent his years travelling, reading, and assimilating the new knowledge of strange societies that had been opened up by the great explorations.

34.   Written, as he indicated, over the course of some twenty years, it was immediately accorded wide acclaim as a major classic, and went through 21 reprintings in its first two years. *N.B.* One long-term effect of Montesquieu's work was to introduce a new method of studying social institutions and practices, thereby effectively initiating what would become the discipline of Sociology.

35.   See Montesquieu, XI, 6 [37], p. 207.

36.   See Carrithers, "Introduction," Montesquieu, p. 76 & Richter, p. 3.

37.   Mansfield, p. 695.

38. Montesquieu, XI, 5 [2], p. 201.

39. See Sabine, p. 560: "In truth, the civil wars had destroyed the vestiges of medievalism that made it appropriate to call England a mixed government, and the Revolution of 1688 had settled the supremacy of Parliament."

40. Randall, p. 943; cf. Carrithers, "Introduction," in Montesquieu, p. 81.

41. As Montesquieu himself said, "It is not my business to examine whether the English actually enjoy this liberty, or not. Sufficient it is for my purpose to observe, that it is established by their laws; and I inquire no further." Montesquieu, XI, 6 [67], p. 213.

42. Strauss, p. 164.

43. See references in Richter.

44. Sabine, p. 552.

45. Montesquieu, II, 1 [1] & 2 [1] [6] [7], pp. 107–8. *N.B.* In this and in subsequent material quoted in archaic language, the spelling of the original work has been retained; the editor, D. W. Carrithers, explains: "In order to preserve the flavor of the eighteenth-century translation, the original spelling and punctuation have been preserved, except in the case of some proper names and place names." See Montesquieu, p. xix.

46. Montesquieu, II, 2, [9] & [10], p. 109.

47. Montesquieu, XI, 6 [24] [25], p. 204, [16], p. 203.

48. Montesquieu, XI, 3 [1] & [2] p. 200.

49. Montesquieu, XII, 2 [1], p. 217.

50. Montesquieu, IV, 5 [2], p. 130.

51. This concern prompted Montesquieu, in Part V, to conduct a detailed examination of the role religion plays in molding civic virtues: urging religious toleration (Montesquieu, XXV, 9, p. 347), he again followed Machiavelli in restricting the examination to "the several religions of the world *in relation only to the good they produce in civil society.*" (Montesquieu, XXIV, 1 [2], p. 321; italics mine).

52. Montesquieu, VIII, 1 [1] & 2 [7], p. 171.

53. Montesquieu, II, 2 [14], p. 109.

54. Montesquieu, IX, 2 [3], p. 185.

55. Montesquieu, XI, 4 [1], p. 200.

56. Montesquieu, XI 4, [2], p. 200, (italics mine).

57. Montesquieu, XI, 6 [4] & [5], p. 202. Cf. the emendations of this in *The Federalist*: Madison, # 47, pp. 323–331, & Hamilton, # 71, pp. 481–86.

58. Montesquieu, XI, 6, (cf. [52], [55] & [56], pp. 210–11.

59. Monetsquieu, IX, 1 [3], p. 183; cf. Hamilton # 9, pp. 50ff..

60. Montesquieu, V, 6 [3], p. 137.

61. Montesquieu, V, 6 [4], p. 138–39.

62.   See Montesquieu, V, 6 [3], p. 137.

63.   Montesquieu, XI, 6 [68], p. 213; (italics mine).

64.   Carrithers, "Introduction," Montesquieu, p. 87; cf., pp. 30–34.

65.   *N.B.* What is claimed in the name of 'reason' and proclaimed as the vision of a new secular religion is not always rationally evaluated. It has been in the name of claims to special 'insight' and consequent secular fanaticism, that most of the horrors of the twentieth century have been wrought: Petrograd beginning in 1917, Berlin in 1933, China in the late 1940s, Cambodia in the 1970s.

66.   Montesquieu, V, 6 [3], p. 137.

67.   *N.B.*, Locke's thesis proclaiming "the one supreme power, which is the legislative." *Second Treatise*, par. 149.

68.   Montesquieu, XI, 6 [66], p. 213.

69.   See Montesquieu, XI, 6 [42], p. 208: "Were the executive power not to have the right of putting a stop to the incroachments of the legislative body, the latter would become despotic; for as it might arrogate to itself what authority it pleased, it would soon destroy all the other powers." Cf. Montesquieu, XI, 6 [43] & [44], p. 208.

70.   See Montesquieu, XI, 6 [40], p. 207, on the dangers of a 'permanent' legislature.

71.   Mosca, pp. 475–76; what Mosca did not envisage was the possibility that the press, as one final defense of a diversity of voices, might itself be corrupted — either by being 'bought' or by being directed by individuals whose primary allegiance was not to the good of the whole but to ideological advantage.

72.   Hamilton, # 34, p. 210.

73.   Madison, # 15, pp. 88–89.

74.   See, e.g., Hamilton, # 6, p. 31; # 12, p. 73; # 24, p. 157.

75.   Richter, p. 105.

76.   See Hamilton # 9, p. 53, citing Montesquieu, [IX, 1], p. 183: "all the internal advantages of a republican, together with the external force of a monarchical government."

77.   See McDonald, p. 281, who notes that this principle "is explicitly confirmed in the Constitution itself by the provision in article 4, section 3, which prevents the states from being divided without their consent, and is implicitly confirmed by article 5 which exempts equal suffrage by state in the Senate from the possibility of amendment." *N.B.* In contrast to the Lockean model which can be understood either as a contract of the poeple with each other, or as an agreement between the people and their ruler(s), the constitutional contract is of the people of the separate sovereign republics with each other.

78.   Madison, #39, p. 254.

79.   *N.B.* Locke's classic usage of 'common-wealth' explicitly derived it, not from *res publica*, but from *civitas*. See Locke's *Second Treatise*, Par. 133.

80. George Washington clearly used it in this sense when, surprised at the insistence of Virginia's landed gentry on a 'bill of rights' for the new Constitution, he marvelled that this demand came from "men of large property in the South . . . [who] are more afraid that the Constitution will produce an aristocracy or a monarchy, than the genuine democratical people of the [North-]East." See Brown, p. 295.

81. Madison, #14, p. 84.

82. Madison, #39, p. 251.

83. Brown, p. 136.

84. McDonald, p. 287, p. 291.

85. Gadamer, p. 376.

86. McDonald, p. 287. *N.B.* That modern dictatorships have appropriated the term is a gross caricature that but trades on its universal appeal.

87. Madison, #45, p. 309.

88. Hamilton, #1, p. 5.

89. Hamilton, #37, p. 234; (italics mine).

90. See Hamilton, #47, p. 324, where he eloquently acknowledged the source of this principle: "The oracle who is always consulted and cited on this subject, is the celebrated Montesquieu."

91. Madison, #47, p. 327.

92. Madison, #47, p. 328; For the further import of the Massachusetts Constitution, see Boorstin, pp. 409–12.

93. Madison, #48, p. 335.

94. Hamilton, #75, p. 503. *N.B.* E.g., The Executive has two legislative functions — the power to veto legislation without its being absolute since it can be overridden by a two-thirds vote in both Houses of the Congress; also, the power to negotiate treaties, which upon ratification by the Senate become law. The Legislature shares in these executive functions: the Senate in concurring on major executive appointments and treaties as well as the judicial authority to sit as a court in impeachment proceedings; the House, of initiating all appropriations for executive activities as well as the prosecutorial function of voting bills of impeachment. The Judiciary shares in both functions by authority to interpret the meanings of laws and their enforcement — an authority which, contrary to many writings, was clearly anticipated (See pp. 164-66.)

95. See, Locke's *Second Treatise*, Par. 134, which proclaims that "*the first and fundamental positive law* of all common-wealths *is* the *establishing of the legislative* power;*"* Par. 136, which speaks of "*The legislative*, or supreme authority . . .;*"* & Par. 149 which insists that "there can be but *one supreme power, which is the legislative* to which all the rest are and must be subordinate . . ."

96. Madison, #48, pp. 333–34; (italics mine).

97. Madison, #47, p. 334 (italics mine); cf. Mosca, p. 157.

98.   Madison, #49, pp. 340–41.

99.   Hamilton, #71, p. 484.

100. Madison, #51, p. 350.

101. See Hamilton, #69, pp. 462ff., for delineation of the differences between the President and the British king, the only comparable 'limited executive' at that time.

102. Hamilton, #71, pp. 482–83. de Tocqueville cited this passage as "animated by a warm and sincere love of liberty," in de Tocqueville, I, p. 153.

N.B. Cf. Rousseau: "The People, submitting to the laws, ought to be their author; . . . But how will they regulate them? . . . Who will give it the foresight? . . . how will a blind multitude, which often does not know what it wants because it rarely knows what is good for it, carry out an enterprise so great and also difficult as a system of legislation [i.e. a constitutional system of "political laws"]? *By itself the people always want the good, but by itself does not always discern it. The general will is always upright, but the judgment which guides it is not always enlightened.* . . . Private individuals see the good they reject; the public wants the good it does not see. All have equal need of guides. It is necessary to obligate the former to conform their wishes to their reason; it is necessary to teach the latter to know what it wants." See, *Social Contract*, Par. 105, pp. 35–36; (italics mine.)

103. Madison (Hamilton?), #63, p. 425.

N.B. Cooke raises the question of whether Madison or Hamilton wrote #63. On the basis of "internal evidence," he assigns this to Madison, even if both claimed authorship. But on the basis of the similarity of the quoted passages in Madison's #63 and Hamilton's #71, and the Rousseauean basis of both, it would seem that, at least, both participated in writing each.

104. Madison, #10, p. 60.

105. Hamilton, #78, p. 523, citing Montesquieu.

106. Boorstin, p. 416.

107. Boorstin, p. 406.

108. Hamilton, #78, p. 524.

109. Hamilton, #33, p. 207.

110. Cf., e.g., Rousseau's landmark distinction between "political laws [that] are also called fundamental laws" on the one hand and, on the other, "civil laws" and "criminal laws." Rousseau, *Social Contract*, pars. 141–145, pp. 50–51.

111. Already evident in the Mayflower compact, this crucial distinction was drawn from the Puritan understanding of Calvinism's Covenant theology. See Smith, p. 27: "By 1634 we find the people of Watertown rising to a constitutional point of their rights under the Charter. In 1639 we have the Fundamental Articles in Connecticut . . . and in 1641 the Bodie of Liberties in Massachusetts. By that time the distinct American trait of Constitution-consciousness was established and channeled."

112. Cf. Boorstin, pp. 409–12: "Not until the Massachusetts Convention of 1780 was *the difference between* the source of *a constitution and that of ordinary legislation* fully and unambiguously illustrated. . . . it was one of the most influential models for the Federal Constitution of 1787 . . . overshadowed in textbook and tradition by the events of 1787. Yet the Massachusetts Constitution of 1780 — in its preparation, discussion, and adoption — was the pioneer." (italics mine.)

113. Cf. Hamilton, #78, p. 523n.: "The celebrated Montesquieu speaking of them says, 'of the three powers above mentioned, the JUDICIARY is next to nothing.' *Spirit of Laws*, vol. I, p. 186. (Publius)."

114. Hamilton, #22, p. 143.

115. Hamilton, #78, pp. 524, 526. *N.B.* Ironically enough, the Supreme Court's acceptance of judicial review, first asserted in 'Marbury vs Madison', sought to restrain, not the legislature but the executive.

116. Madison, #52, p. 360.

117. Hamilton, #78, p. 524.

118. Hamilton, #78, p. 525.

119. Hamilton, #78, pp. 527–528.

120. Hamilton, #81, p. 534.

121. The framers could point, e.g., to the long history of dubious argumentation about the 'true' meaning of the undefined 'rights' spelled out in the First Amendment, e.g., concerning a 'religious establishment' and freedom of speech, as suggesting some validation of their point. *N.B.* Hamilton's specific dissection of a proposed provision for 'liberty of the press' is a lucid case in point. Cf., Hamilton, #84, p. 580, n.

122. Hamilton, #84, pp. 579–81.

123. Friedrich, p. 221.

124. See Madison, #37, p. 234 & #48, p. 334; & Hamilton, #72, p 487.

125. Madison, #10, pp. 56–65.

126. Madison, #10, p. 58.

127. Madison [and Hamilton?], #51, pp. 351–52. *N.B.* Whether Madison or Hamilton wrote this separately or together is a matter of scholarly dispute. Cf. Cooke's comment, p. 634, re "p. 347,"

128. Hamilton, #32, p. 200.

129. Hamilton, #31, p. 195.

130. Hamilton, #71, p. 482, & Madison, #63, p. 425.

131. See note #124 *supra*.

132. Hamilton, #26, p. 164.

133. Madison, #63, p. 428; cf. Montesquieu, XI, 6, [65], p. 213, on the need to moderate the reach of even liberty and reason.

134. Jay, #64, p. 438.

135. See Hamilton, #82, p. 553.

136. Hamilton, #34, pp. 212–13.

137. Hamilton, #85, p. 594, quoting from David Hume's "The Rise of Arts and Sciences."

138. Hamilton, #34, pp. 210–11; (italics mine).

139. No amendments have altered the tripartite system of government. Of all the enacted amendments, only three may be said to have affected the governmental structure itself: the 12th changed the original method for electing the President while leaving its selection in the national body intact; the 22nd restricted any president to two terms of office; and the 17th removed from the state legislatures the responsibility for electing senators and gave it to the people of each state. Four (not counting the repealed 'Prohibition' amendment) expanded the authority of the federal government: the 13th, 14th, and 15th amendments, the settlement of the Civil War, altered the balance of the federal government against the states by prescribing the extension of federally recognized individual rights to the states; and, the 16th opened the door to the dominance of federal authority by authorizing the federal levy of an income tax. Three mandated an extension of the franchise: the 19th, which extended the suffrage to women; the 24th abolished the poll tax (which Hamilton had already opposed in #36); and the 25th reduced the voting age to eighteen.

140. See Aron, p. 193: "The union has endured, having been threatened only once and, as [de Tocqueville] predicted, by slavery. . . . [and] in spite of the advance of centralization and the strengthening of the presidency, a strengthening that de Tocqueville had furthermore declared to be inevitable from the day when the republic would have to face enemies and be engaged in an active foreign policy."

141. Novak, *Democratic Capitalism*, p. 22; see McDonald, pp. 262, 287.

142. Röpke, p. 41.

143. Quoted in Friedrich, p. 34. *N.B.* The respect which the writers of *The Federalist*, the classic exposition of the principles of the Constitution, had for the precedent supplied by the Roman Republic is indicated by the pseudonym which they took in the custom of the time: the name 'Publius', the Roman who, following "Lucius Brutus's overthrow of the last king of Rome, established 'the republican foundation of government'," McDonald, p. 68.

144. See Röpke, p. 97, n. 2.: "the wisdom of the fathers of the American Constitution [is that] they clearly foresaw the danger of democratic tyranny by the majority. . . . Theirs is an excellent example of how, with some intelligence, one can avoid jumping from the frying pan into the fire. . . . To the extent to which one departs in the United States from the spirit of the Constitution, though not from the letter, and reduces the liberal and federal counter-balances, the danger of a totalitarian development with a democracy grows, and this applies also elsewhere."

145. See, e.g., Polanyi, p. 176.

146. Madison, #51, p. 349.

147. Lepage, p. 98.

148. Hamilton, "The Report on the Subject of Manufactures," in (ed.) H. C. Syrett & J. E. Cooke, vol. X, pp. 267, 340, 274.

Chapter 6. *Livelihood*

1. In the American case, the permissions of allowed liberties and the opportunities of freedom were socially grounded from the outset by the continuity of local governments in most of the original states, continuing their legal traditions and religious establishments promoting a standard of public morality.

2. Röpke, p. 46.

3. See McDonald, p. 108.

4. Indeed, the immediate impetus for the American rebellion was the perception of undue British interferences with market-freedom. Significantly, the Revolution, started in Boston, not in Charleston.

5. It was largely the population of the northern states that settled most of what was to become the country. North of the Ohio River (already closed to slavery by the Continental Congress), their children, together with immigrants who joined them, spread westward as far as the Mississippi, and then in a widening arc across the rest of the continent down to southern California.

6. See (ed.) Little, *The Oxford Universal Dictionary*, Third Edition, p. 261, col. 2.

7. Rosenberg & Birdzell, p. vii.

8. Cf. Alexander Hamilton's criticism of the call for minimalist government in his "Report on Manufactures," especially in the footnotes to its earlier pages.

9. It was supplemented in 1914 by the Clayton Act which augmented its provisions and also authorized the early labor unions to negotiate factory working conditions.

10. E.g. One can well argue that, in the economic crisis of the early 1930s, Roosevelt saved capitalism in America by initiating wide-ranging radical reforms of excesses that produced the Great Depression, reforms generally derided by announced partisans of the system he was saving but which, for the most part, would not be repealed by most conservatives today. As one prime example, he refused the call for "the nationalization of banking and currency," and thus effectively *saved what is crucial to any free-enterprise system, private control of private capital.* Cf. the complaint at this particular course by Charles & Mary Beard, p. 212.

11. Additionally, in order to secure income to the state, these mercantilistic governments pre-empted monopolistic controls over some selected commodities (such as tea and tobacco).

12. In the American case, this view, though controversial, was enunciated at the beginning. See Alexander Hamilton's "Report on the Subject of Manufactures" —

which, in its opening pages, presents an incisive dissent from any notion of a government unconcerned with the economic health of the citizenry.

13.   One current source of the drive to improve quality in American production is the recent preference of American consumers for what they discern as the superior quality of imported products. *N.B.* This is one reason why the Marxian concern with 'control of the means of production' so radically misses the point. Historically it missed the point as well: the rise of new production facilites *followed upon, and did not precede*, the Renaissance initiation of banking and international commerce, followed by the Dutch invention of free domestic markets, innovations which opened up new channels for the exchange and *distribution* of goods and hence for their demand.

14.   Rosenberg & Birdzell, p. xi.

15.   Swetz, pp. 11, 25 & 33.

16.   Novak, *Democratic Capitalism*, p. 98.

17.   Rosenberg & Birdzell, p. xi.

18.   Rosenberg & Birdzell, p. 242: ". . . until about 1875, or even later, the technology used in the economies of the West was mostly traceable to individuals who were not scientists, and who often had little scientific training . . ." Cf. p. 23: "The introduction of the industrial research laboratory, toward the end of the 19th century and the beginning of the 20th, systematized [for the first time] the links between science and industry . . ."

19.   Rosenberg & Birdzell, p. 71.

20.   *N.B.* Important to this consideration is the fact that Calvinism was the one wing of the Reformation that was widely accepted by the emerging urban middle classes. Whether Calvinism incorporated the middle-class values of its adherents or that they accepted them because of theological commitment is an open question not easily resolved; in any event, significantly, in both France and England, its proponents were the leaders opposing monarchical absolutism (Cf., e.g., references to *Vindiciae contra tyrannos* of the French Huegenots in Sabine, pp. 377ff.). It could even be argued that 'social contract' theory, so variously voiced by Hobbes, Locke, Rousseau, Kant, and the American Puritans, reflected, in secularized terms, Calvinist 'covenant theology'. As already noted, it also provided the historical source for the principle of 'constitutionalism': cf. pp. 165 ff. above and notes thereto.

21.   Lepage, pp. 59 & 58.

22.   Röpke, pp. 54–55.

23.   China had already, in 221 B.C., seen the perhaps 'premature' abolition of feudalism and its unification into one centralized empire. See, Fung, p. 180.

24.   Johnson, p. 71.

25.   Arciniegas, p. 7. *N.B.* The great age of western imperial conquest and colonization was *not* the product of the Industrial Revolution, as some claim, but its predecessor. The empires of Portugal and Spain, countries hardly touched by the Industrial Revolution, were well in place before it occurred. Dutch, French, and

British imperialism were likewise pre-industrial; Britain lost the heart of its North American empire in the American Revolution as the Industrial Revolution commenced, and then embarked on creating a new one which it dismantled as the second half of the twentieth century began.

26. Lepage, pp. 57 & 45.

27. Rosenberg & Birdzell, pp. 109, 178.

28. Rosenberg & Birdzell, p. 109.

29. Lepage, p. 43.

30. Johnson, p. 71.

31. Berger, p. 73.

32. Rosenberg & Birdzell, p. 229.

33. Novak, p. 98.

34. Rosenberg & Birdzell, p. 15.

35. See Novak, pp. 97–98.

36. Lepage, p. 7.

37. McDonald, p. 127; cf. Hamilton, "On Manufactures." Kant also remarks on the 'novelty' of public debt as a "modern invention;" cf. "Idea for a Universal History" in (ed.) Reiss, p. 51.

38. Johnson, p. 68. Cf. Kant, "Perpetual Peace" in (ed.) Reiss, p. 112–13; cf. pp. 114ff.

39. The word 'monad' meaning "an ultimate unit of being," was derived from the Greek word, '*monas*' meaning a 'single unit' or 'one'; just as any single number contains implicit reference to the entire arithmetic system, so any individual person implies reference to his entire society. Cf. (ed.) Little, *Oxford Dictionary*, p. 1272, col. 1.

40. See Koslowlski, pp. 160–61, 166, 173: "The individual is individuated by the totality of the determinants in its history and in the history of the universe. . . . [They are] Monads, not Atoms . . . [:] Leibniz's ontology of monads clarifies the notion of an idividual as a unique, unrepeatable person and deepens the concepts of methodological individualism." Cf. n. 42 below.

41. And by his most prominent temporal doctrine — that time is 'absolute continuity' of sequence, that it cannot be interrupted by any timeless vacuum, that past-and-present-and-future provide an *absolute continuity* — he sought to explain just how it is possible for us to build today while animated by a vision of the morrow while we yet use the knowledge and skill obtained from selected past experiences in order to do so.

42. Leibniz, cited in (ed.) P. Riley, *The Political Writings of Leibniz*, pp. 23–29.

43. de Tocqueville, II, p. 253.

44. Röpke, p. 103; he adds: "[this is] a perfect proportional system: there is no nullifying of the minorities' will by the majority. . . . [It] is a market democracy, which in its silent precision surpasses the most perfect political democracy."

45.   Polanyi, pp. 112 & 137.

46.   Johnson, p. 68.

47.   See Lepage, p. 45.

48.   See Pericles, p. 147.

49.   See, e.g., *Freedom at Issue*, (New York: Freedom House), # 94, 1987, pp. 19–34, esp. p. 33: & #106, 1989, pp. 47, 56-57.

50.   Novak, *Democratic Capitalism*, p. 22. Cf. (ed.) Novak, *Liberation South, Liberation North*.

51.   In stark contrast to the Russian Czar's dedication to autocracy, the Meiji Restoration, by imperial decrees, dismantled feudalism, effected agrarian reform, instituted a system of 'civil rights', opened the economy to general participation, initiated a system of universal education, inaugurated a modern tax and legal system, and a system of parliamentary government. Cf. W. G. Beasley, *The Meiji Restoration*; & Berger, esp., p. 157.

52.   *N.B.* This was no 'reactionary' government but a progressive coalition of non-Czarist parties that had removed the Czar from power and whose President was Alexander Kerensky, the leader of the Russian Socialist Revolutionary Party.

53.   One can wonder whether the accompanying promises of limited 'democratization' are not a measured response to a newly renascent middle class — although it is not a commercial but a bureaucratic middle class whose authority of governing status must, paradoxically, be curtailed in order to meet its inherently middle-class aspirations to freedom.

54.   Berger, p. 117; *N.B.* Only those *not* subjugated in the name of Marx, after the Second World War, succeeded in relegating this economic condition to their past.

55.   Rosenberg & Birdzell, p. 3.

56.   Berger, p. 35.

57.   Rosenberg & Birdzell, p. 6.

58.   Rosenberg & Birdzell, p. 303.

59.   Lepage, pp. 10–11 & p. 232.

60.   See Berger, pp. 235, n. 5 & p. 183. *N.B.* Berger suggests a comparison of the two Germanies on this count alone, a dramatic contrast between two countries, wrested out of the Second World War, sharing the same cultural heritage. Indeed, the contrast is especially poignant because provinces included in East (Marxist) Germany were among the most dedicated of all to the promises of freedom: Prussia, for example, repudiated National Socialism in the last free election of the Weimar Republic in 1933.

61.   Novak, *Democratic Capitalism*, p. 218.

62.   See Rosenberg & Birdzell, p. 7: Aside from products of new technologies, "the very rich were as well-housed, clothed and adorned in 1885 as in 1986."

63.   *N.B.* its source in the womb of liberalism: see, Locke, *Second Treatise*, par. 28.

64. That this rise has not been merely gratuitous is obvious. In a free society, labor unions have engaged in the struggle with management for economic power and have thus contributed to the free dynamism of a general struggle for power. And so, they have also brought their voices to bear on matters of economic policy, not only in negotiating contracts but also in the political arenas as they properly should in a free society.

65. Cf. Lepage, pp. 232–33: "Technological progress . . . has entered a new phase where . . . it is one of the forces carrying us forward to new social configurations."

66. See, e.g., Berger, p. 125–26: "that the entire Third World might become economically inaccessible would be less dislocating to, say, the United States than the inaccessibility of any one of the other major advanced capitalist societies. . . . to argue that, *in the aggregate*, capitalist penetration has done economic harm to Third World countries is very difficult indeed. Taking Africa as an important test area, countries *least* affected by colonialism (such as Ethiopia) are in the worst economic condition, while countries *most* affected by it (such as Kenya) are in a much better state."

67. Berger, p. 128, (all italics). Cf. Röpke, p. 107: "national frontiers are of no essential importance. The world market is more or less a unit where equal opportunities for selling and buying exist for everyone, regardless of national boundaries of citizenship. There can really be no problems of raw material, colonies or so-called 'living space'."

68. *N.B.* Marx had urged the 'working class' to transcend national boundaries and thus internationalize the world economies. In point of fact, industrial corporations have truly accomplished this; yet, ironically, they are now berated as 'trans-national corporations' that violate the very national loyalties 'workers' had been asked to abdicate.

69. Three points need to be noted: i. free representative government *can be* imposed by force — as in the cases of Austria, (West) Germany, Italy, and Japan; ii. the western demand on *its* conquered territories was not to impose *its* rule — western countries are negotiating with (begging?) Japan to allow their products into the Japanese market — but to insist that their own people, conquered though they might be, had an enforceable obligation to rule in representative form, on the unstated premise that if doing so had not been foreclosed to them, the war would never have occurred; iii. the conquerors of the first three, which had a suppressed heritage of popular rule, authorized them to choose their own representative systems, provided that they were representative and free. Cf. p. 274, n. 38 regarding Italy.

70. Berger, p. 159. *N.B.* Let us, in fact, notice the force of Rousseau's controversial dictum, extended to the international sphere as the countries of the world are becoming increasingly interdependent (which we will face in chapter 7): that, for the sake of the rest of us, each person "shall be forced to be free . . . [for doing so] alone renders legitimate civil engagements, which, without it, would be absurd and tyrannical, and subject to the most enormous abuse." *Social Contract*, Par. 54, p. 18.

71. Berger, p. 157.

72. Cf. McDonald, p. 137: "[Alexander] Hamilton's method was, in the language of modern economists, to structure market alternatives — that is, to make it convenient and advantageous for all people to conduct their economic activity in ways that would lend strength and stability to the national government and to make it difficult, if not impossible, to conduct their affairs in detrimental ways." N.B. Although one generally regards Hamilton as a prophet of American conservatism and Jefferson of American liberalism, it is amusing to note how these retrospective evaluations of them are occasionally altered for ideological purposes. Cf. Beard, p. 258: "the liberal doctrines of Alexander Hamilton and John Marshall [as contrasted to] . . . the narrow doctrines of Thomas Jefferson and John C. Calhoun."

73. Rousseau, *Political Economy*, par. 42, p. 164.

74. Lepage, p. 45.

75. Röpke, p. 178.

76. Röpke, p. 127.

77. Lepage, p. 10.

78. Novak, *Democratic Capitalism*, p. 90.

79. Berger, p. 110.

80. That social mobility is an advantage is a new idea; even Rousseau feared its coming: see Rousseau's *Political Economy*, par. 45, p. 166.

81. |/See Novak, *Democratic Capitalism*, p. 84: "[Democratic capitalism] foments rapid mobility, recognizes that old fortunes decline and new ones arise. In some forms of disparity in wealth and power, it sees utilities from which all benefit. For other forms of disparity, it establishes several correctives: a plural scheme of checks and balances; legislative power in the political system and in the moral-cultural system to restrain, temper and check the economic system; and the stimulation of the due circulation of elites and the economic mobility of individuals."

82. Many among us — artists, professors, perpetual hobbyists — deliberately chose to spend personal time on personal or cultural intersts rather than on seeking the highest monetary compensation the society offers for their talents. To accept or reject the social contribution-value standard of compensation, in favor of some other activity, is an act of personal freedom; complaints about the consequent lack of high income on the parts of those who made this choice would seem to be somewhat disengenuous and even an act of 'bad faith'.

83. Polanyi, p. 158.

84. But see Mosca, pp. 320–21: "But social democracy aspires to absolute justice, to absolute equality, and these can never be attained. Social democracy, therefore, will certainly not disarm in consideration of such benefits [as the amelioration of just grievances]. It will not pardon bourgeois society merely because bourgeois society confesses to some of its sins and does penance. Unlike the God of the Christians, the real socialist, so far as the present economic order is con-

cerned, wants the death of the sinner. He does not want him to reform and live."

85. Berger, p. 110.

86. See Aron, p. 193: "[American] institutions that in [de Tocqueville's] eyes were the expression and guarantee of freedom — the role of citizens in local administration, voluntary associations, the mutual support between the democratic and religious spirit — have survived, in spite of the advance of centralization and the strengthening of the presidency . . ."

87. Mosca designated this principle, that of 'juridical defense', as the fulcrum upon which a free state stands: that the legal authority of the organized community is brought to bear in the defense of each citizen even against any officer of the community who exceeds his proper functions by interfering with the acknowledged liberties or freedoms of any fellow citizen. See Mosca, pp. 120–152.

88. For example, in 1937 the USSR proclaimed a constitution with a full array of individual rights; but by foreclosing all power centers except those incorporated into the state machinery, these assurances and rights, as could have been expected, proved to be tragically meaningless.

89. Berger, p. 3.

90. Marx & Engels, pp. 58–66 (italics mine).

91. That this 'tedium' is universally 'deplored' is open to question. Intellectuals, acting as spectators from their own vantage points, may deplore it; but worker interviews frequently voice the welcome of 'mindless' tedium, as distinct from back-breaking drudgery, so that its participants may be free to think about their own more personally important concerns without being preoccupied by decisional responsibilities.

92. Indeed, free-enterprise economies are, arguably, gradually developing a kind of 'middle-class socialism' by virtue of the increasing ownership of public corporations, at least in the United States, by pension and retirement funds. Even as ownership and directive power have become divorced, this corporate development has had increasing impact on the way management runs industry so as to avoid stockholder problems: increasingly raising the apprehension of whether this development is for the best in view of the interst in immediate 'bottom-line' results, instead of seeking the results of long-range investment. One might note a similar outcome in the management of 'worker-owned' industries in Yugoslavia.

93. N.B. In the process of accomplishing this prosperity, some western societies appear to have developed an 'under-class', to some extent in the United States dangerously along racial lines; the dangers of this social phenomenon are addressed in the sequel.

94. de Tocqueville, p. 50.

95. Rosenberg & Birdzell, p. 7.

96. See, e.g., Rosenberg & Birdzell, p. 173, regarding what the low wages of the early British factories said about the condition of the surrounding countryside: "Victorian England was revolted by the fact that children labored in the factories for a few shillings per week, but when Parliament prohibited child labor, their

places were quickly taken by landless Irish immigrants equally eager to work for a few shillings a week. The low wages, long hours, and oppressive discipline of the early factories are shocking . . . [and] bespeaks, more forcefully than the most eloquent words, the even more abysmal character of the alternatives they had endured in the past."

97.   Just why these regimes have maintained a credibility among some western intellectuals, while being repudiated by their own — and despite their gross suppressions of 'civil liberties' which none of their western suporters would accept at home — is one of the mysteries of life of the contemporary age.

98.   See pp. 199-201 above.

99.   The danger, to which any proponent of freedom needs to be alert, is that a middle class, when threatened by a communist alternative, opts, in the hope of preservation, for a rightist dictatorship. This was classically demonstrated in two prime tragic failures of middle-class dominance: fascism in 1922 Italy and 1933 Germany. Notably power was achieved in both by proclaiming enmity to capitalism which was perceived as having failed the middle class that provided its center. Mussolini, a prominent socialist leader, promptly suppressed democratic freedoms and effectively 'socialized' capitalism in the form of a 'corporate state'. Hitler's National Socialist German Workers' Party immediately initiated a war economy which did much the same; it is doubly ironic to remember that Hitler's 'National Socialsim', announcing its enmity to Leninist 'bolshevism', was proclaimed at the same time as Stalin's Russia, in opposition to 'orthodox' internationalist Marxism, insisted on the Russian right to a national 'socialism in one country'.

100.   See, e.g.,"Vatican Document on Liberation Theology," p. 14.

101.   *N.B.* Franco's Spain is one prime example — as it developed a middle class its members provided the support upon which King Juan Carlos drew to transform a previously fascist state into a democratic republic (albeit in monarchical form).

Chapter 7. *History*

1.   Quoted, Nisbet, p. 23.

2.   Aron, p. 349.

3.   Aron, p. 115; cf. Kant, "What Is Enlightenment," in (ed.) Reiss, p. 55: ". . . a public can only achieve enlightenment slowly. A revolution may well put an end to autocratic despotism and to rapacious or power-seeking oppression, but it will never produce a true reform in ways of thinking. Instead, new prejudices, like the ones they replaced, will serve as a leash to control the great unthinking mass."

4.   Ricoeur, *Political & Social Essays*, p. 40.

5.   Robert Burns, *To a Mouse*, Stanza 7.

6.   Dallmayr, *Politics and Praxis*, p. 175.

7.   Kant, *Perpetual Peace*, in (ed.) Reiss, p. 119.

8.   Cf. Röpke's principle of 'historical interference'; p. 54: "history apparently always takes its course in two phases, a phase of internal mental incubation and a phase of external, physical realization, and as there is a great time lag between these two, the most remarkable and confusing phenomena of interference result from the coincidence of the realization of an already completed mental process of preparation with the incubation of a period that is yet to come."

9.   See, e.g., Kant, *Doctrine of Virtue*, pp. 44–45: "What Ends Are Also Duties? They are *one's own perfection* and the *happiness of others*. . . . For the *perfection* of another man, as a person, consists precisely in *his own* power to adopt his [own] end in accordance with his own concept of duty; and it is self-contradictory to demand that I do . . . what only the other person himself can do."

Cf. Heidegger, *Being and Time*, pp. 158–59: "there is also the possibility of a kind of solicitude which does not so much leap in for the other as *leap ahead* of him . . . not in order to take away his 'care' but rather to give it back to him authentically as such for the first time. . . . it helps the other to become transparent to himself in his care and to become *free for* it. . . . [it] frees the other in his freedom for himself."

Chapter 8. *Agenda*

1.   See Berger, p. 167: "modernization has had an individuating effect . . . in the sense of freeing the individual from the constraints of traditional groupings, such as those of kinship, village, caste, or ethnicity. Put simply, modernization, at least under conditions of capitalism, increases individual autonomy."

Cf. Rousseau, who set out a stringent individuating standard, *Political Economy*, par. 32, p. 157: "Indeed, is it not the commitment of the body of the nation to provide for the conservation of the least of its members wtih as much care as for all the rest? and [is] the safety of a citizen no less the common cause than is the safety of the whole state? . . . Far from any individual being obligated to perish for all, all have engaged their goods and their lives for the defense of each of them, to the end that individual weakness always is to be protected by the public force, and each members by the whole state."

2.   Berger, p. 86.

3.   Jaspers, p. 139.

4.   See, Friedrich, p. 28.

5.   An early forerunner of this present perception may be found in the Monroe Doctrine and, most dramatically, in Lincoln's offer, in the midst of the American Civil War, to assume Mexico's European debts in order to deter the European pretext for any imperial adventure in Mexico.

6.   Rousseau, *Social Contract*, par. 104, p. 35. See *A Project of Perpetual Peace*.

7.   Kant, *Perpetual Peace*, in (ed.) Reiss, pp. 99–100, 102 (italics mine).

8.   A free citizenry, Kant argued, may be expected to oppose any war because "this would mean calling down on themselves all the miseries of war, such as doing the fighting themselves, supplying the costs of the war from their own resources, painfully making good the ensuring devastation, and, as the crowning evil, having to take upon themselves a burden of debt which will embitter peace itself and which can never be paid off on account of the constant threat of new wars." Kant, *Perpetual Peace* in (ed.) Reiss, p. 100.

9.   See Rosenberg & Birdzell, p. 144.

10.   For an incisive examination of the East Asian experience, see Berger, pp. 140–71. *N.B.* The Confucian cultural undercurrent (in Korea, Taiwan, and Singapore) has always been the incipient commercial culture of Chinese civilization which, due perhaps to the very early bureaucratic centralization of China, in contrast to the medieval localism of Europe, was unable to press forward to political expression.

11.   Taiwan, as 'Free China', was always commited to democratization by its 'official' ideological statement, Sun Yat-sen's *San Min Chu I: The Three Principles of the People*, a work unfortunately much neglected but which represents a crucial Asian appropriation of western democratic experience and which, in good measure, inspired the organization of this book.

12.   Cf. Kant: "political prudence, with things as they are, will make it a duty to carry out reforms appropriate to the ideal of public right." in *Perpetual Peace*, in (ed.) Reiss, pp. 118–19n.

13.   Jaspers, p. 150. Cf. Berger, p. 216: "No praxis is possible without value judgments. This . . . is very much true of the social and political praxis commonly called 'policy'. (This implies, incidentally, that the phrase 'policy sciences', contains a *contradictio in adjecto*.)"

14.   Berger, pp. 216–17.

15.   Lepage, p. 84.

16.   I still remember seeing the smoke over Pittsburgh before it was cleaned up. But this seems to have been endemic to rapid industrialization: a few years ago, in both Taiwan and mainland China, I saw clouds of black smoke repeatedly belching froth from groups of factories. And the notorious record of the government of the Soviet Union, in this regard, is just coming into public purview. Every government, it seems, postpones its concerns with pollution as long as possible, while it seeks to encourage its society to reap the quick rewards of rapid industrialization.

17.   This tendency is demagogically encouraged by those who translate problems of economic integration into the volatile language of racial politics. The 'underclass' as it has developed is indeed multi-racial; to treat its members as though their economic alienation were solely due to the question of race or nationality is to subvert the social fabric, discourage effective amelioration, and encourage their psychological outlook as one of hopeless oppression inviting social upheaval rather than of encouraging individual development and social integration. Such demagogic appeals also create a disinterest, if not a 'backlash' in other segments of the popu-

lation, an attitude certainly not conducive to resolving the problem.

18.   In this regard, one can criticize recent American tax legislation that removed lower-income citizens from the tax rolls; politically heralded as the 'massive tax break for the poor' which it is, it also subverts an essential principle of democratic polity: each citizen should experience, in personal terms, the act of contributing to governmental expenses, thereby becoming directly aware of the fact that government consumes, rather than produces, wealth. To the extent that collecting minimal tax contributions from each might cost as much as these contributions might produce, that cost should be regarded as a needed educational expense of a free citizenry.

19.   Jaspers, pp. 181 & 180.

20.   Cf. Montesquieu, XI, 6 [40], p. 207. A Constitutional amendment to restrict the terms of office in the houses of Congress would be at least as justifiable as the twenty-second amendment limiting the Presidency to two terms, an amendment enacted at the behest of shortsighted conservatives who feared presidential power; in terms of Constitutional foresight, as expressed in *The Federalist* concerning 'legislative encroachment', it would seem to be more necessary.

21.   Berger, p. 87.

22.   Lepage, p. 18.

23.   de Tocqueville, II, p. 294n.

24.   In the business community, one sees the American automobile industry, having been run by some of the most vaunted managerial expertise available, which failed to anticipate, much less forestall, radically innovative inroads into its primacy until consumers massively exercised their preferences for superior imported products by foreign competitors. The recent spate of corporate 'takeovers' could be seen as a controversial mode of correction exercised by the capital market against entrenched self-serving business bureaucrats, were it not that these also tend to mitigate against long-run as distinct from immediate-return investment policy, and also tend to consolidate rather than disperse corporate power.

25.   Is it surprising that, since the Second World War, the American liberalist inherited bias for parliamentary government has increasingly denigrated the Presidency while increasingly seeking to augment the authority of progressively permanent legislators who can only rule by fostering bureaucratic encroachments?

26.   Hamilton, "Manufactures," pp. 267, 340.

27.   Schutz, p. 15.

28.   As an excellent critique, though differently focused, see Barrett, *The Illusion of Technique: A Search for Meaning in a Technological Civilization.*

29.   Robert M. Hutchins had already warned against this; cf., e.g., his *The University of Utopia. N.B.* American universities participated in this vocationalization of education by restricting admissions to its graduate schools, even in humanistic studies, a decade or so ago — because of their prognoses, based upon the outlooks of professional associations, of the 'job markets' for their potential graduates.

30.   One has no moral right, while appreciating the import of non-Western cul-

tures and their specific contributions, to ignore one fact that, beyond all relativistic tendencies, glares before us as we proceed to close the twentieth century. It is only out of an often painful development consuming some two thousand years since *first being sparked in the Athenian polis* that the concepts — of freedom, individuality, self-rule, divided government, the wisdom of fragmenting power while still learning how to use it, the virtue of a middle-class society, and a socially responsible free enterprise system to sustain it — have been bequeathed to us. Building on this heritage, western nations have finally begun to learn how to incorporate these lessons into a historically developed workable synthesis of free social organization. It is the example of what this developed system has already done and what it yet promises to do, more than any particular strands from any other courses of cultural developments, that is now finally animating the thrust of all other societies into a common human future in which they seek to find their own.

Is it of no significance that the Chinese students, in Tiananmen Square in June 1989, had no alternative but to choose as their symbol an adaptation of the Statue of Liberty which France had presented to the United States because there was no suitable symbol from Chinese history? (See p. 268, n. 5.)

31.   Encouraging the diversity of religious loyalties, rather than endorsement of any one sect, seems to have been the goal of the First Amendment in foreclosing an ecclesiastical establishment: in point of fact, several of the states ratifying the Constitution and its first ten amendments, had their own establishments during the time of these ratifications. Rooted in a religious heritage, the American tradition has continued to root its faith in freedom in a religious commitment: "In God We Trust" is written on American coinage; each session of the houses of the Congress, as of each political convention, is opened with a chaplain's prayer; and the American Armed Forces maintain chaplains as officers without it being seriously suggsted that they represent an ecclesiastic establishment.

One could do worse than send some 'strict separationists', who question any governmental sanction of religions, back to Machiavelli for lessons on the import of religion to liberty; to Locke, who founded his doctrine of rights on his reading of Scripture; to Rousseau, who had, in the same vein, proposed a 'civil religion' requiring a belief in God as requisite to free citizenship; or to Jefferson's Declaration which appealed to divine sanction for his own country's independence. These 'separationists', who oppose any sanction or recognition of the religious life of the citizenry, should realize that, by not specifying any one religious commitment for all citizens, a free people places a responsibility on its members to provide their own sources for a commitment of at least a quasi-religious nature to the import of freedom, so that their freedom might prosper. Freedom has never prospered without a belief in its sanctity; for freedom requires a faith, which goes beyond any possible verification, a faith in the possibilities to be found by a continuing venture beyond all confirmed knowledge, into the future which is to say into the unknown.

Different citizens will find different roots for this kind of faith; but it is suicidal for a free state to act to destroy, much less fail to encourage, the diversities of outlook to yield what Lincoln had termed that "political religion" necessary for the "perpetuation of free institutions," what Dewey had called "a common faith" in the possibilities of the freedom we share together. However grounded in the outlook of each individual citizen — and the plurality of such grounds serves to enhance the freedom of commitment — official recognition of the diverse forms of such a common faith is necessary to guard the sense of public morality and of virtuous citizenship upon which free citizenship depends..

32. de Tocqueville, p. 329.

Chapter 9. *Pragmatics*

1. Kant, *Perpetual Peace*, in (ed.) Reiss, pp. 124; (italics mine). *N.B.*Noteworthy is the fact that Kant, the foremost of rigorous philosophers, who deemed the concept of freedom to be the *a priori* ground of all evaluative judgments, commended *a pragmatic mode of prudential reasoning* whenever we enter into political questions. Cf. e.g., the two appendices to *Perpetual Peace* in (ed.) Reiss, pp. 116–130.

2. Peirce, "What Pragmatism Is," pp. 281–82.

3. If this pragmatic maxim had been observed, utopian projects would not have so often entailed prison camps or extermination for those who declined to share the privileged insight; the *heirs* of untold millions — who declined Leninsit visions only to die in 'gulags' and Maoist visions only to suffer the wrath of 'cultural revolution', whether in their own countries or in others that mimic them — would be among us today to enjoy the fruit of that social progress we all claim to seek to carry forward. Would that those among us who justify themselves by decrying these 'excesses' could bring themselves to face the pragmatic logic of what their favored revolutions entailed!

4. *N.B.* Although these strictures are not presented in the order mandated by a strict reading of Peirce's "three modes of being," I believe they are generally commensurate adaptations of the spirit of his three categories as he variously presented them.

5. See Kant, *Principles of Virtue*, pp. 97–98n.; cf. Montesquieu, XI, 6 [68], p. 213.

Works Cited

Apel, Karl Otto. *Charles S. Peirce: From Pragmatism to Pragmaticism.* Trans. by J.M. Krois. Amherst: University of Massachusetts Press, 1981.

Arciniegas, German. *America in Europe: A History of the New World in Reverse*, Trans. by C. Arciniegas & R. V. Arana. New York: Harcourt Brace Jonanovich, 1986.

Arendt, Hannah. "What is Freedom?" in *Between Past and Future: Six Exercises in Political Thought.* New York: Viking, 1961.

Aristotle. *Politics & Nichomachean Ethics.* Trans. by W. D. Ross. Oxford: Oxford University Press, 1942.

Aron, Raymond. *History, Truth, Liberty: Selected Writings of Raymond Aron*, Ed. by F. Draus. Chicago: The University of Chicago Press, 1965.

Barrett, William. *The Illusion of Technique: A Search for Meaning in a Technological Civilization.* Garden City: Doubleday, 1978.

Beard, Charles & Mary. *America in Midpassage.* New York: Macmillan, 1939.

Beasley, W. G. *The Meiji Restoration.* Stanford: Stanford University Press, 1972.

Bentham, Jeremy. *The Works of Jeremy Bentham.* Edinburgh: William Tait, MDCCCXLIII. vol. X.

Berger, Peter L. *The Capitalist Revolution: Fifty Propositions About Prosperity, Equality and Liberty.* New York: Basic Books, 1986.

Bergson, Henri. *Creative Evolution*. Trans. by Arthur Mitchell. New York: Henry Holt and Co., 1911, 1937.

Berlin, Isaiah. *Four Essays on Liberty*. London: Oxford University Press, 1969.

Boorstin, Daniel J. *The Americans: The National Experience*, New York: Random House, 1965.

Brown, Catherine Dinker. *Miracle at Philadelphia*. Intro. by Warren Burger. Boston: Little Brown, 1966, 1986.

Burke, Edmund. "Speech on . . . the Representation of the Commons in Parliament" (1782), in (ed.) Peter J. Stanlis, *Selected Writings and Speeches*. Chicago: Henry Regnery Company, 1963.

Crankshaw, Edward. *The Fall of the House of Habsburg*. New York: Viking Press, 1963.

Dallmayr, Fred R. *Polis and Praxis: Exercises in Contemporary Political Theory*. Cambridge: The MIT Press, 1984

——. "Introduction," Michael Theunissen, *The Other: Studies in the Social Ontology of Husserl, Heidegger, Sartre, and Buber*. Trans. by C. Maccann. Cambridge: The MIT Press, 1984.

Descartes, René. *The Philosophical Works of Descartes*. Trans. by Haldane & Ross. Cambridge: Cambridge University Press, 1968, two vols.

Fraser, J. T. *Of Time, Passion and Knowledge*. New York: George Braziller, 1975.

Friedrich, Carl Joachim. *The Philosophy of Law in Historical Perspective*, Second Edition. Chicago: The University of Chicago Press, 1963.

Fung, Yu-lan. *Short History of Chinese Philosophy*. New York: The Free Press, 1948.

Gadamer, Hans-Georg. *Truth and Method*. New York: The Seabury Press, 1975.

Gastil et al, (ed.) Raymond. "Freedom Around the World: The Map of Freedom," in *Freedom at Issue*, No. 94, 1987, No. 106, 1989. New York: Freedom House.

Green, Thomas Hill. *Lectures on the Principles of Political Obligation*, in *Works*, vol. II. London: Longmans, Green, 1911.

——. "Liberal Legislation and Freedom of Contract," in *Works*, vol. III. London: Longmans, Green, 1911.

——. "On the Different Senses of 'Freedom'," in *Works*, vol. II. London: Longmans, Green, 1911.

——. "Popular Philosophy in Relation to Life," in *Works*, vol. III. London: Longmans, Green, 1911.

Griffin, Donald R. *Animal Thinking*. Cambridge: The Harvard University Press, 1984.

Gurvitch, Georges. *The Spectrum of Social Time*. Dordrecht: Dr. Reidel, 1964.

Hamilton, Alexander. "The Report on the Subject of Manufactures," in (ed.) H. C. Syrett & J. E. Cooke, *The Papers of Alexander Hamilton*. Vol. X, New York: Columbia University Press, 1966.

Hamilton Alexander, John Jay & James Madison. *The Federalist*. Ed. by Jacob E. Cooke. Middletown: Wesleyan University Press, 1961.

Heidegger, Martin. *Being and Time*. Trans. by J. Macquarrie & E. Robinson. New York: Harper & Row, 1962.

——. *Vom Wesen des Grundes*. Frankfurt: Vittorio Klostermann, 1965.

Heisenberg, Werner. *Physics and Beyond: Encounter and Conversations*. Trans. by A. J. Pomerans. New York: Harper & Row, 1971.

Hutchins, Robert M. *The University of Utopia*. Chicago: The University of Chicago Press, 1953.

Jaspers, Karl. *The Origin and Goal of History*. Trans by M. Bullock. [First German edition, 1949.] New Haven: Yale University Press, 1953.

Johnson, Paul. *Enemies of Society*. New York: Atheneum, 1977.

Kant, Immanuel. *Anthropology from a Pragmatic Point of View*. Trans. by M. J. Gregor. The Hague: Martinue Nijhoff, 1974.

——. *Critique of Pure Reason*. Trans. by N. K. Smith. New York: St. Martin's Press, 1968.

——. *The Doctrine of Virtue*. Trans. by M. J. Gregor. Philadelphia: University of Pennsylvania Press, 1964.

——. *The Metaphysical Elements of Justice*. Trans. by J. Ladd. Indianapolis: Bobbs-Merrill Company, 1965.

——. *An Answer to the Question: 'What Is Enlightenment'; Idea for a Universal History with a Cosmopolitan Purpose; & Perpetual Peace: A Philosophical Sketch*, in (ed.) H. Reiss, *Kant's Political Writings*. Trans.

by H. B. Nisbet. Cambridge: Cambridge University Press, 1970, 1985.

Koslowski, Peter. "Maximum Coordination of Entelechial Individuals: The Metaphysics of Leibniz and Social Philosophy." *Ratio*, XXVII, 2 December 1985.

Landes, David S. *Revolution in Time: Clocks and the Making of the Modern World*. Cambridge: Harvard University Press, 1983.

Laski, Harold J. *The Decline of Liberalism*, London, 1940.

Leibniz, G. W. "New System of Nature," in (ed.) Wiener, *Leibniz Selections*. New York: Charles Scribner's Sons, 1951.

————. (ed.) Patrick Riley, *The Political Writings of Leibniz*. Cambridge: Cambridge University Press, 1972.

Lepage, Henri. *Tomorrow Capitalism: The Economics of Economic Freedom*. Trans. by S. C. Ogilvie. La Salle: Open Court, 1982.

Little, William. (ed.) *The Oxford Universal Dictionaray on Historical Principles*, Third Edition, Oxford: Clarendon Press, 1955.

Locke, John. *Second Treatise of Civil Government*/Any edition/or/ (ed.) C. L. Sherman, New York: D. Appleton-Century, 1937.

Machiavelli, Niccolò. *The Prince and Discourses*. Intro. by Max Lerner, New York: The Modern Library, 1940.

Mansfield, Jr., Harvey. "Edmund Burke," in (ed.) Leo Strauss & Joseph Cropsey, *History of Political Philosophy*, Third Edition. Chicago: The University of Chicago Press, 1987.

Marcel, Gabriel. *Royce's Metaphysics*. Trans. by V. & G. Ringer, Chicago: Henry Regnery Company, 1956.

Marx, Karl & Friedrich Engels. *The Communist Manifesto*, Trans. by S. Moore. Ed. by J. Katz. New York: Washington Square Press, 1964, 1974.

McDonald, Forrest. *Novus Ordo Seclorum: The Intellectual Origins of the Constitution*. Lawrence: University Press of Kansas, 1985.

Mill, John Stuart. *Utilitarianism, Liberty, and Representative Government*. J.M. Dent & Sons, 1910, 1936.

————. "Bentham" & "Coleridge" in *Mill's Essays on Literature and Society*, (ed.) J. B. Schneewind. New York: Collier Books, 1965.

Montesquieu, Charles le Secondat, Baron de la Brède et de. *The Spirit of the Laws: A Compendium of the First English Edition*, Ed. & Intro. by David Wallace Carrithers. Berkeley: University of California Press, 1977.

Mosca, Gaetano. *The Ruling Class*, Trans. by H. D. Kahn. New York: McGraw-Hill, 1939.

Mussolini, Benito. "The Doctrine of Facism," in (ed.) Michael Oakeshott, *The Social and Political Doctrines of Contemporary Europe*. Cambridge: Cambridge University Press, 1939.

Nisbet, Robert. *Conservatism*. Minnespolis: University of Minnesota Press, 1986.

Novak, Michael. *The Spirit of Democratic Capitalism*. New York: Simon & Schuster, 1982.

———. (ed.) *Liberation South, Liberation North*. Washington: American Enterprise Institute for Public Policy Research, 1981.

Orr, Robert. "The Time Motif in Machiavelli," in (ed.) M. Fleisher, *Machiavelli and the Nature of Political Thought*. New York: Atheneum, 1972.

Packe, Michael St. John. *The Life of John Stuart Mill*. London: Secker and Warburg, 1954.

Paul & Peter, Sts. *The New Testament*, Revised Standard Version. New York: Thomas Nelson & Sons, 1901, 1946.

Peirce, Charles S. "What Pragmatism Is," in (ed.) C. Hartshorne & P. Weiss, *Collected Papers of Charles Sanders Peirce*, vol. V. Cambridge: Harvard University Press, 1963.

Pericles. "Funeral Oration," in Thucydides, *The History of the Peloponnesian War.* Trans. by Rex Warner. London: Penguin Books, 1954, 1972.

Plato. "Crito." Trans. by H. Tredennick, in (ed.) Hamilton & Cairns, *The Selected Dialogues of Plato*. Princeton: Princeton University Press, 1963, 1985.

Polanyi, Michael. *The Logic of Liberty: Reflections and Rejoinders*. Chicago: The University of Chicago Press, 1951, 1980.

Randall, John Herman. *The Career of Philosophy*, vol. I. New York: Columbia University Press, 1962.

Richter, Melvin. *The Political Philosophy of Montesquieu*, Cambridge: Cambridge University Press, 1977.

Ricoeur, Paul. *History and Truth*. Trans. by C. A. Kelbley. Evanston: Northwestern University Press, 1965.

———. *Political and Social Essays*. Ed. by D. Stewart & J. Bien. Athens: Ohio University Press, 1974.

Riley, Patrick. *The General Will Before Rousseau: The Transformation of the Divine into the Civic*. Princeton: Princeton University Press, 1986.

Röpke, Wilhelm. *The Social Crisis of Our Time*. Trans. by A. & P. S. Jacobsohn. Chicago: The University of Chicago Press, 1950.

Rosenberg, Nathan & L. E. Birdzell, Jr. *How the West Grew Rich: The Economic Transformation of the Industrial World*. New York: Basic Books, 1986.

Rousseau, Jean-Jacques. *Of the Social Contract: or Principles of Political Right & On Political Economy*. Trans. & Ed. by C. M. Sherover, New York: Harper & Row, 1984.

———. *Project of Perpetual Peace*. Trans. by E. M. Nuthall. in (ed.) M. C. Jacob, *Peace Projects of the Eighteenth Century*. New York: Garland Publishing, 1974.

Royce, Josiah. *Studies of Good and Evil*. New York: D. Appleton & Co., 1902.

———. *The World and the Individual*. Two vols. New York: Macmillan, 1904.

———. *The Problem of Christianity*. Two vols. New York: Macmillan, 1913.

Sabine, George H. *A History of Political Theory*. New York: Henry Holt & Co., 1937.

Schutz, Alfred. in (ed.) Richard Grathoff, *The Theory of Social Action: Alfred Schutz and Talcott Parsons*. Bloomington: Indiana University Press, 1978.

Sherover, Charles M. "Royce's Pragmatic Idealism and Existential Phenomenology." in (ed.) Corrington, et al, *Pragmatism Encounters Phenomenology*. Washington: Center for Advanced Research in Phenomenology & University Press of America, 1987.

———. *The Human Experience of Time: The Development of Its Philosophic Meaning*. New York: New York University Press, 1975.

Smith, Chard Powers. *Yankees and God*. New York: Heritage House, 1954.

Spencer, Herbert. *The Man versus the State*, Boston: The Beacon Press, 1950.

Spinoza, Benedict de. *The Ethics*, in *On the Improvement of the Understanding, The Ethics, Correspondence*. Trans. with Intro. by R. H. M. Elwes. New York: Dover Publications, n.d.

Strauss, Leo. *Natural Right and History*. Chicago: The University of Chicago Press, 1950, 1953.

Sullivan, William M. *Reconstructing Public Philosophy*. Berkeley: University of California Press, 1982.

Sun, Yat-sen. *San Min Chu I: The Three Principles of the People*. Trans. by F. W. Price. Chungking: Information Ministry of the Republic of China, 1943.

Swetz, Frank J. *Capitalism and Arithmetic: The New Math of the 15th Century*. LaSalle: Open Court, 1987.

Tapie, Victor L. *The Rise and Fall of the Habsburg Monarchy*. Trans. by S. Hardman. New York: Praeger, 1971.

Theunissen, Michael. *The Other: Studies in the Social Ontology of Husserl, Heidegger, Sartre, and Buber*. Trans. by C. Macann, Intro. by F. R. Dallmayr. Cambridge: The MIT Press, 1984.

Tocqueville, Alexis de. *Democracy in America*. Two vols. Ed. by P. Bradley. New York: Alfred A. Knopf, 1980.

Vatican. "Key Sections from Vatican Document on Liberation Theology," in *New York Times*, April 6, 1986, p. 14.

Whitehead, Alfred North. *The Concept of Nature*. Ann Arbor: The University of Michigan Press, 1957.

Index